The Blue Guides

Please write in with your comments, suggestions and corrections for the next edition of the Blue Guide. Writers of the most helpful letters will be awarded a free Blue Guide of their choice.

City Guide
Kraków

Jasper Tilbury

A&C Black • London
WW Norton • New York

First edition September 2000

Published by A & C Black (Publishers) Limited
35 Bedford Row, London WC1R 4JH

ISBN 0–7136–5308–6

Published in the United States of America by
WW Norton and Company, Inc
500 Fifth Avenue, New York, NY 10110

Published simultaneously in Canada by
Penguin Books Canada Limited
10 Alcorn Avenue, Toronto, Ontario M4V 3B2

ISBN 0–393–32138–X USA

The author and the publishers have done their best to ensure the accuracy of all the information in *Blue Guide Kraków*; however, they can accept no responsibility for any loss, injury or inconvenience sustained by any traveller as a result of information or advice contained in the guide.

Jasper Tibury was born in London. He graduated in modern history from the University of St Andrews. Since 1989 he has lived in Kraków, where he works as a freelance journalist and translator.

Cover picture: a detail of the Cloth Hall (Sukiennice) in the Market Square © Phil Robinson. Title page illustration: Wawel Cathedral

Printed in Great Britain by Martins of Berwick.

Contents

The Guide

Maps and plans

Introduction

Kraków (population 755,000), Poland's fourth largest city, lies in a broad valley on the banks of the Vistula river. Its focal point is the Market Square, or *Rynek Główny*, situated at the heart of the Old Town (*Stare Miasto*)—the city's historic centre. This compact area, with an urban plan dating back to the Middle Ages, is a treasure-trove of architectural monuments, given recognition in 1978 when it was included on **UNESCO's World Heritage List**. Seen from a distance, the city's skyline is dominated by the twin towers of St Mary's Church, from which the famous bugle signal, or *hejnał*, is sounded on the hour. To the south of the Market Square, perched on a hill, lies the magnificent Wawel Castle, the former seat of Poland's rulers which overlooks the Vistula at a point where the river turns at almost 90 degrees.

Kraków ceased to be the capital of Poland in the early 17C, but its royal legacy is still everywhere to be found: in the ancient colleges of the Jagiellonian University, funded by Queen Jadwiga (1385–99), in the tombs and monuments that fill Wawel Cathedral, and in the 'new' district of Kazimierz, established by the Polish monarchy in the 14C. Yet the city also has a distinctly provincial side. In the Old Town's quiet, narrow backstreets, almost totally devoid of modern buildings, life generally seems to proceed at a slower pace. The area is ideal for walking, and this is one of the great advantages that Kraków has over many cities: you will hardly ever need to use public transport, let alone a car, to get to the major sites. Kraków has a vast number of attractions, and most are located in and around the Old Town.

Geographical location has played an important role in the history of Kraków. For centuries it rivalled the great Central European cities of Budapest, Prague and Vienna, like them becoming a centre of cultural development in the region. The affinities have remained strong. Even today, some Cracovians wistfully refer to themselves as 'Galicians' to underline the uniqueness of their cultural legacy. There is indeed some truth to this claim: for the best part of the 19C Kraków was ruled by the Austrian Habsburgs, while Warsaw, for instance, was part of a wholly different domain—Czarist Russia.

Nowadays, Kraków is Poland's most visited city, and it is easy to see why. In summer, the *Rynek* really comes alive with concerts, fairs, processions and scores of other festivities. Crowds fill the open-air cafés, which form an almost continuous line around the periphery of the square. Kraków is still regarded as the country's cultural capital, playing host to a variety of events including **Music in Old Kraków** (August), the **International Short Film Festival** (May/June), **Festival of Jewish Culture** (June), and **International Graphic Art Triennale** (September). Along with eight other cities—Avignon, Bergen, Bologna, Brussels, Helsinki, Prague, Reykjavik, Santiago de Compostela—it was chosen as the European Capital of Culture for the year 2000, with numerous festivals and events taking place in the millennium year and beyond.

In the decade since the fall communism, Kraków has been developing at breakneck speed. A modern city is emerging: old state-owned enterprises have been closed down or privatised, their place taken by new businesses, and a plethora of new restaurants, cafés and cellar bars has appeared. Today, the city can boast a nightlife that is the envy of visitors from other parts of Poland. Construction is struggling to keep up with the rapid pace of change. There is an acute shortage of both residential housing and tourist accommodation, and finding a room is not always easy, especially in peak season. Despite this, ambitious new buildings—banks and churches, hospitals, offices and houses—are being designed by a new generation of architects. Today's graduates of the city's academic institutions are young enough not to remember the communist period. The grim certainties of the past have been consigned to the history books along with the 'dour', 'grey' eastern bloc stereotype. Besides, there has been a sea change in attitudes towards Kraków's architectural heritage. Municipal authorities no longer see the city's ancient monuments and illustrious past as a financial and ideological burden, but as a means of generating revenue through tourism. The 1000th anniversary of the Kraków diocese (in 2000) has given a new impetus to the conservation of historic monuments, and already the Cloth Hall, Church of St Mary and Town Hall Tower on the Market Square have undergone thorough renovation. The end result is impressive to say the least.

Pollution, once the scourge of the city, has vastly improved in recent years. The iron and steel works in Nowa Huta has changed its production profile, with the most polluting sections being closed down, and modern filters have been installed at the industrial plant in nearby Skawina. Nowadays, most air pollution is caused by the persistence of coal stoves in many homes and increasing car use—the promised ring road for lorries and through traffic is still awaiting completion. But while Kraków's air could hardly be called pristine, the days when even a short stay in the city was considered a health hazard are thankfully long gone.

Few would claim that the transition period has been easy. Certainly it has entailed social costs in the form of unemployment, poverty and crime, but as most Cracovians agree, the changes of the past decade have, overall, been for the better. Thanks to modernisation and development, they argue, Kraków can enter the 21C not only with a rich thousand-year heritage, but with a youthful optimism and the prospect of a rosy future. One thing is for sure: Kraków will remain, as it has done over the centuries, one of Europe's most beautiful and captivating cities.

Acknowledgements

The publication of this, the first Blue Guide Kraków, would not have been possible without the help of many people. Their names are too numerous to mention, but I would like to thank, in particular, all the staff at A & C Black, especially Miranda Robson for her meticulous editorial work and Gemma Davies for her customary patience. A special word of gratitude is due to Dr Paweł Pencakowski of the Academy of Fine Arts in Kraków, who provided many insightful comments on the text and removed some of the more serious errors. Needless to say, any remaining errors are entirely my own. I am also indebted to the staff of the Małopolska School of Public Administration, who gave me free and unlimited access to their state of the art office equipment. Several people were directly involved in the research for this book: many thanks to Karolina Stępniewska and Małgorzata Segda for their indispensable assistance in compiling the Practical Information section, Aleksander Janicki for his insider's view on Cracovian art galleries, Jerzy Skoczylas for his amusing digressions on politics and vodka, and Marek Król, whose in-a-nutshell accounts of famous Cracovians were of great benefit. Last but not least, I wish to thank Dagmara for her constant encouragement and support.

How to use the Guide

The Guide is structured around eighteen, self-contained walks. Seven of these describe the Old Town and its environs, beginning on or close to the **Market Square**. Nine walks explore districts outside the perimeter of the Old Town and a further two venture out of the city centre.

The first **names of Polish monarchs and saints** have not been translated (thus avoiding clumsy Anglicisations such as 'Laidslaus' or 'Boleslaus') but their epithets have. Thus, 'Kazimierz the Great' is preferred to 'Kazimierz Wielki' or 'Casimir the Great'. Where possible, names have been kept in the original. Exceptions include names of famous personages that have a conventional English (Latin) spelling. Thus, 'Copernicus' is preferred to 'Kopernik'.

Stars have been used in this Guide to indicate places or buildings of special interest. Places and buildings prefixed by two stars (the maximum) are considered to be of major importance on a European or world scale.

Road distances are given in kilometres and are based on official publications. **Times** are given according to the 24-hour clock, as is conventional in Poland.

Abbreviations

c	circa	al. (aleja)	avenue
C	century	pl. (plac)	square/plaza
km	kilometre	ul. (ulica)	street
m	metre	Os. (osiedle)	estate
ha	hectare	Św. (święty)	saint/holy

Highlights

The vast number of sites and attractions in Kraków means that visitors staying for only a few days cannot hope to see all the city has to offer. If your time is limited, you should not miss the **Castle and Cathedral** on Wawel hill (walk 5), which could take up the best part of a day, the **Church of St Mary** on the Market Square (walk 1), and the University Quarter (walk 6), with its oldest college building—**Collegium Maius**. Equally fascinating are two of the walks beyond the Old Town which follow a specific theme: walk 1, taking you through the former **Jewish district of Kazimierz**, and walk 6, which looks at Kraków's Stalinist legacy in the suburb of **Nowa Huta**. On a fine day, you could climb the **Kościuszko Mound** (walk 9) for a panoramic view of the city, or head upstream along the Vistula to the secluded **monasteries at Bielany and Tyniec** (walks 1 and 2; *Beyond the city*).

Some visitors to Kraków come for one reason only: to see the **Nazi concentration camp of Auschwitz-Birkenau**, 50km to the west. However, several other interesting day trips are listed in this Guide. A mere 12km to the southeast lies Wieliczka with its extraordinary **11C salt mine**, another UNESCO World Heritage site, while to the northwest extend the grottoes and cliff-top castles of the **Ojców National Park**. Hikers and skiers might spend a weekend in **Zakopane**, a popular resort at the foot of the picturesque Tatra Mountains. Further to the east lies a lower, but no less spectacular range—**the Pieniny**—where you can navigate the dramatic Dunajec gorge by raft, or go on walks through beautiful landscape.

PRACTICAL INFORMATION

 Planning your trip

When to go

Kraków has a temperate climate which is more continental than Britain's, with colder winters and warmer summers. The average daytime temperature in July, the hottest month, is 23°C, though in recent years daily temperatures in excess of 30°C have been common. Summer (July/August) is not the best time to visit due to the large volume of tourist traffic. Accommodation is scarce, the air is hot and humid, and the pollution makes itself felt. Early autumn (September) is attractive due to the numerous cultural events and mild temperatures, but it also has the highest rainfall. The first snowfalls usually come in November, and 'white Christmases' are the rule. January and February are the coldest winter months, when average temperatures drop to below freezing. During exceptionally cold winters temperatures as low as minus 20°C have been recorded. If you visit at these times, warm clothing is essential. Winter tourism (December–March) is popular in Kraków due to the proximity of the Tatra Mountains. There is usually plenty of snow there for skiing enthusiasts, though the few resorts and inadequate infrastructure cannot cope with all the tourist traffic, and the more determined will often go further afield to Slovakia. Spring (April–June) is the best season for sightseeing. May and June have many sunny days with clear skies, and there is usually much in the way of cultural events and entertainment.

Entry requirements

Visas are no longer required of EU and US citizens to enter Poland. The maximum period of stay is six months for UK citizens and three months for US citizens. To extend this period, you should apply to the Passport Office (*Urząd Paszportowy*), Visa Department (*Oddział wiz*), ul. Św Sebastiana 9–11, ☎ 422 0913, ☎ 422 7170, fax 422 3019). You will need to show proof of temporary residence in Poland (if you are renting an apartment, this should be arranged through your landlord).

Canadian and Australian citizens must have a tourist visa to enter Poland. These are issued for a maximum of ninety days, but cannot be extended within Poland. Tourist visas are single-, double- or multiple-entry and may be used up to six months from their date of issue. Applicants must have a full passport that is valid for at least one month after the expiry date of the visa.

Transit visas, which may be purchased at the border, are valid for 48 hours and are only issued if you can show a visa (if required) for your next country of destination; you must also enter and leave Poland through different border crossings.

Polish tourist boards

The Polish National Tourist Office (addresses below) will provide you with information on visiting Kraków.

- **UK** Remo House, First Floor, 310–312 Regent St, London W1N 5AJ, ☎ (020) 7580 8811, fax (020) 7580 8866, www.pnto.dial.pipex.com.

- **USA** 275 Madison Ave, Suite 1711, New York, NY 10016, ☎ (212) 338 9412, www.polandtour.org.

Tour operators

Listed below are Polish-run tour operators with a proven track record in travel and tourism:

UK

- *Polorbis*, 82 Mortimer St, London W1, ☎ (020) 7637 4971, fax (020) 7436 6558.
- *Danube Travel*, 45 Great Cumberland Place, London W1H 7LH, (202) 7724 7577, fax (020) 7224 8959, e-mail:holidays@danubetravel.freeserve.co.uk
- *Gem Tazab Travel*, 273 Old Brompton Rd, London SW5 9JB, ☎ (020) 7341 2600, fax (020) 7373 1141.
- *Martin Randall Travel Ltd*, 10 Barley Mow Passage, London W4 4PH, (202) 8742 3355, fax (020) 8742 7766, e-mail:info@martinrandall.co.uk

USA

- *Orbis*, 342 Madison Ave, Suite 1512, New York, NY 10173, ☎ (212) 867 5011.

Polish embassies and consulates abroad

- **UK** 73 New Cavendish St, London W1N 4HQ, ☎ (020) 7580 0476; 2 Kinner Road, Edinburgh EH3 5PE, ☎ (0131) 552 0301.
- **USA** 2640 16th St NW, Washington DC 20009, ☎ (202) 234 3800; Madison Ave, New York, NY 10016, ☎ (212) 889 8360.
- **Australia** 10 Trelawny St, Wollahara, Sydney, NSW 2025, ☎ (02) 9363 9816.
- **Canada** 443 Daly St, Ottawa, Ontario K1N 6H3, ☎ (613) 789 0468, ☎ (789) 3376/77; 1500 Pine Ave West, Montreal, Quebec, H3G 1 B4, ☎ (514) 937 9481.

Consulates in Kraków

- **UK** Honorary Consulate, ul. Św. Anny 9, ☎ 421 7030, fax 422 4264.
- **USA** ul. Stolarska 9, ☎ 429 6655, fax 421 8292, www.usconsulate.krakow.pl

Customs

Import regulations Visitors can bring the following items into Poland duty free: articles for personal use connected with the length and purpose of stay, including one of each of the following: a personal computer, VCR, cassette player, radio, TV etc., together with accessories such as cassettes/video tapes/CDs/diskettes (10 of each), a portable musical instrument, surfboard, kayak, bicycle, tent, binoculars and one pair of skis. Two still cameras and one cine/video camera together with accessories and ten rolls of film are allowed. Permits issued by a Polish consulate are needed for sporting or hunting guns, hand guns and air pistols. Visitors may import precious jewellery provided its total weight does not exceed 50g as well as gifts and souvenirs not exceeding 100 $US in total value. In addition, adults may bring in the following alcoholic beverages and tobacco products: 0.5 litre of spirits, 0.75 litre of wine, 1 litre of beer, 250 cigarettes or 50 cigars or 250g of tobacco.

Export regulations Gifts and souvenirs not exceeding 100 $US in total value may be taken out of Poland duty free. The export regulations for alcoholic beverages and tobacco products are the same as for import. Special export licences are required for any items (including works of art, furniture etc.) manufactured prior to 9 May 1945. The licences are issued by the Conservator-General (*Generalny Konserwator Zabytków*) in Warsaw, ☎ (0-22) 826 5751, but the procedure can be time-consuming. You will be charged a flat rate of 25per cent on the value of the item you intend to export.

Currency and banks

There is no compulsory currency exchange in Poland. You may bring in as much foreign currency as you wish, but you will not be able to (re)export more than the equivalent of 5000 Euro unless you fill out a currency declaration upon arrival. If you have money sent directly to you in Poland, you will need a bank certificate (equivalent to a customs declaration) to take it out of the country again, if the sum exceeds 5000 Euro. As Polish currency—the **złoty** (abbreviated to zł or PLN)—is only internally convertible, there is no point in exporting it. Before leaving Poland, you should convert all your złoty into pounds/dollars or some other foreign currency. It is a good idea to have a small amount of złotys on arrival as the exchange rates at the airport are invariably bad. Most high-street banks will order Polish currency for you, though this may take a day or two.

The Polish złoty comes in the following denominations: banknotes: 200, 100, 50, 20, 10; coins: 5, 2, 1. One złoty contains 100 grosz (gr.), denominated as follows: 50, 20, 10, 5, 2, 1. You should be careful when handling Polish banknotes, and on no account accept any note that has three zeros or more—this is the old money that went out of circulation in January 1997. The best place to change cash is at a *kantor* (private exchange office), as they offer better rates than banks and are plentiful in the city. The following are all located in the Old Town: ul. Szewska 21 (open Mon–Fri 08.00–21.00, Sat 08.00–18.00), ul. Grodzka 13. (open Mon–Fri 09.00–19.00, Sat 09.00–15.00), Rynek Główny 9 (open Mon–Fri 09.00–18.00, Sat 10.00–15.00), Rynek Główny Pasaż Hawełka (open Mon–Fri 09.00–19.00, Sat 09.00–16.00, Sun 10.00–14.00), ul. Floriańska 40 (open Mon–Sat 09.00–20.00, Sun 10.00–18.00). There is a *kantor* inside the main railway station (open Mon–Fri 08.00–18.00, Sat 0800–12.00) and another one on the square opposite (open daily 06.00–20.00). If you are bringing cash to Poland, be careful not to bring any marked or damaged foreign notes, as banks and *kantors* will often refuse to accept them.

Nowadays, credit and debit cards are widely used, and indeed Polish banks offer Visa and Mastercards to their customers. Most hotels and travel agencies, many supermarkets and some shops and restaurants now accept plastic. Transactions are basically secure. Selected banks and hotels will give cash advances on most major cards, but it may be simpler to use a cash dispenser (*bankomat*). There are dispensers at ul. Wiślna 6, ul. Karmelicka 9, Rynek Główny 41, Rynek Główny 47, ul. Szpitalna 38, ul. Basztowa 15, ul. Sienna 14, ul. Sławkowska 20 and ul. Floriańska 6. In case of loss or theft of a **credit card**, you should immediately stop the card by phoning your bank's emergency number, or by contacting PolCard Ltd, Warsaw, ☎ (0-22) 827 4513, ☎ 827 3040 (24hr service).

Banks offer a slightly worse rate on travellers cheques than on cash and charge up to two per cent commission; hotels charge even more, and *kantors* do not accept them at all. You will always need proof of identity to change travellers cheques. The American Express desk inside the Orbis office at Rynek Główny 41 issues, cashes and refunds travellers cheques and will arrange **international**

money transfers for American Express cardholders. The latter can also be arranged through Western Union at ul. Dietla 68 (☎ 422 7672; inside the Prosper Bank) and at ul. Miodowa 11 (☎ 422 4202).

Health and insurance

Britain (but not the US) has a reciprocal agreement with Poland which entitles British citizens to free medical and dental care in case of accidents or emergencies, including transport to hospital. Proof of ID is required. All other medical and dental care will be charged. It is best to take out private travel/health insurance for your stay in Poland as the costs are minimal compared to the potential benefits.

For minor ailments it is best to go to a private clinic (*klinika prywatna*) or medical co-operative. *Medicover* at ul. Krótka 1 (☎ 421 7038, ☎ 429 4130) has English-speaking doctors, who also do home visits, payable in cash. There are also two good clinics on the Market Square: *Lekarska Spółdzielnia Pracy*, Rynek Główny 37 (open Mon–Fri 7.00–19.00, ☎ 422 8821, ☎ 422 2933, ☎ 422 2953) and *Profimed*, Rynek Główny 6, 1st floor (open Mon–Fri 8.00–20.00, Sat 09.00–13.00, ☎ 421 7997). Hotels often have their own medical services and will arrange visits for you if they do not.

There are no compulsory inoculations required of people arriving from the EU or US, although some doctors advise getting a hepatitis A vaccination. The tapwater is officially drinkable, but it doesn't taste too good. Boil it before use, or, better still, simply stick to mineral water, which is easily obtained in shops, restaurants and hotels.

Pharmacies (*apteki*) are run by qualified staff and have a wide selection of foreign and domestic medications. Prescriptions made out by doctors abroad are usually honoured. The pharmacies at ul. Mogilska 21 and ul. Kalwaryjska 94 are open 24hrs, seven days a week. Other pharmacies operate weekend and night shifts according to a rota system. For details, check the notices posted outside—the keyword is (*nocny*) *dyżur* (night) shift. The following chemists are all located in the city centre: Rynek Główny 13 (Market Square; open Mon–Fri 09.00–21.00, Sat and Sun 10.00–16.00); ul. Szczepańska 1 (open Mon–Fri 08.00–20.00, Sat 08.00–14.00); ul. Lubicz 7 (near the main railway station; open Mon–Fri 08.00–20.00, Sat 08.00–15.00); ul. Mikołajska 4 (open Mon–Fri 08.00–20.00, Sat 08.00–15.00).

Disabled travellers

Poland is well behind Western countries in terms of provision for disabled travellers. In Kraków, the main post office, a few museums, cinemas and modern hotels have wheelchair access, but in general facilities are few and far between. The information centre for the disabled (*Polskie Towarzystwo Walki z Kalectwem*, ul. Dunajewskiego 5) takes calls on Mon and Wed 15.00–17.00 (☎ 422 2811). One 'radio taxi' company (☎ 96-33) has special cars for disabled travellers, but you will need to book a day in advance. For more information on travel abroad, contact the Royal Association for Disability and Rehabilitation, 12 City Forum, 250 City Road, London, ☎ (020) 7250 3222.

Getting there

By air

Both *LOT* and *British Airways* run daily flights between London and Kraków. The journey time is approximately 2 hours 35 minutes. *LOT* has direct, twice-weekly flights to Kraków from New York (7 hours 30 minutes) and Chicago (8 hours 30 minutes). There are also direct connections between Kraków and many European cities. If all the direct flights are fully booked, the obvious option is to fly to Warsaw and then on to Kraków by *LOT*'s domestic service (twice daily, 40 minute flight time) or by train (2 hours 30 minutes). Flights to Warsaw are more plentiful and may be cheaper than to Kraków. *British Midland* runs cheap flights from the UK to Warsaw during the summer months. It is worth checking other airlines for similar deals.

Information about reservations and tickets is available at *LOT* offices abroad: London, 313 Regent St, ☎ (020) 7580 5037; New York, 500 Fifth Ave, Suite 408, NY 10110, ☎ (212) 869 1074. You can also make reservations on-line at www.lot.com and www.britishairways.com. The cheapest tickets are Apex, which must be bought well in advance and have various restrictions including fixed journey dates. If you change these dates at a later stage you will lose the Apex discount and the penalties are harsh if you cancel altogether. Regular economy class tickets are valid for up to one year but can be twice as expensive as Apex. It is worth checking the press for operators offering one- or two-week package deals, as these can often work out cheaper than the price of a regular ticket. 'Bucket shops' are also an option. All ticket prices vary with the season. In general, they are lowest in February/March and October/November.

On arrival

Kraków airport is at Balice, 15km west of the city centre (☎ 411 1955). Though recently modernised, it does not have all the services found at large international airports. Notably, there is no duty free shop for departing passengers, although on the first floor you can buy gifts and souvenirs, including Polish vodka. The electronic billboard in the main hall gives up-to-the-minute information on available rooms in hotels around the city. This is very useful if you have no pre-booked accommodation. A special metro line from the airport to the main railway station is under construction, but for the moment you will have to rely on buses or taxis. The quickest way to reach the centre of Kraków by public transport is on bus no. 152, which goes to the *Cracovia* Hotel and then to the main railway station; no. 208 runs from the airport to pl. Nowy Kleparz, 15 minutes' walk from the Market Square (for ticket details, see *Getting around*). A journey by 'radio taxi' (see *Taxis*) into the centre should take around 25 minutes. Provided you summon it by phone, it should cost you approximately 30 PLN (8 $US). Taking a taxi from the rank may cost significantly more, though you could try to negotiate a set price with the driver. Many taxis now accept credit cards.

By rail

The journey from London to Kraków, via Brussels (Eurostar), Cologne and Berlin, takes about 24 hours. It is marginally cheaper to take the long ferry crossing between Harwich and the Hook-of-Holland, but this will add to your journey time. Taking the train only pays if you are under 26, as the standard ticket costs more than an Apex flight, although unlimited stopovers are allowed. An increasingly popular option is to fly to Vienna, Prague, Budapest or Berlin and then continue by train to Kraków. This cuts down on journey time and may even be cheaper than travelling direct, as bargain flights to these cities are plentiful. Train tickets can be bought at *Rail Europe*, Victoria Station, London SW1, ☎ 0990 848 848, and *Usit Travel*, 52 Grosvenor Gardens, London SW1, ☎ (020) 7730 3402. Inter-Rail passes are valid in Poland.

On arrival

The **main railway station** is Kraków Główny (pl. Kolejowy, ☎ 9313, ☎ 422 4182 domestic, ☎ 422 2248 international). It has been recently refurbished and has all the usual facilities, including money exchange, left luggage lockers, and two clean and modern restaurants, one self-service. The electronic billboard in the main hall gives up-to-the-minute information on available rooms in hotels around the city. There is a post office on the square opposite the station, as well as numerous stalls selling food and miscellaneous goods. Walk through the underpass to get to the Market Square (10 minutes). The whole area around the station is being redeveloped, with the first stage of work set to finish in 2002. When complete, the complex will include a multi-storey car park, hotels, offices, supermarkets etc.

By coach

This is the cheapest way of getting to Kraków, but also the most exhausting. The journey from London can take up to 36 hours depending on the company and route. *Eurolines* (a branch of National Express), 52 Grosvenor Gardens, London SW1, ☎ (020) 7730 8235, has air-conditioned coaches with video and toilets and provides the most comfortable and reliable service from the UK. Alternatively, you could try one of the Polish-run companies, such as *White Eagle Lines*, 200 Earls Court Rd, London SW5, ☎ (020) 7244 0054, which offers a good service at competitive rates, as do the tour operators Gem Tazab and Fregata (see *Tour operators*).

On arrival

The **main bus station** (☎ 9316 domestic, ☎ 421 0240 international) is situated next to the main railway station. Coaches leave from here to many domestic and foreign destinations. There are also private mini-bus services to nearby towns and villages. The bus station has not been modernised for years and has few modern facilities. A new one is being built under the redevelopment programme.

By car

From the UK, the quickest route to Kraków is via Brussels, Hannover and Berlin, crossing the Polish border at Forst-Olszyna (but beware that the first stretch of the E-30 on the Polish side is in poor condition). The distance from the French or Belgian coast to Kraków is about 1500km and the journey takes roughly 24 hours. Petrol is cheaper in Poland than in Germany, so it is best to fill your tank on the Polish side of the border. If entering from Slovakia, the fastest crossing is at Trstená–Chyżne, but alternatively you could try the scenic crossing at Javorina–Łysa Polana in the heart of the Tatra Mountains. Another picturesque crossing is at Harrachov (Czech Republic)–Jakuszyce. All the above border crossings are open 24 hours.

To drive a foreign-registered car in Poland you must have: a driving licence, car registration documents, a country sticker and Green Card insurance (see, also,

Getting around). The latter can be purchased at the **Polish Motoring Association** (**PZM**), which has offices at all border crossings. The PZM also sells maps and guides and provides general information on travel in Poland. At all times your car should also carry, by law, a warning triangle for breakdowns, a fire extinguisher, and a first aid kit. Until recently, an international driving licence was required to drive a foreign-registered car in Poland, but nowadays licences from EU countries and the US are respected. However, you will need an international licence if you intend to drive abroad in a car registered in Poland.

On dual carriageways be warned that overtaking on the inside is common, so care should be taken when changing lanes. Seatbelts are compulsory in the front and back seats and children under 12 must sit at the back. The speed limit is 60kph in built-up areas including villages (operative from the white sign with the place name), 90kph on open roads (and when travelling through villages if the place sign is green), 110kph on expressways, and 130kph on motorways (minimum speed is 40kph). Radar speed traps are common. From 1 November to 30 March headlights must be switched on at all times, regardless of weather conditions. The allowable alcohol limit for driving is very low (a small beer) and the penalties are high if you're caught with more. Random breathalyser tests are used. All accidents should be immediately reported to the police to determine damage and liability. If your car breaks down, contact the **Polish Motoring Association** (**PZM**), which has a nation-wide emergency breakdown service (☎ 981).

 Where to stay

Hotel accommodation can be booked direct (see the listings below for addresses and telephone numbers) or through British- and US-based agencies before arrival (see *Tour operators*). Reservations can also be made through the Internet at www.pol-hotels.com, a good website with up-to-date prices and information. The busiest period is June to September, and if you visit at this time you should always book in advance. Prior booking is also recommended at other times, especially if you visit during major festivals (eg Kraków 2000). For a double room with breakfast in a superior Kraków hotel you should expect to pay upwards of $US130 per night. The price for a similar room in a bottom-end hotel starts at around $US50. Guest houses (pensions) start at around $US30 per night. Most hotels are located within the Old Town or close by. Even the out-of-town ones, such as the **Orbis-Continental**, are only a matter of minutes from the centre of Kraków by bus or taxi.

Hotel categories Polish hotels follow the international classification system, with categories ranging from one to five stars. This is misleading, however, as most two-star hotels in Kraków are well-located, clean, comfortable and perfectly adequate to most visitors' needs. Four-star hotels are much larger and will inevitably offer a wide range of services and facilities, but many of these (eg conference rooms, computers, modems, faxes) are geared towards business travellers and are rarely used by the average visitor. If you are looking for a hotel with basic facilities, and don't have unlimited funds, then two- or three-star establishments are the best bet. All hotels from two-star upwards have private bathrooms. The hotels listed below are arranged by price category (expensive, moderate, inexpensive).

Hotel charges Due to the general shortage of accommodation in Kraków (construction doesn't keep up with the tourist influx), hotels have few single rooms and often charge the same rate for singles as for doubles. All hotels charge per room, not per person. However, if you are travelling alone and are put in a double room, it is worth trying to negotiate the price. Many hotel staff speak English and/or other foreign languages, so communication shouldn't be a problem. Some hotels offer cheaper rates in winter or for long stays. Check-out time is usually 12.00, but you will normally be allowed to leave your luggage at reception if required. Restaurants and cafés in Kraków rarely offer extensive breakfast menus, so if you are used to having a substantial morning meal, it may be best to reserve a room with breakfast. In any case, when booking you should always ask if breakfast is included in the price. Telephone calls from hotels may be expensive, and it is usually cheaper to use a public card phone (available at kiosks and post offices). International calls arranged through *AT&T, MCI* or *Sprint* are even cheaper. Before you arrive, ask your phone company for up-to-date numbers of their operators in Kraków. Most hotels have extra beds which can be put into rooms so that children can be with their parents. Some will charge for this, others not—ask when making your reservation. For English-speaking babysitters, a reputable agency is *Agencja Topolino*, ul. Friedleina, ☎ 633 0662 (10.00–16.00).

Recommended hotels
The listed prices are for a double room with bathroom.

Expensive
☆☆☆☆
Elektor ul. Szpitalna 28, ☎ 423 2317, fax 423 2327. Luxury hotel contained inside a 19C town-house. Centrally located between the station and the Market Square. Guarded car park nearby. Business services. 15 rooms, some overlooking the Słowacki Theatre (see p. 139). Good, reasonably-priced restaurant and wine bar. The hotel annexe at ul. Św. Marka 29 has four one-bedroom and two studio-type apartments. Ask at the main reception desk for details. **$US190–250** (depending on the floor).

Orbis-Forum ul. M. Konopnickiej 28, ☎ 261 9212, fax 269 0080. Huge 1970s building situated on the south bank of the Vistula, overlooking Wawel Castle. Nine conference rooms, business centre, travel services, air conditioning, wheelchair access, car park, swimming pool, sauna, tennis courts, night club, top-floor café. 276 rooms. **$US189**.

Grand ul. Sławkowska 5/7, ☎ 421 7255, fax 421 8360. Situated a few metres from the Market Square. Plush restaurant with turn-of-the-century decor. Wheelchair access. 60 rooms. **$US189**.

Copernicus ul. Kanonicza 16, ☎ 431 1044, 431 1055, fax 431 1140. Very elegant hotel situated in a beautiful street leading up to Wawel Castle. Painstakingly restored, the 14C building was opened as a hotel in the spring of 2000. Original 16C frescoes and ceilings are preserved in some of the rooms. Air conditioning, business services, fitness club. 29 rooms. **$US162**.

☆☆☆
Orbis-Continental ul. Armii Krajowej 11, ☎ 637 5044, or ☎ 423 8622, fax 637

5938. Situated in an out-of-town residential district, within easy reach of the E-40 motorway (16km from the airport, 4km from the city centre). The largest hotel in Kraków. Travel office, indoor swimming pool, sauna, casino, car park, business services, air conditioning, wheelchair access. 304 rooms (including two for disabled guests). Views onto the Kościuszko Mound (see p. 158). **$US130.**

Ester ul. Szeroka 20, ☎ 429 1188, fax 429 1233. Newly-opened hotel situated in the heart of Jewish Kazimierz (see p. 140). Air-conditioned restaurant serving European and Jewish cuisine. Wheelchair access. Conference room, parking space on the square (ul. Szeroka). 24 rooms, some facing the Old Synagogue (see p. 141). **$US135.**

Orbis-Francuski ul. Pijarska 13, ☎ 422 5122, fax 422 5270. Elegant, turn-of-the-century building in a quiet, Old Town location. Business services, car rental. Pets permitted. French restaurant. 42 rooms. **$US153.**

Moderate

☆☆☆☆

Demel ul. Głowackiego 22, ☎ 636 1600, fax 636 4513. Recently opened establishment located in the suburb of Bronowice, 4 km from the city centre. Car park, two conference rooms, swimming pool, sauna, fitness club, wheelchair access, air-conditioned apartments. 58 rooms. **$US110.**

☆☆☆

Orbis-Cracovia al. Focha 1, ☎ 422 8666, fax 421 9586. Grandiose, communist-style building situated opposite the National Museum (see p. 156 and next to a noisy thoroughfare (al. Krasińskiego). Orbis travel office, car rental, car park, business services, laundry, wheelchair access. Pets permitted. 309 rooms, some overlooking the Błonia common (see p. 156). Ten minutes' walk from the Market Square. **$US116.**

FM Pod Kopcem al. Waszyngtona 1, ☎ 427 0355, or ☎ 427 1355, fax 427 0101. Situated by the Kościuszko Mound, within the walls of a 19C Austrian fort (see p. 158). In the same building is the RMF FM radio station. Quiet, leafy surroundings. Car rental, car park, wheelchair access. Restaurant currently under renovation. 11 rooms. **$US120.**

Kazimierz ul. Miodowa 16, ☎ 421 6629, fax 422 2884. A small and inconspicuous hotel located in the former Jewish district (see p. 140). 16 rooms. **$US90.**

Logos ul. Szujskiego 3, ☎ 632 3333, fax 632 4210. Modern establishment situated in a quiet side-street just outside the Old Town. 115 rooms. **$US96.**

Piast ul. Radzikowskiego 109, ☎ 636 4600; fax 636 4774. Situated on a busy roundabout, 5km from Balice airport. Conference facilities, tennis court, guarded car park. 158 rooms (including rooms for disabled guests). **$US92–129.**

Pod Różą ul. Floriańska 14, ☎ 422 1244, fax 421 7513. Historic 16C building (see p. 104) situated on the Old Town's busiest street. Two restaurants, including the *Amarone* serving Italian cuisine (see *Restaurants*). Air-conditioned apartments. Nearest car park on pl. Szczepański. 54 rooms. **$US102.**

Polski Pod Białym Orłem ul. Pijarska 17, ☎ 422 1144, fax 422 1426. Central location, opposite the medieval city walls. 54 rooms. **$US105.**

Rezydent ul. Grodzka 9, ☎ 429 5018, ☎ 429 5410, fax 429 5576. Located on one of the city's showpiece streets, south of the Market Square. Eight one-bedroom apartments contained in 14C–15C interiors. Business centre. **$US90.** In the cellars of the same building is the excellent *Krew i Róża* restaurant (see *Restaurants*).

Royal ul. Św. Gertrudy 26-29, ☎ 421 3500, fax 421 5857. Known for many years as the *Garnizonowy* (garrison), the *Royal* was originally built as a hotel for Austrian army officers, and is today still frequented by the military. The building retains much of its Art Nouveau elegance and is situated opposite Wawel Castle. ✩✩✩ rooms at **$US107**, ✩✩ rooms at **$US70**.

Orbis-Wanda ul. Armii Krajowej 15, ☎ 637 1677, fax 637 8518. A motel situated next to the *Orbis-Continental*. Car park, swimming pool, garden, wheelchair access. Pets permitted. 80 rooms. **$US90–108**.

✩✩

Ibis ul. Przy Rondzie 2, ☎ 421 8188, fax 411 4794. Modern hotel situated in an ugly part of Kraków, east of the main railway station. Car park, business facilities. 221 rooms. **$US127**.

Inexpensive
✩✩✩

Europejski ul. Lubicz 5, ☎ 423 2510, fax 423 2529. The best of the hotels close to the main railway station. Recently refurbished, but often full. 56 rooms. **$US83**.

Fortuna Bis ul Piłsudskiego 25, ☎ 430 1025, fax 430 1077. Slightly more expensive than its sister hotel, the *Fortuna* (see below), but immaculately clean and with a good, on-site African restaurant—the *Kassumay*. Central location, 5 minutes' walk from the Market Square. 23 rooms. **$US70**.

Pollera ul. Szpitalna 30, ☎ 422 1044, ☎ 422 1128, fax 422 1389. Early 19C building with slightly poky rooms and basic facilities, but excellent value nonetheless. Guarded car park nearby. Restaurant contained inside a former ballroom. 42 rooms, some overlooking the Słowacki Theatre (see p. 139). **$US91**.

Polonia ul. Basztowa 25, ☎ 422 1233, fax 422 1621. Recently modernised and conveniently located (3 minutes' walk from the main railway station). Air-conditioned apartments. Underground car park. Travel office. 69 rooms. **$US50**.

Wawel Tourist ul. Poselska 22, ☎ 422 1301, fax 422 0439. Situated in a side-street close to the Market Square. Modern, unpretentious, and excellent value. Prior booking essential. 23 rooms. **$US50**.

Wit Stwosz ul. Mikołajska 28, ☎ 429 6026, fax 429 6139. Small, church-owned hotel with stylish interiors, situated right opposite the *Planty*. Friendly atmosphere. Nearest car park by the *Dom Turysty Hotel* (50m). No wheelchair access. **$US50–65**.

✩✩

Alef ul. Szeroka 17, ☎ 421 3870. Situated in the heart of Jewish Kazimierz. Good restaurant serving non-kosher Jewish cuisine. 5 apartments with pre-war furnishings. Prior booking essential. **$US70**.

Fortuna ul. Czapskich 5, ☎/fax 422 3143, ☎ 430 1004, ☎ 411 0806. A small hotel with stylish interiors in a quiet central location (5 minutes' walk from the Market Square). Good value. 25 rooms. **$US65**.

Dom Turysty ul. Westerplatte 15, ☎ 422 9566, ☎/fax 422 5719. Ugly 1970s building, 5 minutes' walk from the main railway station. The recently refurbished interiors have been converted from hostel accommodation into a hotel proper. Travel agency, car park, bingo hall, fitness centre (see *Fitness Clubs*). 384 rooms. **$US70**.

Klezmer Hois ul Szeroka 6, ☎ 411 1245, fax 411 1622. Quiet, atmospheric hotel with 19C furnishings, situated in the building of the former Jewish *mikvah* (ritual bath). 10 rooms. Prior booking essential. **$US70**.

Mini pl. Wolnica 7, ☎ 656 2467, fax 656 5956. With only 4 rooms, the *Mini* certainly lives up to its name. Situated opposite Kazmierz's 16C Town Hall (see p. 145). *Thien Long* Vietnamese restaurant in the same building (see *Restaurants*). **$US55**.

Saski ul. Sławkowska 3, ☎ 421 4222, fax 421 4830. Somewhat overshadowed by the neighbouring *Grand*, but good value considering its location. Chinese restaurant. 62 rooms. **$US69**.

Pensions (pensjonaty)

Pensions, or guest houses, are a cheap alternative to hotels. Unfortunately, very few are located in the city centre. The better ones will offer private bathrooms and half or full board. Some have basic catering facilities. Local travel agents can make reservations.

☆☆

Rycerska pl. Na Groblach 22, ☎ 422 6082, fax 422 3399. Close to Wawel Castle. 16 rooms, some with fine views. **$US35**.

Jagiellonian University Guest House (*Dom Gościnny UJ*), ul. Floriańska 49, ☎ 421 1225. Very central. Small, well-run, but usually full. Book well in advance. 22 rooms. **$US65**.

☆

Krystyna ul. Lusińska 9B, ☎ 654 7165, ☎ 654 7191, fax 654 7856. Situated in the southern suburb of Swoszowice. 60 rooms. From the city centre, take tram nos 8, 19, 22 or 23 to the terminus in Borek Fałęcki, followed by bus nos 101, 145, or 225. **$US33**.

Pensjonat Stowarzyszenia Architektów Polskich SARP, ul. Floriańska 39, ☎/fax 429 1778. Very central. Reception on the fourth floor. Run by the Polish Architects' Association. 6 rooms with catering facilities and shared bathrooms. Book well in advance. **$US44**.

Perła ul. Zakopiańska 180B, ☎ 267 3192. Situated on the Zakopane road (see p. 176). Restaurant, car park. From the city centre, take tram nos 8, 19, 22 or 23 to the terminus in Borek Fałęcki, followed by bus nos 101, 145, 165, 235, 245, 255, 275 or 285. **$US35**.

Private rooms

Private rooms are usually part of the owner's house or flat, but normally you will be given your own key and have full freedom of movement. The Waweltur office at ul. Pawia 8 (☎ 422 1921) and some tourist agencies (see *Tourist Information*) can arrange accommodation in private lodgings.

Student dormitories

Cheap summer accommodation in student dormitories can be arranged through the *Almatur* student organisation (ul. Grodzka 2, ☎ 422 4668, ☎/fax 428 4520; open Mon–Fri 09.00–18.00, Sat 10.30–14.30). Some dormitories also offer rooms to tourists throughout the year, but out of season (i.e. during term time) you should book in advance. Facilities are basic, with shared toilets and bathrooms, but standards are continually improving. There will usually be at least some double rooms with private bathroom, for which you should expect to pay around **$US20–40**. Curfews may apply—ask at reception.

All the places below (except **Bratniak** and **Instytut Polonijny**) are located in or close to the student campus (*miasteczko studenckie*), west of the city centre.

Bratniak ul. Jabłonowskich 10/12, ☎ 422 6100. Dormitory run by the Academy of Agriculture. Excellent location, 3 minutes' walk from the Market Square.

Hotel Nauczycielski, ul. Lubelska 23, ☎ 633 4169. Teachers' hotel with shared catering facilities on each floor.

Instytut Polonijny (Polonia Institute), Przegorzały, ul Jodłowa 13, ☎ 429 9211, fax 429 9351. High-standard dormitory scenically located on a hill in the suburb of Przegorzały. For transport details, see p. 158. 70 rooms.

Letni, ul. Bydgoska 19, ☎/fax 423 7932. 500 beds. From the main railway station, tram nos 4, 12, 14 or bus no. 208.

Nawojka, ul. Reymonta 11, ☎ 633 5205, fax 633 3936. Student dormitory situated near the Wisła football stadium. 300 beds, some available all year round. From the main railway station, bus nos 139, 159, 179 or 208.

Piast, ul. Piastowska 47, ☎ 637 4933, fax 637 2176. Large student dormitory with 50 rooms available all year round and many more in summer. Café, bar, Chinese restaurant, post office, laundry. From the main railway station, tram nos 4, 12, 14, or bus no. 208.

Żaczek, al. 3 Maja 5, ☎ 633 5477, fax 633 1914. Large and lively dormitory overlooking the Błonia common (see p. 156). 600 beds. Holders of *Euro 26* cards are entitled to a 10 per cent discount. From the main railway station, tram no. 15 or bus nos 119 or 179.

Youth hostels

Youth Hostels (*schroniska młodzieżowe*), the cheapest form of accommodation, are run by the PTSM, a national organisation affiliated to the **International Youth Hostel Federation** (IYHF). Holders of IYHF cards are eligible for a 25 per cent discount. Facilities are very basic, with multi-person rooms and shared bathrooms. Curfews apply. Some hostels are open all year round, others in summer only. Visitors of all ages are welcome. For more information, contact the local office of the PTSM at ul. Oleandry 4, ☎ 633 8822, fax 633 8920. You should expect to pay around $US6 for a bed in a triple room.

Schronisko młodzieżowe, ul. Oleandry 4, ☎ 633 8822. Round the corner from the *Żaczek* student dormitory (see above). Rooms for 3, 6, 8 and 16 people.

Schronisko młodzieżowe, ul. Kościuszki 88, ☎ 422 1951. On the way to Salwator (see p. 156). 15–20 mins walk from the Market Square. Rooms for 18, 20 and 36 people.

Schronisko młodzieżowe, ul. Szablowskiego 1c, ☎ 637 2441. Close to the **Orbis-Continental** (see p. 18). From the main railway station, tram no. 4 or bus no. 208. Rooms for 14 people. July–August only.

Camp sites

Most camp sites are open in summer only (May–September), though some offer accommodation all the year round. Holders of FICC-AIT-FIA international camping carnets may get discounts.

Clepardia, ul. Mackiewicza 14, ☎ 415 9672. Open-air swimming pool.
Krak, ul. Radzikowskiego 99, ☎ 637 2957, ☎ 637 2122, ☎ 637 2532. Open all year. On site motel and caravan facilities.
Krakowianka, ul. Żywiecka Boczna 4, ☎ 266 4191. On site hotel.
Smok, ul. Kamedulska 18, ☎/fax 421 0255. Well-managed and scenically located in the suburb of Przegorzały (see p. 159).

Getting around

Maps

Maps in English, usually in dual-language versions, are readily available from the PTTK bookshop at ul. Jagiellońska 6° (*Sklep Podróżnika*; open Mon–Fri 11.00–19.00, Sat 10.00–15.00) as well as from bookshops and kiosks. A Kraków city map is definitely worth buying (ask for *plan miasta*) as it will provide additional information not covered in this Guide. Old city maps should be used with caution, as many street names honouring famous communists have been abandoned since 1989 in favour of original pre-war names or, in some cases, wholly new ones.

If you intend to go hiking in the Tatra Mountains (see p. 175) you should equip yourself with the *Tatrzański Park Narodowy* (Tatra National Park) topographical map, which covers the most important part of the Tatra Mountain region as well as the town of Zakopane. The scale is large enough to show hiking trails, shelters, and much else. Likewise, the *Pieniński Park Narodowy* and *Ojcowski Park Narodowy* maps are a must for hiking in the Pieniny Mountains (see p. 169) and Ojców National Park (see p. 172).

Public transport

Public transport—trams and buses—is cheap and efficient. In addition to normal services, there are: 'fast' buses (numbers beginning with a '5'), which stop at fewer places; night buses (numbers beginning with a '6'), which run from roughly 23.00–05.00, although it is always best to travel by taxi at night—safe, cheap and reliable; and suburban buses (numbers beginning with '2'), for which tickets cost 50 per cent more. There are also private minibus companies, useful for getting to out of town places (see *Days Out*).

Day services run from around 05.00–23.00 and can get very crowded at peak hours. Regular tickets can be bought in advance from any kiosk, or directly from the driver for a small surcharge (no change given). All public transport tickets are flat-rate and interchangeable (buses and trams), but cannot be used in other cities. You will need an extra ticket for each large piece of luggage. Tickets should be validated in the punching machines immediately after boarding. 'Plain clothes' inspectors will make fare dodgers pay an on-the-spot fine and will call the police if they cannot pay. Regular tickets (*bilet normalny*) are valid for one journey (if you change bus or tram you will need a new ticket). One-day (*bilet dzienny*), weekly (*bilet tygodniowy*), group (up to 20 people, *bilet grupowy*) and period tickets (*bilet czasowy*, expires one hour after validation) are available from the MPK (Municipal Transport Authority) office at the corner of ul. Studencka and ul. Dunajewskiego, or from any MPK booth—

there is one at the corner of ul. Szewska and ul. Podwale. Photographs are not required (only for monthly tickets). Smoking is forbidden on all forms of public transport.

Driving

Unless you know your way around, driving in the centre of Kraków can be a frustrating experience. There are many one-way streets, frequent road works and diversions, and three traffic zones (A, B and C). Zone A (basically the Market Square) is for pedestrians only. To drive in zone B (most of the Old Town) you need a special permit, which is only available to local residents. You may drive freely through zone C, but in order to park you have to buy a special pay-and-display ticket (*karta postojowa*), available from kiosks. These restrictions apply Mon–Fri 09.00–18.00. Do not at any time park in zones A or B—your car will be clamped or towed away. However, guests of hotels located in zone B are allowed to park outside their hotel during check-in and check-out (max. 15 minutes).

The two car parks closest to the Market Square are on pl. Szczepański (often full) and pl. Św. Ducha. There is also a large one above the platforms at the main railway station. It is usually best to leave your car where you are staying and travel into the centre by public transport, or simply walk. During the afternoon rush hour (15.00–18.00) the centre of Kraków gets very congested, though the situation may improve when the city's ring road is finally completed. Parking on the pavement is allowed, unless stated otherwise, provided at least 1.5m of walking room is left for pedestrians. Car theft is common and it is not advisable to leave your car unattended overnight. Use your hotel's own parking facilities or any guarded car park (*parking strzeżony*), such as at: ul. Powiśle (next to Wawel Castle); ul. Straszewskiego 14–16; main railway station; pl. Św Ducha; pl. Szczepański; al. Focha (in front of the *Cracovia* hotel); ul. Kałuży (next to the Cracovia stadium); al. Krasińskiego (in front of the National Museum). Valuables should never be left in your car at any time.

Fuel Most filling stations belong to the state-owned CPN chain, but an increasing number are owned by foreign companies. *BP* (al. 29 Listopada 39b), *Statoil* (al. Jana Pawła II 200), *Texaco* (al. Pokoju 65) and *Arge* (ul. Zakopiańska 290) all are open 24 hours. Other filling stations are usually open 06.00–22.00. Three types of petrol are available: regular (86 octane, only for very old vehicles), super (94 and 98 octane) and unleaded (95 and 98 octane). Diesel oil is called *olej napędowy* (look for the black ON symbol). Liquid gas refills can be bought at: *TG*, ul. Pachońskiego 5 (open Mon–Fri 06.00–20.00, Sat 06.00–16.00) and *BP*, ul. Wadowicka 4 (Mateczny roundabout, 24 hours).

Car hire

All the major international car-rental agencies have offices in Kraków (see below). You can book a car from abroad, but only a few agencies will allow you to return it outside of Poland. Rates are generally very high and it is worth checking the local press for cheaper domestic agencies, although bottom-end Polski Fiats should definitely be avoided. *Hertz* has an office at the airport, and some travel offices, such as *Orbis*, offer car rental services. To rent a car you will normally need a passport, credit card and a national driving licence that has been valid for at least a year (international licences are not required). The minimum age for car rental is 21 years.

Car-rental agencies

Amigo-Tourist, ul. Karmelicka 6, ☎ 422 2500.

Ann Rent-a-Car, Balice airport, ☎ 090 216 466 (www.ann-rent-a-car.com.pl). Unlimited mileage, payment by credit card only, long term rentals for companies, mini leasing, mini-bus service for VIPs and delegations.

Avis Poland, ul. Basztowa 15, ☎/fax 421 1066, or ☎ 422 7078. Fly & Drive, one-way service, mini-leasing.

Budget Car Rental, Motel Krak, ul. Radzikowskiego 99/101, ☎/fax 637 0089.

Europcar, ul. Krowoderska 58, ☎/fax 633 7773.

Express Rent-a-Car, ul. Konopnickiej 28 (Hotel *Forum*), ☎ 266 6468, fax 266 7913. Prices range from around $US65 per day (Ford Fiesta) to around $US110 (Ford Galaxy).

Hertz Rent-a-Car, al. Focha 1 (*Cracovia Hotel*), ☎ 637 1120, ☎ 429 6262, fax 422 2939 (www.hertz.com).

Joka Rent-a-Car, ul. Kałuży 1 (next to the Cracovia stadium), ☎/fax 429 6630, or ☎ 0601 545 368 (mobile).

Taxis

Taxis are cheap and plentiful and are a good way of getting around the city. Ranks are found at the airport, railway station and most hotels. Taxis can also be hailed in the street, but it is better to phone for a 'radio taxi' (which has the company name and telephone number displayed on top of the vehicle or along its side), as these are cheaper and more reliable than private taxis. Popular companies include: *Barbakan*, ☎ 9661, *Lajkonik*, ☎ 9628, *Mega*, ☎ 9625, *Metro*, ☎ 9667, and *Wawel*, ☎ 9666 (a full listing is given in the local press). When phoning, give your location address and the number from which you are calling. You can also ask for an English-speaking driver. Most taxis will take no more than 10 minutes to arrive, often less. On Sundays, public holidays, and between 22.00 and 06.00, the standard fare increases by 50 per cent. Meter rates do not apply on out-of-town journeys. This is the case, for instance, when travelling to the airport from town: the driver may try to charge you for the return journey, even if you are only going one way. In such instances, it is best to agree on a set price beforehand. By law taxis are not allowed to take more than four passengers and no amount of persuasion will help. The private cabs at the rank by the main railway station may charge twice as much as a 'radio taxi'. 'Radio taxis' are not allowed to queue at this rank, but they can pick up and drop passengers there. You can call for a 'radio taxi' from the public pay phones inside the station, or simply go up to the car park above the platforms, where the 'radio taxi' companies have their own rank.

 # Eating and drinking

Meal times reflect the working day, which can begin as early as 06.00, ending at 14.00 or 15.00. **Breakfast** (*śniadanie*) is usually solid, consisting of bread or rolls (*bułki*) served with sausage (*kiełbasa*, infinite in variety; try the local brand— *kiełbasa krakowska*), frankfurters (*parówki*), cheese and ham. Due to the proximity of the Tatra Mountains (the only sheep farming region in Poland), two traditional varieties of sheep's cheese are common in Kraków: *oscypek* (either smoked or non-smoked) and *bryndza* (cream cheese). Fried or scrambled eggs are often combined with bacon (*boczek*) or, in season, with wild mushrooms such as ceps (*borowiki*) or chantarelles (*kurki*). The excellent home-made jam (*konfitura*) is made from a variety of woodland fruits and berries.

Places on the Market Square serving breakfasts and morning snacks include the **Europejska**, **Hawełka** (see *Restaurants*) and the **Dom Polonii**, Rynek Główny 14 (open 09.00–22.00). The **Grand Hotel** (see p. 18) does a breakfast buffet from 07.00 to 11.00, also available to non-guests.

Most Cracovians eat their **main meal** (*obiad*) after work, at around 15.00, though in recent years the concept of 'lunch' has come into vogue. A standard *obiad* begins with soup, followed by a main dish and sometimes a dessert. **Soups** are tasty, nourishing—if a little oily—and usually a safe bet in restaurants. The two classic varieties are: *barszcz* (borscht), made of beetroot stock (fresh or fermented), and *żurek*, a delicious sour soup made from fermented rye flour. Restaurant menus vary with the season, and if you visit in late spring or summer you could try *zupa szczawiowa* (sorrel soup), or *chłodnik*, a speciality from the east of Poland, made from beetroot, cucumber, hard-boiled eggs, buttermilk and sour cream, and served cold. Another good starter is *śledź* (herring) in sour cream or oil, traditionally accompanied by a vodka aperitif. Some menus will list herring as '*po Krakowsku*' (Kraków-style), but this is really just gloss. Most dishes termed '*po Krakowsku*' rarely differ from their non-Cracovian equivalents, though duck Kraków-style (*kaczka po Krakowsku*), roasted with wild mushrooms and/or apples and served with boiled buckwheat, is unique to the region. Dedicated carnivores might try *talerz wédlin*—a platter of smoked meat usually comprising pork loin and varieties of smoked sausage.

The most commmon **main dishes** are beef, veal, pork and chicken. Lamb (*jagniécina*) and mutton (*baranina*) sometimes appear on restaurant menus thanks to Kraków's close links with the Polish highlands—the classic dish is baked leg of lamb (*udziec jagniécy*) served with potatoes. Meat and poultry are usually fried in batter, less often grilled (*z rusztu*), and served with a side salad consisting of fresh or marinated vegetables. The former is usually referred to as *sałatka*, the latter as *surówka*. Of the traditional dishes, best-known are *bigos* (meat stewed in sauerkraut), *kaszanka* (black pudding), *kiszka* (Polish haggis), *kasza gryczana w sosie* (buckwheat in a meaty sauce), *gołąbki* (stuffed cabbage leaves), and the formidable *golonko* (pork knuckle, baked or stewed in beer) for those with a mighty appetite. As with fish dishes, *golonko* is usually sold by weight, so the menu will specify the price per gram, not the price of what you are served. Trout, grilled or baked, is a popular local dish, but only worth ordering if fresh (*świeży*), not frozen (*mrożony*).

Dumplings (*pierogi*) are a Polish speciality and come in a variety of forms. The most popular savoury fillings are mince, cabbage, and cottage cheese mixed with mashed potatoes. The latter are known as *pierogi ruskie* ('Russian' dumplings), which, despite their name, have no particular connection with Russia or the east. In season, you will also get a choice of delicious fruit fillings, such as strawberries, blueberries, etc.

There is no better place to eat pierogi than the **Jadłodajnia U Pani Stasi** on ul. Mikołajska, just off the Market Square (see *Restaurants*).

For **dessert** you could try *sernik krakowski*, a locally-made cheesecake flavoured with vanilla, or *makowiec*, a traditional poppyseed cake. Like *pierogi*, pancakes (*naleśniki*) come with a choice of fillings, both sweet and savoury, and are often served with a cream, ice-cream or chocolate topping. Cafés (*kawiarnie*) are often the best place to eat cakes or desserts. **Coffee** comes in three *forms*—*parzona*, i.e. boiling water added directly to ground coffee, *z expresu* (expresso), and *rozpuszczalna* (instant). If you want cream, ask for *biała kawa* (white coffee). Tea is taken plain or with lemon, but never with milk—the latter combination is seen as a quaint British invention.

Supper, or *kolacja*, is a lighter meal, and usually eaten at around 19.00 or 20.00. The format is similar to breakfast, with bread and a selection of meats and cheeses, perhaps followed by cake or a sweet dessert.

Regional cooking

Despite the efforts of some culinary journalists to promote Cracovian cuisine as unique in Poland, the fact of the matter is that regional differences are not particularly strong. Certainly, the preponderance of *gulasz* (goulash), and *Wiener schnitzel* (*sznycel po wiedeńsku*) seems to support the view that Kraków's Austro-Hungarian heritage (see *History*) has had an important and lasting effect on its food, but the case is nearly always overstated. Polish cuisine, in general, is highly eclectic, combining domestic tradition with an assortment of foreign influence, and this is hardly surprising: until the Second World War, the country was home to sizeable German, Jewish, Lithuanian, Ukrainian, and Russian minorities, all of which made a strong contribution to national cuisine. Nowadays, though, the food served in restaurants does not differ much from city to city or region to region. You are just as likely to find 'regional' dishes from the south served in other parts of the country and vice-versa. No doubt, half a century of central planning has played its part in levelling diversity. Visitors expecting to find restaurants specialising in regional cooking, as in, say, France or Spain, will be disappointed. *Chłopskie Jadło*, **Wentzl** and **Pod Aniołami** (see *Restaurants*) all serve a few local specialities, but that's about as far as it goes.

Drinking

Vodka, the Polish national drink, comes in many varieties. The best clear vodkas are currently *Bols* (produced in Poland under Dutch licence) and *Cracovia*. If you want to buy a bottle as a gift, *Chopin* may be a good choice, too. It's classic case of 'paying for the label'—the very fancy packaging includes an engraved image of Chopin—but the quality is excellent. Slightly further down the scale are *Luksusowa* and *Krakus*, the latter, despite its name, produced in the city of Wrocław. *Wyborowa* and *Żytnia* were the prize vodkas of the communist period, but are now decidedly mid-range. Generally, all kosher (*koszerna*) vodkas are a good bet, especially those produced by Polmos Bielsko-Biała, as quality-control standards (including water purity) are more rigorous. At a frightening 180°, *Spirytus rektyfikowany* is the strongest spirit on the market and one that even many hardened Poles will keep well away from. If you wish to sample this fiery concoction, be warned that it should always be diluted first. A curiosity is a brand called *Siwucha*, made by Polmos Zielona Góra. Initially produced as a limited-edition joke to celebrate the company's 40th anniversary (the colour, consistency and taste are deliberately designed to suggest that something has gone wrong in the fermentation process), it soon proved to be a major commercial success. The taste is indeed acquired, but it has legions of admirers. Genuinely poor vodkas include the insipid *Czysta* (another leftover from the People's Republic) and barely drinkable *Lodowa* and *Stołowa*. Sample these at your peril.

Some of the best vodkas available on the market are flavoured varieties. The classic one is called *Żubrówka*, seasoned with a blade of sweet-scented grass (hierchloe) found only in the Białowieża Forest in northeastern Poland (hence its association with bison, or *żubry*, natives of the forest). Similar, but slightly sweeter in taste, is *Dzięgielówka*, made from angelica fruit and thus claimed to have medicinal qualities (Cracovians swear by it as the best cure for colds). *Cytrynówka* (lemon vodka) and *Orzechówka* (nut vodka) are both palatable, if slightly less exotic in taste. Also worth looking out for are sweet vodkas, such as *Wiśniówka* (wild cherry vodka), which comes in two strengths (40 per cent and 28 per cent), *Żołądkowa Gorzka* ('*gorzka*' actually means 'bitter', but it is anything but), *Goldwasser*, which contains flakes of real gold and when shaken creates the effect of a snowstorm in miniature, and *Śliwowica paschalna* (Passover Slivovitz), an aromatic plum brandy. There is also a strong (68 per cent), non-kosher version of *Śliwowica* made by the Polish highlanders. It is unlicensed, and therefore not available in shops, but if you ask around in Zakopane (see p. 175) you may be able to get hold of a bottle or two—it's worth the effort!

Clear vodka is served neat, in tumblers (*kieliszki*), and is best when ice-cold. Shots come in 50 or 100 gramme measures, and are preceded by a simple '*na zdrowie!*' (cheers!) or perhaps a more elaborate toast, as the occasion permits. Flavoured vodkas should be served lightly chilled, sweet ones at room temperature, the exceptions being *Krupnik* and *Starka*, which are often mixed with boiling water or added to tea. Diluted hard spirits were until recently considered a heresy, but nowadays ordering a 'vodka and orange' in a Kraków pub won't raise any eyebrows. In general, the trend in the 1990s has been towards milder drinks at the expense of hard spirits.

Decent foreign wines are now commonplace on restaurant tables, but often ridiculously overpriced. Anything that advertises itself as Polish wine is best avoided. Local beer is strong and full-bodied, with a distinctive flavour that is not always to the liking of visitors weaned on Western lagers. Famous brands include *Żywiec* and *Okocim*—both of long Habsburg tradition—and you will invariably find these on tap in Kraków bars.

A standard menu (*Jadłospis*)

Starters (*przekąski/zakąski*)

befsztyk tatarski	steak tartare
flaki	tripe served in bouillon
śledź w oleju	herring in oil
śledź w śmietanie	herring in sour cream
jajko w majonezie	hard-boiled egg in mayonnaise
smalec	dripping mixed with pork scratchings
bryndza	cream cheese made from ewe's milk
oscypek	sheep's cheese, either smoked or non-smoked

Christmas and Easter celebrations

To sample Polish home-cooking at its best, you would do well to attend a Christmas meal on 24 December (*wigilia*). The culinary customs connected with this event are rooted in a Catholic tradition of abstinence from meat on that day. The courses, of which there can be up to twelve, vary from home to home, but the following ingredients are always present: fish (mainly carp), mushrooms, cabbage, and *kutia*, an ancient and popular dish from the east, made from boiled wheat flavoured with poppyseeds, honey, nuts and raisins. Typical dishes might include borscht with dumplings filled with dried wild mushrooms (*uszka*), wild mushroom soup, carp fried in batter, cabbage with mushrooms or peas, marinated herring in apple purée, onion and cream, carp in aspic (often in the Jewish version with vegetables, almonds and raisins), dumplings filled with mushrooms and cabbage, plain dumplings (*kluski*) with poppyseeds, honey cake, and poppyseed cake. The *wigilia* meal traditionally begins when the first star appears in the night sky. Close family members will gather around the Christmas table in an atmosphere of good-will and reconciliation. This is manifested in the tradition of sharing the holy wafer with all present and wishing them well for the coming year. There are also pagan customs associated with the meal: straw is put under the tablecloth, and the holy wafer is also shared with animals. Poles are prover-bially hospitable ('a guest in the house is God in the house'), and it is cus-tomary to leave an empty place at the table for unexpected guests.

During the carnival (*karnawał*), which begins after the New Year, it is cus-tomary to eat *chrust*, a biscuit of made of dough deep-fried in lard, also known as *faworki*. On Maundy Thursday (*tłusty czwartek*), the whole nation traditionally gorges itself on doughnuts. Shrove Tuesday (*ostatki*) marks the official end of the *karnawał* and is traditionally a day of raucous parties and guilt-free gluttony. Lent begins on Ash Wednesday, when the standard dish is herring, served in a number of elaborate forms. Nowadays, the fasting period usually lasts only two days. No meat or alcohol are consumed on Good Friday, while on Saturday food is blessed in preparation for the most important meal of the Easter period: Sunday breakfast. The latter is preceded by a ceremonial sharing of Easter eggs, another pagan custom—the eggs symbolising the beginning of life. A cold buffet is normally served, consist-ing of sausage, ham, eggs, cold roasts and horseradish.

Soups (*zupy*)

żurek	traditional sour soup made from fermented flour
barszcz	borscht (beetroot soup, either clear or with sour cream)
barszcz z krokietem/ paszteçikiem	beetroot soup with croquette/small pastry
barszcz z uszkami	borscht with meat dumplings
rosół	bouillon with noodles
kapuśniak	cabbage soup with sauerkraut
pomidorowa	tomato soup
ogórkowa	cucumber soup
szczawiowa	sorrel soup
jarzynowa	vegetable soup

grochowa	pea soup
grzybowa	mushroom soup
fasolowa	bean soup
cebulowa z grzankami	onion soup with croutons
botwinka	baby beetroot soup
chłodnik	iced beetroot soup, made with buttermilk and sour cream
krupnik	pearl barley soup with diced meat and potatoes

Main courses (*dania drugie/potrawy główne*)

Meat dishes (*dania mięsne*)

bigos	meat stewed in sauerkraut and French cabbage
kotlet schabowy	pork chop fried in batter
kotlet mielony	mince cutlet
sztuka mięsa w sosie chrzanowym	boiled beef in horseradish sauce
polędwica	sirloin
fasolka po bretońsku	beans in a tomato and meat sauce
kasza gryczana w sosie	buckwheat in a meat sauce
pieczeń wołowa	roast beef
żeberka	spare ribs
golonko	pork knuckle
gulasz	goulash
rumsztyk	rump steak
eskalopki cielęce	veal scallops
kotlet de volaille	cutlet de volaille
schab pieczony	roast pork loin
zrazy	beef olives
wątróbka wieprzowa	pork liver
gołąbki	cabbage leaves stuffed with rice and meat
parówki	frankfurters
kiełbasa	sausage
pasztet (z dzika)	(wild boar) pâté
kaszanka	black pudding
kiszka	Polish haggis
udziec jagnięcy	leg of lamb
pierogi z mięsem	dumplings with meat filling
kołduny	Lithuanian dumplings with meat filling
pyzy/kopytka	traditional potato noodles, often served with a meat sauce
kluski	plain dumplings
łazanki z kapusty	plain noodles served with mince meat and cabbage

Poultry dishes (*drób*)

kurczę pieczone	roast chicken
kurczę gotowane	boiled chicken
kurczak	chicken (usually fried)
wątróbka drobiowa	chicken liver
filet z kurczaka	chicken fillet

indyk	turkey
kaczka	duck
gęś	goose

Fish dishes (*dania rybne*)

pstrąg	trout
łosoś	salmon
węgorz	eel
szczupak	pike
sandacz	pike-perch
sardynki	sardines
makrela	mackerel
... *wędzony*	... smoked

Vegetarian dishes (*dania/potrawy jarskie/wegetariańskie*)

pierogi ruskie	dumplings with cottage cheese, onion and potato filling
pierogi z grzybami i kapustą	dumplings with mushroom and sauerkraut filling
pierogi leniwe	cottage cheese dumplings
knedle	round dumplings with fruit filling
knedle ze śliwkami	dumplings with plum filling
knedle z truskawkami	dumplings with strawberry filling
knedle z jagodami	dumplings with bilberry filling
placki ziemniaczane	potato pancakes
naleśniki	pancakes
jajecznica	scrambled eggs

Side dishes (*dodatki*)

zestaw surówek	selection of marinated side salads
zestaw sałatek	selection of fresh side salads
frytki	French fries
ryż	rice
ziemniaki (młode)	(new) potatoes
fasolka szparagowa	green beans
szpinak	spinach
szparagi	asparagus
kalafior	cauliflower
grzyby marynowane	marinated wild mushrooms
pieczarki smażone	fried field mushrooms
kapusta zasmażana	stewed cabbage
kapusta kiszona	sauerkraut
pieczywo/chleb	bread
bułka	bread roll

Salads (*sałatki/surówki*)

mizeria	sliced cucumber in sour cream or vinegar
ćwikła	mashed beetroot and horseradish
ogórki kiszone	cucumbers in brine
ogórki marynowane/ korniszony	pickled cucumbers

ogórki małosolne	fresh salted cucumbers
sałatka mieszana	mixed salad
sałatka jarzynowa	vegetable (Russian) salad
sałatka z tuńczyka	tuna salad
sałatka z białej kapusty	white cabbage salad
sałatka z czerwonej kapusty	red cabbage salad
sałatka z porów	leek salad
sałatka z marchwi	carrot salad
sałatka z selera	celery salad

Desserts (*desery*)

sernik	cheesecake
pascha	creamy (Passover) cheesecake
makowiec	poppyseed cake
szarlotka	apple and cinnamon cake
piernik/miodownik	dark-brown honey cake
pierniki	gingerbread
pączki	doughnuts
mazurek	shortcake layered with jam
lody	ice cream
owoce	fruit
ciastko	cake/tart
tort	(birthday) cake with layers of cream and a topping

Drinks (*napoje*)

piwo	beer
wino	wine (*słodkie*—sweet, *pół-słodkie*—semi-dry, *wytrawne*—dry)
wino białe	white wine
wino czerwone	red wine
wino grzane	mulled wine
sok	fruit juice
napój owocowy	fruit squash
kefir	kefir (thick soured milk)
kompot	traditional drink made from stewed fruit
woda mineralna	mineral water (*gazowana*—carbonated, *nie gazowana*—non-carbonated)
herbata z cytryną	lemon tea
kawa parzona	Turkish-style coffee
kawa z ekspresu	expresso coffee
kawa rozpuszczalna	instant coffee

Restaurants

Since 1989, the standards and choice of restaurant food have dramatically improved, and eating out is no longer the exasperating experience it was during communist times. The most noticeable change has been the arrival of foreign cuisine, particularly Chinese, Vietnamese, Italian, Mexican and Middle-Eastern, providing an alternative to traditional Polish fare. Western fast-food chains and pizzerias are also commonplace. Nowadays, Kraków has a wide range of eating establishments, beginning with the most basic *bary mleczne* (also called *jadłodajnie*), self-service 'milk bars' serving mostly dairy-based food where you can get a simple but nourishing three course meal for as little as 10 PLN. These are often the best places to sample traditional cuisine, but they are usually only open during the day.

For a slightly more up-market meal with waiter service you could try one of the many mid-range restaurants, such as the *Cechowa*, or the somewhat smarter *Krew i Roza*, both of which serve tasty local dishes. Mid-range establishments are probably the best bet for visitors; they are, after all, the places most Cracovians will head for when going out to eat. Exclusive restaurants are a gamble and you may be disappointed. This is especially true of the *Wierzynek*, where standards of service and food quality hardly justify the inflated prices. As a rule, exclusive restaurants have an intense snob appeal which is reflected in the type of customer they attract, and this means a fair share of sleazy mafia-types eager to flaunt their wealth.

Generally, Western visitors will find restaurants to be significantly cheaper than their equivalents at home. Ordering drink can be expensive, though, due to the high import duty on alcohol. If you're on a limited budget, avoid foreign wines and spirits and stick to Polish beer (5 PLN in a pub, up to 8 PLN in a restaurant) or vodka. As a rule, always ask for the drinks menu/wine list in advance. Like pubs, restaurants in Kraków are often located in historic interiors. Gothic cellars are common and have a special ambience, but ventilation can be a problem.

Tipping. A tip of 10 per cent is standard in restaurants. It is customary to include the tip when paying the bill, rather than to leave it on the table.

Vegetarian food

Today, the average Polish diet is still fatty and extremely meat-based, but times are changing and vegetarian food is no longer dismissed with derision. A few vegetarian eateries have sprung up in recent years, and many restaurant menus will usually offer at least some meat-free dishes. *Chimera* and *Vega*, for instance, do good salads and fresh fruit juices. Most salads are made with vegetables that are in season. For simple snacks you could try one of many stalls in and around the Market Square selling corn-on-the-cob, broad beans and a local speciality—*bajgle* (pretzels seasoned with salt or poppyseeds).

Restaurants listed in this Guide have been divided into three price categories. In 'exclusive restaurants' you should expect to pay from 70–150 PLN for a three course meal, not including alcohol; in 'medium price' restaurants, anything from 20–70 PLN is standard. In bottom-end *bary mleczne* (milk bars) or 'cheap eateries' you can get a three course meal for as little as 10 PLN.

Exclusive restaurants

Cyrano de Bergerac, ul. Sławkowska 26 (☎ 411 7288). Possibly the best French restaurant in Poland. Excellent and imaginative dishes made by the resident French chef, whose speciality is *foie gras* infused in red wine. Friendly service and a pleasant atmosphere, slightly spoilt by overly loud music and rather cramped seating in the entresol at the back—when booking ask for a table in the main room or summer patio. Good wine, but ridiculously overpriced.

Na Wawelu, Wzgórze Wawelskie 9 (☎ 421 1915). Situated on Wawel hill, inside a former Austrian barracks. Expensive and pompously arranged, but convenient if you need a rest whilst visiting the castle and cathedral.

Tetmajerowska, Rynek Główny 34 (☎ 422 0631). Upstairs from the Hawełka (see below). One of the most expensive restaurants in Kraków, frequently used for official ceremonies and banquets. Named after the late 19C artist Włodzimierz Tetmayer, who painted the frieze (see p. 102) in the back room. Polish and international cuisine served by fussy waiters. In-house wine cellar.

Villa Decius, ul. 28 Lipca 17a (☎ 425 3390). In the suburb of Wola Justowska. Exclusive restaurant inside a historic villa (see p. 162). Polish and French/Italian cuisine. Live Renaissance music.

Wierzynek, Rynek Główny 15 (☎ 422 9896). Poland's most famous restaurant on account of its connection with a historic feast held in 1364 (see p. 98). The interiors are worth a look, but the food is overrated and unjustifiably expensive. Polish and international cuisine.

Medium-price restaurants

A Dong, ul. Brodzińskiego 3 (☎ 656 4872). Situated in the Podgórze district (see p. 147), just across the Piłsudski bridge. Has a reputation as the best Chinese/Vietnamese restaurant in Kraków. Seafood specialities. Could be combined with a visit to the nearby Starmach Gallery (see *Contemporary Polish Art*, p. 53).

Amarone, ul. Floriańska 14 (☎ 422 1244). Situated at the back of the **Hotel Pod Różą** (enter from ul. Św Tomasza). Very elegant, Italian-style interior under a glass roof. Two menus, continental and Italian, both good. Extensive wine list, with more on offer in the downstairs wine bar.

Alef, ul. Szeroka 17 (☎ 421 3870). Vaulted interiors with a stylish pre-war feel. Jewish (non-kosher) specialities of varying quality, including excellent *pascha* (Passover) cheesecake. Ideal location if you're sightseeing in Kazimierz. Frequent Klezmer nights. A few guest rooms available (see *Where to stay*).

Avanti, ul. Karmelicka 7 (☎ 430 0770). Opposite the Bagatela Theatre. Despite the suspect decor, the food is made by a resident Italian chef and is more than palatable. Large selection of Italian and French wines.

Cechowa, ul. Jagiellońska 11 (☎ 421 0936). Unpretentious, good quality Polish food. House specialities include *żurek* (see p. 26) and white sausage in horseradish sauce. Sometimes closed at weekends for private parties.

Cherubino, ul. Św. Tomasza 15 (☎ 429 4007). Situated in a side street between two popular bars—**Dym** and **Loch Camelot**. Simple, well-prepared Polish and Italian (Tuscan) cuisine, a cheap alternative to the **Amarone** opposite. Large choice of wine. Quirky interior—you can eat your meal inside an old-fashioned stagecoach. Basement area for banquets and receptions. Gets very crowded in summer.

Chimera 2, ul. Gołębia 2. The only Georgian restaurant in Kraków. Filling, reasonably priced food, but limited choice. Daily concerts.

Chłopskie Jadło, ul. Św Agnieszki 1 (☎ 421 8520). Very popular establishment (booking essential) and recent winner of the *Teraz Polska* award for best cuisine. As its name ('Peasant Grub') suggests, the restaurant concentrates on country specialities, or at least what the Polish middle class understands these to be. The menu is a nutritionist's nightmare, but if you're partial to rich, fatty food, you won't be disappointed. Older readers may appreciate such curiosities as the hors d'oeuvre of dripping (*smalec*) served in a tin cup with wholemeal bread (*razowiec*). Worth trying, too, are the roast pork in plums and garlic and the seasonal dishes like cep soup and fruit dumplings. The 'captain's cabin' decor is compensated by friendly service and an upbeat atmosphere, which includes live highland music on most nights.

At the back is a separate restaurant—**Baba Ryba** (☎ 421 8774)—serving fish specialities. The original **Chłopskie Jadło** restaurant (same format) is located out of town on the Zakopane road (Głogoczów 196; ☎ 090 315 813)—convenient if you're returning from the Tatra Mountains by car.

Corleone, ul. Poselska (☎ 429 5126) A new Italian restaurant that scores high points for decor and atmosphere, but somewhat less for food quality and service.

Europejska, Rynek Główny 35 (☎ 429 3493). Refurbished in the 1990s to look like a cross between a Central European coffee house and an English pub. The lunches/dinners (12.00–23.30) are expensive for what you get and very oriented towards tourists. Specialities include Astrakhan black caviar with Russian yeast rolls (*bliny*), Salmon in thyme sauce, and especially good pancakes with a choice of sweet fillings. English and Viennese breakfasts are also offered.

Da Pietro, Rynek Główny 17 (☎ 422 3279). Italian restaurant contained inside a typically Cracovian interior. The vaulted Gothic cellar is charming, but could really do with some air conditioning. Best are the hors d'oeuvres, including tasty *pepperonata*, *carpaccio*, and cream of tomato soup, followed by fairly standard pasta dishes. In summer you can sit upstairs on the square, but the menu there is limited to pizzas.

El Paso, ul. Św. Krzyża 13 (☎ 421 3296). A *Tex-Mex* joint done up like a cowboy saloon. Your best bet: a spicy *burrito* washed down with a cold Corona beer and lime. Twelve brands of tequila available. Run by the same management as the **Taco Mexicano** (see below). Saturday booking essential.

Ganges, ul. Krakowska 7 (☎ 292 0262). The first Indian restaurant to be opened in Kraków. Food of varying quality. No clay oven, hence no *nan* bread. Not exactly London's Brick Lane, but if you're fed up with bland Polish food, this makes a welcome change.

Gospoda CK Dezerter, ul. Bracka 6 (☎ 422 9731). Situated next door to **Guliwer** (see below), just off the Market Square. Central European cuisine. Czech beer on tap.

Guliwer, ul. Bracka 6 (☎ 439 2466). A mixture of Polish and French cuisine, with the latter predominant. Live accordion music. A favourite haunt of the writer Sławomir Mrożek (see p. 135). Slightly more up-market than **Gospoda CK Dezerter**.

Hotel Elektor, ul. Szpitalna 28 (☎ 421 8025). A hotel restaurant somewhat lacking in atmosphere. Cheap set lunch menus. Polish cuisine. Good wine bar.

Hotel Francuski, ul. Pijarska 13 (☎ 422 5122). Once the best French restaurant in Kraków, but nowadays eclipsed by the **Cyrano de Bergerac**.

Lemon, ul. Floriańska 53 (☎ 0501 413747). An inconspicuous grill bar with tables in the courtyard in summer. The menu, very-meat based, offers Balkan specialities including country soup, steak, kebabs, and various salads. For drinks, try the potent Croatian *Rakija*.

Hawełka, Rynek Główny 34 (☎ 422 4753). Not as elegant (or expensive) as the **Tetmajerowska** upstairs (see above). Ground floor room with portrait of Emperor Franz Josef I and copies of famous Polish paintings hung on the walls. Polish cuisine, including duck Kraków-style (with buckwheat and mushrooms), wild boar steak, venison in cream, pheasant and other game specialities. Polish breakfasts also served.

Kartagina, pl. Dominikański 6 (☎ 422 5227). Tunisian self-service bar and restaurant. Filling, if rather bland food. Specialities of the house include Berber veal and couscous.

Krew i Róża, ul. Grodzka 9 (☎ 422 9694). Run by the same management as *Chłopskie Jadło* (see above), with slightly more concessions to healthy eating. The decor is also much better, with striking murals in the banquet room and eerie mannequins that look like props from a Kantor play (see p. 115). Renaissance music.

Na Kazimierzu, ul. Szeroka 39 (☎ 422 6790). Located in a modern building renovated by the US Nissenbaum Foundation. The only kosher restaurant in Kraków. Polish/Jewish cuisine. Café downstairs.

Nowina, Głogoczów, off the Zakopane road, half an hour's drive from Kraków (☎ 273 1226). Run by the descendants of a famous noble family. Traditional Polish cuisine served inside the vaulted cellars of a former brewery. Lots of game dishes, smoked meats, pâtés and meat pies. The speciality is 'Royal Bigos', made from two types of cabbage and ten types of meat, which takes five days to cook! Excellent desserts, including rum omelettes and a variety of cakes. Winner of the Golden Jackdaw statuette, awarded annually to the best restaurant in the Kraków region.

Orient Express, ul. Poselska 22 (☎ 422 6672). International cuisine from countries through which the Orient Express passes. You get to sit in your own 'train compartment', complete with luggage rack and suitcases. Good main courses and desserts, reasonably priced.

Paese, ul. Poselska 24 (☎ 421 6273). One of the best restaurants in Kraków. Tasty, well-prepared Mediterranean (Corsican) cuisine at very reasonable prices. Excellent steak in green pepper sauce. Seafood specialities including moules and lobsters (when available), washed down with French or Corsican wine. Low-key atmosphere and discreetly efficient service. Booking essential.

Pod Aniołami, ul. Grodzka 35 (☎ 421 3999). Gothic cellars with a clay oven and grilling areas. Standard Polish menu, enlivened with a few highland specialities. Palatable, if overpriced.

Pod Baranem, ul. Św Gertrudy 21 (☎ 429 4022). Situated opposite the *Hotel Royal*. Surprisingly good Polish cuisine. Specialities include roast salmon, stuffed chicken, duck, and wild mushroom soup served in a hollowed-out loaf. Good selection of vegetarian dumplings and pancakes.

Taco Mexicano, ul. Poselska 20 (☎ 421 5441) Run by same management as the *El Paso* (see above), with an almost identical menu. Filling, but nothing special. Four rooms, including one for non-smokers, and a patio. Latin American sounds.

Bombay Tandoori, ul. Mikołajska 11. The better of the two Indian restaurants in Kraków. More choice than in the *Ganges* (see above) and the curries are genuinely hot. Cheap set lunches on weekdays between 12.00 and 15.00.

U Pollera, ul. Szpitalna 30 (☎ 421 8061). Inside the *Hotel Pollera*. Converted from a ballroom, which explains the high ceiling and glass roof. Standard Polish cuisine, of average price and quality.

U Ziyada, ul. Jodłowa 13 (☎ 429 7105). Recommendable primarily for its location: a 1930s hill-top villa in the suburb of Przegorzały (see p. 159), with great views from the terrace onto the Vistula and monasteries of Bielany and Tyniec (see p. 160). Frequented by Polish-American students from the nearby dormitory. Kurdish and Polish food, not in itself justifying the journey.

Wentzl, Rynek Główny 19 (☎ 429 5712). Elegant restaurant, one of the best in Kraków. A mixture of French and Central European cuisine. Live jazz on Fridays and Saturdays.

Cheap eateries

Akropolis, ul. Grodzka 9. Self-service Greek restaurant, situated very close to the Market Square. Large portions but decidedly bland.

Bar Grodzki, ul. Grodzka 47. Recently renovated and now slightly more up-market. Traditional Polish cuisine. Good potato pancakes.

Chimera, ul. Św. Anny 3. Popular salad bar in a smoke-free basement. A choice of 40 salads and different sauces. In summer you can sit out in the pleasant courtyard. Frequent evening concerts. The upstairs restaurant of the same name (facing the street) serves Polish cuisine, including various roast meats and good soups.

Hoang Hai, ul. Stradom 13. Chinese and Vietnamese cuisine. Cramped interior with uncomfortable seating, but very popular nonetheless. Within easy walking distance of Wawel Castle. The same management runs a larger establishment (same name) at ul. Zamkowa 1, just across the Dębnicki bridge.

Jadłodajnia, ul. Sienna 11. Established in 1934, this tiny self-service bar does unpretentious meals at unbeatable prices.

Jadłodajnia Kuchcik, ul. Jagiellońska 12. Self-service bar, popular among students.

Jadłodajnia u Pani Stasi, ul. Mikołajska 16. The best dumpling bar in Kraków, if not Poland. Open on weekdays from 12.30 until the food runs out (usually 16.00). You will normally have to queue in the courtyard, but it's well worth the wait. Excellent home-made soups and famously good dumplings with a choice of sweet and savoury fillings. Ridiculously cheap—you can get a whole meal (soup, dumplings, side salad, plus *kompot* or *kefir*) for less than 10 PLN (!). Waitress service, but you pay at the cash desk. No alcohol, no smoking, no tea or coffee—just eat and leave.

Kassumay, ul. Piłsudskiego 25. African cuisine. Intriguing dishes like Bongo-Bongo salad.

King Pie, ul. Sławkowska 20. Take-away pies.

Piccolo, ul. Jagiellońska 2 (corner of pl. Szczepański). Unlike other self-service bars, this one stays open until 22.00. Chicken and chips, but not much else.

Różowy Słoń, ul. Straszewskiego 24. Popular student bar situated opposite Collegium Novum (see p. 133). Unmistakable for its cartoon murals inspired by TV shows from the 1970s and 1980s. Good pancakes. Two other branches at ul. Szpitalna 38 and ul. Sienna 1.

Thien Long, pl. Wolnica 7. Vietnamese cuisine. If you're exploring western Kazimierz and need a quick meal, this is the place.

Vega, ul. Św. Gertrudy 7. Strictly vegetarian (not vegan). Good choice of pancakes, dumplings and salads. Pleasant atmosphere. Artistic decor and classical music. Two other branches at ul. Szeroka 3 (in Kazimierz) and ul. Krupnicza 22.

Cafés

As in other Central European cities, café culture was an integral part of social life in Kraków from the late 19C onwards. Some of the establishments listed below have a long history behind them as meeting places for artists, writers, intellectuals etc, and still preserve an atmosphere suggestive of the past. This is especially true of *Jama Michalika* and *Noworolski*, which have impressive turn-of-the-century decor, but also *Krzysztofory* and *U Literatów*, both associated with the post-war avant-garde. Café society remained in vogue throughout the communist period for the simple reason that pubs and clubs, which today are taken for granted, simply didn't exist. That has all changed in the last decade, and, faced with new competition, cafés have been forced to change their profile in order to win customers. Most now serve alcohol and food, and many stay open late into the evening.

In summer, bars and cafés put seats out in their courtyards (*ogródki*), or simply spill onto the street. At this time the Market Square looks like one big café, with an almost uninterrupted line of chairs and tables around its periphery—it's hard to tell where one café ends and the next one begins.

The list below is necessarily subjective. It gives preference to long-established and/or popular places, but there are, of course, hundreds more.

Arka Noego, ul. Szeroka 2. Friendly café with elegant, pre-war furniture. Food also served. In the same building is the *Jarden* bookshop for those interested in Jewish culture and history.

Bambus, Rynek Główny 27. Ground floor of the Rams' Palace (see p. 99). One of the most popular cafés on the Market Square. The interior is not too exciting, but a good place to sit in summer, when the wicker chairs are moved outside.

Botanica, ul. Bracka 9. New(ish) establishment, crowded with students during the day. The main area has lots of plants and is no-smoking.

Gołębnik, ul. Gołębia 5. Smoke-free tea room, often crowded with students. If there's nowhere to sit, try the similar *Mozaika* or *Gołębia 3* further along the street.

Graffiti, ul Św. Gertrudy 5. A mandatory port of call for patrons of the *Wanda* cinema next door. On summer evenings, free open-air film shows are held in the courtyard at the back.

Jama Michalika, ul. Floriańska 45. One of the most famous cafés in Kraków, contained in historic interiors (see *Cabaret* and p. 105).

Konsulat, ul. Stolarska 13. More a beer garden than a café, set in a beautiful courtyard with lots of plants.

Krzysztofory, ul. Szczepańska 2. A typical Cracovian *piwnica* with a long history behind it (see p. 102).

Larousse, ul. Św. Tomasza 22. The walls of this tiny establishment are covered in pages of the famous encyclopaedia (hence the name). Four tables, usually occupied.

Loch Camelot, ul. Św. Tomasza 17. Stylish café with original works by the celebrated Polish naïve painter, Nikifor of Krynica (1895–1968) on the walls. Young(ish), arty crowd. Highland bread sandwiches and good salads. English/American newspapers available for guests (see *Cabaret*).

Manggha, ul. Starowiślna 10. Outside the Old Town. Small café named after the writer and explorer Feliks Jasieński (see p. 149). Frequented by students and staff from the Academy of Music across the street. Enter from the courtyard.

Noworolski, Rynek Główny 1 (Cloth Hall). Spacious, ground floor coffee house with Viennese-style, turn-of-the-century decor, especially impressive in the 'Red Room'.

Pożegnanie z Afryką, ul. Św. Tomasza 21. A non-smoking café and coffee shop, with the best and broadest selection of coffee in town.

Redolfi, Rynek Główny 38. One of the more up-market cafés on the Market Square, established in 1823. Good salads and lunches, reasonably priced.

TriBeCa Coffee Co., ul. Karmelicka 6. A typical American-style coffee shop, offering a wide range of coffee, sweets and sandwiches (eat in or take away). No smoking.

U Literatów, ul. Kanonicza 7. Once a favourite haunt of writers and artists. Low key interiors complemented by a summer patio and secluded garden.

Late-night eating

Restaurants usually close at around midnight, sometimes later, depending on the number of guests. After this time your choice will be limited. The *Akropolis* at ul. Grodzka 9 stays open late, but don't expect more than a stomach filler. Another Greek place—the nearby *Dionisos* at pl. Dominikański 4—is open 24 hours, but the food is pretty dreadful. Marginally better is the *Kawiarnia Grill* under the arcades on ul. Stolarska, which does greasy steak and chips until 03.00. Of the Western fast-food chains, only *McDonald's* has late opening until 02.00 at ul. Floriańska 55, and a 24 hour drive-in at ul. Wadowicka 2a (near the Mateczny roundabout). The self-service bar and restaurant at the main railway station are also open 24 hours. There is a kebab stall just off pl. Wszystkich Świętych, and many more on the Market Square selling hot snacks. If you like Polish sausage (*kiełbasa*), head for the stall by the viaduct on ul. Dietla. It's a bit of a journey but well worth the effort. Locals claim this is the best grilled *kiełbasa* in the city.

Late-night bars and clubs

With over 400 pubs and clubs in Old Town alone, you won't have to walk far to get a drink in Kraków. Most of the bars listed below are well-established, but bankruptcies occur at an alarming rate. Some places close and then re-open under a new name and management; others become intensely fashionable for a few months and then sink without trace. Consequently, any list of recommended establishments becomes out-of-date almost as soon as it's written. The best policy is simply to ask the locals for suggestions. If you don't like a bar, move on: there's bound to be a couple of good ones just round the corner.

The most common type of drinking establishment is the cellar bar, or *piwnica*, where ventilation can be a major problem. Non-smokers, in particular, may find these airless caverns too much to bear. A few places have basic air-conditioning (i.e. fans), but even here your clothes will probably reek of cigarettes in the morning. The situation is not helped by the fact that Poles are committed smokers (in Europe, second only to the Greeks).

Licensing hours are extremely liberal. Cracovians, who even among Poles have a reputation as heavy drinkers, take full advantage of this. Pubs will often close when the last guest leaves—03.00 in the morning is not uncommon—while some places will stay open as late as 06.00. If there is live music, you may be charged a small entrance fee. Cracovian pubs don't have the same sort of social mix as pubs in the UK. Most bars attract young clientele (20–30), some cater to an older crowd, but rarely will you find a place with a cross-section of ages.

Alchemia, ul. Estery 5. A new rival to the *Singer* down the street. The tatty and eclectic furnishings only add to its charm. Friendly service and a view onto the square.

Black Gallery, ul. Mikołajska 24. Dark, dirty cellar bar with overly loud music, but the upstairs marquee (summer only) is much better. The Gallery's flagship drink—the 'kamikaze' (vodka, Blue Curaçao, lemon juice, served in 6 or 12 tumblers) is not as potent as it sounds. It also comes in a red version—the 'scorpion'.

Bull Pub, ul. Mikołajska 2, just off the Market Square. Originally the *John Bull Pub*, but the name had to change when the management lost the franchise. Expensive and frequented by Polish yuppies, for whom it has snob appeal. If you can't live without English bitter, this is the place to be.

CK Browar, ul. Podwale 7, underneath the Elefant department store. A large cellar bar keen to promote its Habsburg heritage—a portrait of Emperor Franz Josef I hangs above the entrance. Depressingly bad decor, but good beer, brewed on the premises, and excellent bar snacks. Adjoining disco.

Dom Wina, ul. Pijarska 11 (next to the *Hotel Francuski*). One of very few wine bars in Kraków.

Dym, ul. Św. Tomasza 15. Tiny bar exhibiting works by local photographers. Gets crowded in summer, when the tables spill out onto the street.

Fischer Pub, ul. Grodzka 42 (under the arches). Mixed Polish/foreign crowd. Good choice of beer. Downstairs bar and disco.

Free Pub, ul. Sławkowska 4. Popular cellar bar, just of the Market Square. Funny signs from the communist period stuck on the walls. Late closing at weekends (06.00–ish), thus a haven for sundry desperadoes. Occasional fights, but foreigners never involved.

Kapsuła, Rynek Główny 6. In a courtyard off the Market Square. Odd design that's supposed to resemble a boat, complete with an upper deck. Tables outside in summer.

Klinika 35, ul. Św. Tomasza 35. Situated at the end of the street, by the *Planty*. Cellar bar with frequent rock, jazz and blues concerts.

Klub Kulturalny, ul. Szewska 25 (by the *Planty*). Policed by a huge bouncer ('The Leader'), and thus possibly the safest bar in Kraków. Mixed crowd of locals and foreigners. A successor to the *Roentgen* (see below).

Klub U Louisa, Rynek Główny 13. Popular cellar bar frequented by a teenage/twenty-something crowd. Lech, Budweiser, Guinness and Kilkenny on tap. Snacks, including good *pierogi*. Live music on Thursdays and Fridays. Internet room at the back (see *Internet*) and tables in the courtyard in summer.

Kredens, Rynek Główny 12. A chain of underground rooms, somewhat incongruously filled with old armchairs and sofas. Two bars and a dance floor, packed at weekends.

Maska, ul. Jagiellońska 1. One of the few bars to attract a middle-aged crowd (40+). Co-owned by Tadeusz Huk, an actor from the Old Theatre upstairs (see p. 134), and hence frequented by thespians, filmmakers etc. You'll either love or hate the prize-winning art deco(ish) decor. Good cocktails and food. Up-market, but not overpriced.

Miasto Krakoff, ul. Łobzowska 3. Spacious ground floor pub/disco situated just beyond the *Planty* ring. Arty decor and frequent concerts. Techno, funk, rock, soul. Newly-opened and (for now) extremely popular. Be sure to leave your coat/bag in the cloakroom, as thefts are common.

Molier, ul. Szewska 4. Dark, ground floor room, with a small patio at the back. Quiet atmosphere. Snacks available.

O'Morgan's, ul. Garncarska 5. The first unashamedly ex-pat bar in Kraków. Clientele primarily of English teachers and company staff. Big screen for live football matches. Celtic sounds and decent Guinness on tap. Foreigners most welcome.

Music Bar 9, ul. Szewska 9. Studenty bar with downstairs disco.

Paparazzi, ul. Mikołajska 9. New American-style bar with a decidedly nouveau riche clientele. Walls decked out in newspaper clippings (hence the name) and photographs of the rich and famous. Snacks available.

Pasja, ul. Szewska 5. Yuppyish bar with a lively disco and pool room.

Piwnica pod Ogródkiem, ul. Jagiellońska 6. Two large rooms that on Fridays become a sweaty teenage disco. Occasional live music. Gallettes, crêpes and other snacks available. The upstairs courtyard, with it's own bar, is much nicer.

Podium, ul. Bracka 4. Entrance from the passage. Friendly, studenty cellar bar sponsored by Radio Zet. Small stage for concerts.

Piwiarnia Pod Jemiołą, ul. Floriańska 20. Literally, 'under the mistletoe'. One room with country-style tables and benches, and seating in the summer courtyard at the back. Following a spate of drug busts, it now has a much cleaner image.

Pod Papugami Irish Pub, ul. Św. Jana 14. Cellar bar with a pool table and Kilkenny on tap. Not to be confused with the *Pod Papugami* disco on ul. Szpitalna.

Pod Złotą Pipą, ul. Floriańska 30. A relatively clean and well ventilated cellar bar offering Czech Budweiser on tap. Tends to attract a forty-something clientele. If you don't mind the gaudy Austro-Hungarian decor, it's a good place to come for a quiet drink and/or snack.

Propaganda, ul. Miodowa 20. A tongue-in-cheek monument to Socialist Realism, complete with portraits of Stalin, 1950s radios, and edifying tributes to the heroes of yesteryear.

Ratuszowa, Ryneck Główny, underneath the Town Hall Tower (see p. 92). Same ownership as the *Maska*. Slightly damp interior. Adjoins a tiny theatre—a branch of the *Ludowy* in Nowa Huta.

Roentgen, pl. Szczepański 3. Traditionally, the last port of call when everywhere else is shut. Loud and smoky, but since a recent revamp—no longer squalid. Occasional live bands. As regulars like to point out, the Fertility Clinic sign in the passageway refers to an establishment in the courtyard.

Shakesbeer, ul. Gołębia 2. One of the first Western-style bars in Kraków. Nowadays somewhat less popular, perhaps because the pool tables and chrome fittings no longer impress.

Singer, ul. Estery 20. Not quite same since the departure of its founder–owner, but still retains a cosy, slightly bohemian atmosphere. The furnishings include a set of old pedal-driven Singer sewing machines used as tables (hence the name). While away the night hours to Jacques Brel and Edith Piaff, or stop in for coffee during a tour of Kazimierz.

Strawberry Club, ul. Św. Tomasza 1 (corner of pl. Szczepański). Basement bar with pool tables and a very young clientele.

Teatr Bückleina, ul. Lubicz 5a. A converted Austrian barracks with a dark, warehouse-like atmosphere. Used as a theatre and concert venue by day, and a bar/disco by night (entrance fee on Fridays). Opposite the main railway station.

Trelkowski, ul. Czarnowiejska 55. In the west of town, on the way to the student campus. Named after the main protagonist of Polański's *The Tenant*. Three, low-lit basement rooms and an old upright piano. Run by the former owner of the *Singer*, and hence similar in ambience.

Vinoteka (*Hotel Pod Różą*), ul. Floriańska 14. Wine cellar with an extensive choice of wine, mostly Italian.

Vis-à-Vis, Rynek Główny 29 (next to the police station). An untypical bar for the Market Square, completely lacking in pretension and not at all oriented towards tourists. Once a favourite haunt of members of the *Piwnica pod Baranami Cabaret* (see p. 99, and nowadays still attracts its fair share of crazed artists and heavy vodka drinkers. Sit outside in summer and watch the crowds, or chat to the two charming waitresses—Pani Zosia and Pani Krysia—who've worked there for the last thirty-odd years.

Telephone and postal services

Post offices (*urzédy pocztowe*, or *poczty* for short) are usually open 08.00–18.00 or 20.00 on weekdays and 08.00–14.00 on Saturdays. The **main post office** at ul. Westerplatte 20 (entrance from ul. Wielopole; open Mon–Fri 08.00–20.00, Sat 08.00–14.00, Sun 09.00–11.00) has a 24 hour telephone service, so even when the main section is closed you can still make national and international calls. Other branches include Rynek Główny 19 (Market Square; open daily 08.00–22.00) and ul. Lubicz 4 (opposite the main railway station). If you just want to buy stamps or send postcards, you can do this at the mock stagecoach on the Market Square, near the Italian House (see p. 98; summer only).

Telephone calls. The best way to make international calls is to buy a magnetic phone card (*karta telefoniczna*; 25, 50 or 100 units; phone cards and tokens can also be bought at certain kiosks and hotels) and dial direct from a blue or silver pay phone. You should break the perforated edge of the card before use. To make an international call, dial 0, wait for the tone, then dial 0 again followed by the country code (44 for the UK; 1 for the US and Canada; 61 for Australia), next the area code (dropping the zero), and then finally the subscriber's number. For long-distance calls in Poland, dial 0 followed by the area code (eg 22 for Warsaw; 12 for Kraków) and the subscriber's number. The older pay phones take tokens (*żetony*), also available from post offices: 'A' for local calls (3 minutes), 'C' for national calls. Rates for national (but not international) telephone calls are cheaper after 19.00 and at weekends; they are cheapest between midnight and 06.00. **To call Kraków from the UK, dial 00 48 12**, followed by the number.

Other services provided at the main post office include: registered mail, telegram, telex, fax, poste restante and operator-assisted calls to areas which do not have automatic exchanges. There is also a good courier service (*EMS Pocztex*; entrance from ul. Westerplatte, ☎ 422 6696, info-line 0-800-120-091), including international door-to-door parcel delivery (☎ 655 2214). Postage stamps, envelopes and postcards are available at all post offices. Out-of-town and international mail should be put into the red post boxes; the green ones are for local mail. A letter takes about one week to reach European countries, two weeks to the US.

Useful telephone numbers

Long-distance operator	☎ 900	Speaking clock	☎ 9226
Telegrams	☎ 905	International area codes	☎ 9310

Internet

Polish Telecommunications (*Telekomunikacja Polska*) offers free access to the Internet dial 0202122 (you will be charged for a local call) to connect to a public access PPP server (username: ppp, password: ppp). If you have a laptop, you may be able to log on from your hotel room. If not, try one of the Internet cafés in the city, such as *Looz* at ul. Mikołajska 13 (surfing: 1hr—8 PLN, videophone 1hr—10 PLN, www.looz.com.pl), *Magiel* at ul. Librowszczyzna 4 (surfing: 1hr—6 PLN, fast connections, friendly staff, www.netcom.net.pl/~magiel), or *U Louisa* at Rynek Główny 13, the first Internet café in Kraków (surfing: 1hr—10 PLN, slow connections, very busy).

Entertainment, cultural events and festivals

- **Kraków 2000** Numerous events are taking place in the year 2000 and beyond. For details, contact the festival bureau: Biuro Organizacyjne Kraków 2000, ul Św. Krzyża 1, ☎ 421 8693, www.krakow2000.pl

The best place to get information about cultural events in Kraków is the **Cultural Information Centre** (*Centrum Informacji Kulturalnej*) at ul. Św. Jana 2, just off the Market Square (open Mon–Fri 10.00–19.00, Sat 11.00–19.00, ☎ 421 7787; www.karnet.krakow2000.pl). The office publishes a very useful listings magazine called *Karnet* in both English and Polish. Tickets for some events can be purchased directly at the office. If not, the friendly, English-speaking staff will tell you how and where to book.

Exhibitions, concerts, film shows, seminars, etc., some in foreign languages, are organised by various **cultural institutions** in Kraków:

- **Austrian Consulate** ul. Krupnicza 41, ☎ 421 9766, fax 421 6737.
- **British Council** (newly-opened) Rynek Główny 26, ☎ 428 5930.
- **French Institute** ul. Wiślna 2, ☎ 421 4610.
- **Goethe Institute** Rynek Główny 20, ☎ 422 6902, fax 422 5829, fax 422 8276.
- **International Cultural Centre** Rynek Główny 25, ☎ 421 8601, fax 421 8571.
- **Italian Institute** ul. Grodzka 49, ☎ 421 8946, fax 421 9770.
- **Jewish Cultural Centre** ul. Meiselsa 17, ☎ 423 5595, fax 423 5034.
- **Manggha Centre of Japanese Art and Technology** ul. Konopnickiej 26, ☎ 267 2703, fax 267 4079.

Other publications listing cultural events The Friday edition of *Gazeta Wyborcza*, a national daily, has previews (in Polish) of events in Kraków over the coming weekend, as well as extensive listings of films, plays, exhibitions, restaurants, live music, bars etc. Of the English-language magazines, by far and away the best is *Kraków in Your Pocket* (www.inyourpocket.com), published monthly. You could also check *Kraków What, Where, When* (www.inter.com.pl), *Welcome to Cracow & Małopolska*, and *Kraków Insider*, but their information is not always up-to-date.

Events calendar

Film, theatre, cabaret
March *International Advertising Festival*. Kijów cinema. A review of the best TV, radio and press advertisements from the previous year.
March *International Alternative Theatre Festival*. Rotunda student club. The oldest alternative theatre festival in Poland, with performers from home and abroad.
April *Cabaret Review*. Rotunda Student Club.
May/June *International Short Film Festival*. Kijów cinema and Rotunda

student club. There are two parallel competitions—for foreign and Polish short films—with the prize-winners being shown a second time at the Kijów.

July *International Festival of Street Theatre*. Mime artists, clowns, stilt walkers etc. Market Square.

November *Etiuda International Film Festival*. A review of the best work done by film students from home and abroad. Rotunda student club.

Dance

May/June *Kraków Ballet Festival*. Słowacki Theatre.

Music

March/April *Ludwig van Beethoven Easter Festival*. A relatively recent initiative (1997), inaugurated by Elżbieta Penderecka, wife of the composer Krzysztof Penderecki. So far, the couple have managed to attract top musicians from around the world, such as Anne Akkiko Meyers and Boris Pergamenschikov, making this one of the most important events in the city's classical music calendar. Concerts are held at the Philharmonic Hall, Słowacki Theatre, Cloth Hall, and the Academy of Music's 'Florianka Hall' at ul. Basztowa 8.

March *Organ Music Festival*. Oratorios and organ recitals performed at the Philharmonic Hall and churches around the city.

June *International Military Band Festival*. Parades on the Market Square.

July *Opera and Operetta Festival*. Słowacki Theatre.

July *Kraków Summer Jazz Festival*. Polish and foreign jazz played at open-air venues and in clubs. Recent Polish performers have included Tomasz Stańko, Michał Urbaniak and Urszula Dudziak. An especially memorable concert in 1998 was given by the all-star quartet of Joe Lovano (sax), John Scofield (guitar), Al Foster (percussion) and Dave Holland (bass) in the courtyard of Wawel Castle.

July/August *Tyniec Organ Recitals*. Held at the Benedictine Abbey in Tyniec (see p. 163).

July/August *Old Jazz in Kraków* (traditional jazz). Venues include the Kornet Jazz Club, Arts Pavilion (*Bunkier Sztuki*), and café by the Town Hall Tower.

August *Music in Old Kraków*. An International classical music festival, with events held inside courtyards, churches, and other historic buildings.

October/November *Early Music Festival*. Renaissance and Baroque music played on original instruments in churches around the city.

November *Zaduszki* (All Souls') *Jazz Festival*. Philharmonic Hall (day), jazz clubs (night).

November *Audio-Art Festival*. Art and experimental music combined. Venues include the Bücklein Theatre, Goethe Institute, Arts Pavilion (*Bunkier Szuki*), and Krzysztofory Art Gallery.

December *Jazz Juniors* (international amateur jazz festival). Rotunda student club.

Art

August Folk art fair. Market Square.

August/September *International Graphic Art Triennale* (next one in 2000).

Religious festivals

Easter This is the holiest period in the Polish calendar, with numerous religious events taking place in and around the city. The most extraordinary of these is the annual **Passion play** in the town of Kalwaria Zebrzydowska, west of Kraków (see

Days Out). A couple of pleasant hours can be spent at the Emaus fair, held on Easter Monday at the Premonstratensian Convent in Salwator (see p. 158). This is a good place to buy religious items, trinkets and Polish gingerbread (*pierniki*). For a description of culinary traditions at Easter, see *Eating and Drinking*.

8 May *Feast of St Stanisław*. This religious event is connected with the cult of St Stanisław (see p. 146), one the first martyrs of the Polish Catholic Church. A procession headed by bishops and cardinals brings the reliquary containing the saint's remains from Wawel Cathedral to the 'Skałka' church (see p. 146). Crowds of believers sing religious songs as the cortège proceeds slowly down ul. Stradom and ul. Krakowska. The event culminates in an open-air mass said by the Primate of Poland (presently Cardinal Glemp).

June/July *Festival of Jewish Culture*. Established in 1988, the aim of the festival is to bring Jewish culture to a wider Polish audience and to tackle the thorny issue of Polish-Jewish relations by promoting dialogue, understanding and informed tolerance. A series of concerts, lectures, workshops and meetings are held all over the city (details at the Jewish Cultural Centre, ul. Meiselsa 17). All the bands play at the final, open-air concert (usually Saturday) held on ul. Szeroka in Kazimierz (see p. 141). The atmosphere is wonderful, and when the main show is over the crowds move into the local bars to continue the festivities. Not to be missed.

December *Christmas (Nativity) crib competition*. The best ones are displayed by the Mickiewicz monument on the Market Square and then in the Historical Museum (see p. 102). A Nativity scene with a live tableau of humans and animals is shown in front of Franciscan Church (see p. 110) over Christmas. For a description of culinary traditions at Christmas, see *Eating and Drinking*.

Miscellaneous

Easter Monday is also the day that young men carry on the tradition of *śmigus-dyngus*. This originally involved showering peasant girls with buckets of water, but these days all women are potential targets. Worse still, your assailants will take greatest pleasure in catching you completely off your guard—be especially vigilant when getting on/off trams or buses. If getting drenched is not your idea of fun, stay indoors.

May *Juvenalia Student Festival*. A tradition reaching back to the Middle Ages. Krakow's student community is symbolically handed the keys to the city for three days. Lots of concerts (in clubs and on the Market Square) and drinking.

June *Wianki* (Midsummer's Eve, nearest weekend to 21 June). A spectacular show, with live music and fireworks, on the riverside by Wawel Castle. The main events take place in the evening (19.00–22.00), but come early if want to get a good view. During the festivities candlelit wreathes (*wianki*) are cast into the river. This ancient Slavic custom was originally performed by young women to determine when they would marry.

Cabaret

Loch Camelot ul. Św. Tomasza 17. Small stage in the cellar of a chic café. The newest and possibly best cabaret in Kraków. Open until midnight, with shows on Fridays at 20.15. Tickets can be bought at the Cultural Information Centre (see above), or reserved by phone direct from the cabaret (☎ 421 0123).

Jama Michalika ul. Floriańska 45. Plush, smoke-free café set in beautiful fin-de-siècle interiors. The oldest cabaret in Poland (see p. 105), with a puppet show based on early 20C texts by Tadeusz Boy-Żeleński. Saturdays at 20.00, provided there is a minimum audience of 30 guests. For reservations, ☎ 656 5381.

Feniks (Café Cabaret) ul. Św. Jana 2. The Feniks is a self-advertised 'dancing bar'—a wonderful throwback to the communist period. 'Dancing bars' were endemically tacky establishments—actually a restaurant, disco and drink bar rolled into one—where Party functionaries would take their spouses for a night on the town. The special atmosphere of these halcyon days is continued in the dance evenings for the over 40s held on Tuesdays to Sundays, 17.00–21.00, complete with apathetic waiters, glitterballs, a repertoire of Barry Manilow, Demiss Rousoss and other 70s favourites or, worse still, a live band. The main entertainment takes place between 21.00 and 03.00, usually a cabaret (frequent performances by Jan Pietrzak's *Kabaret Pod Egida*), more dancing and/or the occasional stripper. For current shows, check the posters outside; for reservations, ☎ 421 9637, ☎ 421 5093.

Piwnica Pod Baranami Rynek Główny 27. Poland's most famous cabaret (see p. 99), contained in a cellar bar off the Market Square. Though officially closed in 1996, there are intermittent performances, sometimes at alternative venues (eg the Słowacki Theatre). Ask at the Cultural Information Centre for details. Prior booking essential (☎ 421 2500). Saturdays at 21.00. There is also a disco in the cellars (open 20.00 till late, turn left at the bottom of the stairs).

Cinema

Mainstream Hollywood films are shown in Polish cinemas soon after their release in Western Europe. Unfortunately, current Polish films are pretty dire, with most trying to imitate American action movies and not really succeeding. Now and again good films are made by established directors like Andrzej Wajda (see p. 150), but they rarely enjoy commercial success outside of Poland. A notable exception is Krzysztof Kieślowski's widely acclaimed *Three Colours* trilogy of the early 1990s. Foreign films are subtitled in cinemas; on television they are narrated as proper dubbing is considered too expensive. The largest and most comfortable cinema in Kraków is the *Kijów* (al. Krasińskiego 34, next to the *Cracovia Hotel*), which tends to show Hollywood blockbusters. Good, centrally located cinemas include the *Wanda* (ul. Św. Gertrudy 5, near the Vega restaurant), *Apollo* (ul. Św. Tomasza 11a) and *Sztuka* (ul. Św. Jana 6, with two other affiliated cinemas in the same building). Two 'art-house' cinemas often showing alternative/older firms are the *Mikro* (ul. Lea 5) and *Pod Baranami* (Rynek Główny 27), both with small screens and rather cramped seating.

Music

Classical music Contemporary Polish music has achieved international renown through such composers as Witold Lutosławski, Krzysztof Penderecki, Andrzej Panufnik and Henryk Górecki. Their works are often performed in Kraków (Penderecki is a native of the city). The principal concert venue is the **Filharmonia**, or Philharmonic Hall (ul. Zwierzyniecka 1, ☎/fax 422 9477, ☎ 422 4312, box office open Mon–Fri 14.00–19.00 and one hour before performances). There is a varied annual programme, including music performed by, among others, the excellent *Capella Cracoviensis*. Classical concerts are often held inside historic buildings (eg the Cloth Hall, St Catherine's church), or in spectacular open-air settings, such as the courtyards of Wawel Castle and Collegium Maius (summer only). Tickets are still very cheap—you can hear top-class performers for as little as $US5.00 There are numerous annual music events in the city (see *Festivals*), which are usually of high standard and always well attended.

In July and August an attractive option is to combine a boat trip along the Vistula with a visit to the Benedictine Abbey in Tyniec (see p. 163), where organ recitals are held (ask at the Cultural Information Centre for details). Another attractive venue is the Villa Decius (*Willa Decjusza*) in the suburb of Wola Justowska, where your night-out could be combined with a meal at the exclusive *Villa Decius* restaurant.

Live Music Polish **jazz** has been held in high regard ever since musicians like Tomasz Stańko and Michał Urbaniak made their names in the West. Kraków plays host to four annual **Jazz festivals**: Jazz Juniors (December), the Kraków Summer Jazz Festival (July), Old Jazz in Kraków (July–August), and the 'Zaduszki' (All Souls) Jazz Festival (November). The most well-established jazz club in the city is *U Muniaka* (ul. Floriańska 3), named after its founder and chief performer, Janusz Muniak, which has trad jazz concerts on Fridays and Saturdays at 21.30. Other good venues include the *Kornet* (ul. Krasińskiego 19, opposite the *Kijów* cinema), with New Orleans jazz on Wednesdays and the Old Metropolitan Band and others on Fridays, the *Harris Piano Jazz Bar* (Rynek Główny 28), which has concerts almost every day, and the recently-opened *Indigo* (ul. Floriańska 26), fast-becoming the best club, where concerts are broadcast live on Jazz FM.

Polish **pop music** is vastly more diverse now than it was a decade ago. The pre-1990s 'old guard' (solo artists like Maryla Rodowicz and Czesław Niemen, or bands like Maanam and Budka Suflera) are still top of the popularity ratings, but they are now having to share the limelight with a crop of talented younger performers. The latter include Kayah, whose recent album with Serbian composer Goran Bregovic went platinum before reaching the shops!, the cattish Justyna Steczkowska, who composes as brilliantly as she performs and can boast a huge vocal range, Anna Maria Jopek, also an excellent jazz singer, Kazik, an original Polish 'rap' artist who performs with his band *Kazik na Żywo* (Kazik Live), and finally Grzegorz Turnau, a member of the *Piwnica pod Baranami Cabaret* (see p. 99), whose poetic lyrics and acoustic sets are something of a rarity.

Large open-air rock concerts are usually held at the *Hala Wisły* (ul. Reymonta 22). Bands with less pulling-power play at the indoor *Rotunda* (ul. Oleandry 1), a student club which also has jazz on Tuesdays and rock/grunge music on other nights. A number of bars in the city centre offer live music of various kinds (see, also, *Late-night bars and clubs*): *Miasto Krakoff* (ul. Łobzowska 3, Polish alternative bands), *Klinika 35* (ul. Św. Tomasza 35, mainly rock and blues), *U Louisa 10,5* (Rynek Główny 13, jazz and blues on Fridays and Saturdays and occasional jam sessions), *Alef* (ul. Szeroka 17, Klezmer nights attended by an older crowd, daily in summer), and *Pod Jaszczurami* (Rynek Główny 8, jazz and rock, also doubles as a student disco). When there is a band playing you will normally be charged a nominal fee for entry into a bar or club. Check the posters around town for venues and times.

Theatre

Contemporary Polish theatre enjoys a better reputation than cinema. A major problem for visitors is, of course, the language barrier. Plays are sometimes staged by foreign theatre companies, during festivals for instance, but in general non-Polish productions are a rarity. The two oldest and most reputable theatres in Kraków are the *Stary* (pl. Szczepański, see p. 134) and the *Słowacki* (pl. Św. Ducha 1, see p. 139), both contained inside historic buildings that are well worth seeing in themselves. They have a predominantly classical repertoire, concentrating on the greats of the Romantic era, such as Fredro, Krasiński, Wyspiański, etc, but plays by modern writers are also staged. The *Słowacki* tends to put on large-scale productions. It hosts the Kraków Ballet Festival in May/June and also serves as an opera house. Indeed, its design is based on that of the Paris Opéra.

Alternative theatre is a better bet as regards overcoming the language barrier. Two places to try are the *Bücklein* (ul. Lubicz 5a), which employs a young cast and has occasional performances by foreign companies (it is also a concert venue), and the *Łaźnia* (ul. Paulińska 28) in Kazimierz, which is the closest you'll get to 'underground' theatre in Kraków.

For an altogether different experience, you could visit the *Teatr Lalki i Maski Groteska* (ul. Skarbowa 2), whose excellent **puppet shows** are enjoyed by children and adults alike.

Amusement parks

The best amusement park is **Cricoland** (summer only), Rondo Grunwaldzkie (tram nos 18, 19, 22, bus nos 103, 194). Get off just after the Grunwaldzki Bridge. Bumper cars, ferris wheel, and a rather tame rollercoaster. There is another funfair on al. Focha, just past the *Cracovia Hotel*, which was closed at the time of writing.

Zoo

Located in the Wolski Forest, a good area for walks (see p. 160). At weekends the road up to the Zoo (al. Kasy Oszczędności m. Krakowa) from Wola Justowska is only accessible by bus (no. 134, last stop) or taxi. Cars may enter on weekdays, but a small toll is charged. Open 09.00–18.00 (spring), 09.00–19.00 (summer).

Botanical gardens

Situated at the end of ul. Kopernika (no. 27), next to departments of the city's Medical Academy. A small but well-managed garden with a wide variety of Central European and tropical plants, as well as a 500-year old oak (open Sat–Thur 09.00–19.00; greenhouses 10.00–13.00).

 # Museums and galleries

As a rule, museums are open six days a week and are **closed on Mondays**. They open at around 10.00 and close at around 17.00, but may stay open longer on certain days of the week. Times may also vary with the season—museums usually operate shorter hours in winter (Oct–Mar). In the Guide, **opening times are given for the summer season** only. Last entrance is usually 30 minutes before closing. Tickets are cheap by Western standards, with concessions for students (proof of ID is required), and there is usually one free day. Exhibits are often marked in English or German. Foreign language booklets about the displays are usually available from ticket offices. At major sites (eg Wawel Castle), you can arrange for an English-speaking guide, given prior notice. Very few museums have provision for people with mobility difficulties. For more information, contact the museum directly or the *Polskie Towarzystwo Walki z Kalectwem* (see *Disabled travellers*).

The list below is only intended as a basic guide to museums and galleries in Kraków. More detailed descriptions can be found in the main text. Private and commercial art galleries are listed separately under *Contemporary Polish Art* (see p. 53).

Archaeological Museum (*Muzeum Archeologiczne*):

- **Main Branch** ul. Poselska 3 (open Mon–Wed 09.00–14.00, Thur 14.00–17.00, Sun 11.00–14.00). There are four sections: Mediterranean culture in antiquity; the ancient and medieval history of Małopolska; Nowa Huta in prehistoric times; and the history of the museum building.

- **Church of St Adalbert** (*Kościół Św. Wojciecha*) Market Square (open Mon–Sat 12.00–16.00, May–Sept). This branch of the Archaeological Museum is devoted to the life of St Adalbert, the first martyr of the Polish Catholic Church.

Archdiocesan Museum (*Muzeum Archidiecezjalne*) ul. Kanonicza 19 (open Tues–Sat 10.00–15.00). A small display of liturgical vestments and religious art from various churches in Kraków. You can also visit the room where Pope John Paul II once lived.

Arts Pavilion (*Bunkier Sztuki*) pl. Szczepański 3 (open Tues–Sun 11.00–18.00). Exhibitions of modern art. Also the venue of the International Graphic Art Triennale in September.

Cricoteka ul. Kanonicza 5 (open Mon–Fri 10.00–14.00). Exhibits connected with the work of the artist and playwright Tadeusz Kantor.

Ethnographical Museum (*Muzeum Etnograficzne*) pl. Wolnica 1 (open Mon 10.00–18.00, Wed–Fri 10.00–15.00, Sat–Sun 10.00–14.00). Folk art, mainly from the south of Poland. The museum has a tiny **exhibition centre** at ul. Krakowska 46 (open Mon–Fri 09.00–15.00).

Gallery of Ukrainian Art (*Galeria Sztuki Ukraińskiej*) ul. Kanonicza 15 (open Thur–Sun 12.00–16.00). A small collection of 17C–19C icons, and paintings by Jerzy Nowosielski.

Geological Museum (*Muzeum Geologiczne*) ul. Senacka 1–3 (open Tues 10.00–17.30, Wed–Fri 10.00–15.00, Sat–Sun 10.00–14.00).

Ghetto Museum (*Muzeum Pamięci Narodowej 'Apteka pod Orłem'*) pl. Bohaterów Getta 18 (open Mon–Fri 10.00–16.00, Sat 10.00–14.00). Situated across the river in the district of Podgórze. A small display documenting life in the Płaszów ghetto during the Second World War.

Palace of Art (*Pałac Sztuki*) pl. Szczepański 4 (open daily 08.15–20.00). Exhibitions of graphic art, sculpture and painting, often the best in Kraków.

Historical Museum of Kraków (*Muzeum Historyczne Miasta Krakowa*):

- **Barbican** at the exit of ul. Floriańska (open Mon–Fri 09.00–12.45, 13.15–18.00, Sat–Sun 09.00–17.00). A unique example of medieval defensive architecture. No exhibition as such, but a venue for summer concerts and plays.

- **Hippolitus House** pl. Mariacki 3 (open Wed, Fri–Sun 09.00–15.30, Thur 11.00–18.00). Temporary exhibitions, though a permanent display of 19C interiors is being prepared.

- **House under the Cross** (*Dom Pod Krzyżem*) ul. Szpitalna 21 (open Wed 11.00–18.00, Thur–Sun 09.00–15.30). An exhibition on the history of theatre in Kraków.
- **Krzysztofory** Market Square 35 (open Thur 11.00–18.00, Wed and Fri–Sun 09.00–15.30). Rather lacklustre display tracing the history of the city. An exhibition of clocks on the second floor.
- **Old Synagogue** (*Stara Synagoga*) ul. Szeroka 24 (open Wed–Thur, Sat–Sun 09.00–15.00, Fri 11.00–18.00). An exhibition devoted to the history and culture of Kraków's Jews.
- **Town Hall Tower** Market Square (open Wed–Fri, Sat–Sun 09.00–16.00, summer only). Fine views over Kraków from the third floor rooms.

Jagiellonian University Museum (*Collegium Maius*) ul. Jagiellońska 15 (open Mon–Fri 11.00–14.30, Sat 11.00–13.30; guided tour in English). The exhibition traces the history of the Jagiellonian University. You can visit the rooms where its most famous student, Nicholas Copernicus, studied. The highlight is a collection of astronomical instruments, some used by Copernicus.

Museum of Pharmacy (*Muzeum Farmacji*) ul. Floriańska 25 (open Tues 15.00–19.00, Wed–Fri 11.00–14.00; entry for group tours only, by prior arrangement; ☎ 421–9279). The history of Polish pharmacy from medieval times until the present day.

National Museum (*Muzeum Narodowe*):

- **Cloth Hall Gallery** Sukiennice (open Tues–Wed, Fri–Sun 10.00–16.00, Thur 10.00–18.00). One of the best galleries in Kraków, with the emphasis on 19C Polish painting.
- **Czartoryski Collection** ul. Św. Jana 19 (open Tues–Fri 09.00–17.00, Sat–Sun 10.00–15.30). The main permanent displays cover the history of Poland from the 14C to the 18C (mainly armoury, weaponry and royal memorabilia), European decorative art, and European sculpture and painting (13C–19C), including Leonardo da Vinci's **Lady with an Ermine**. Temporary exhibitions are held on the ground floor.
- **House of Józef Mehoffer** ul. Krupnicza 26 (open Tues, Thur–Sun 10.00–15.30, Wed 10.00–18.00). A small biographical display devoted to one of the major Polish painters.
- **Manggha Centre of Japanese Art and Technology** ul. Konopnickiej 26 (open Tues–Sun 10.00–18.00). An excellent permanent exhibition of Japanese art, comprising 18C woodcuts, Samurai weaponry, porcelain and jewellery.
- '**New Building**' ul. 3 Maja 1 (open Tues, Thur–Sun 10.00–15.30, Wed 10.00–18.00). Polish painting and sculpture from the 'Young Poland' period to the present day, including a rich collection of works by Wyspiański.
- **Szołayski House** pl. Szczepański 9 (open Tues 10.00–18.00, Wed–Sun 10.00–16.00). Polish sculpture and painting, with particular emphasis on medieval art from the Małopolska region. The building was closed for renovation at the time of writing.
- **Wyspiański Museum** ul. Kanonicza 9 (open Mon–Fri 10.00–15.00). A biographical display tracing the life and work of Stanisław Wyspiański, one of the greatest figures in Polish art and literature.

Theatre Museum (*Muzeum Starego Teatru*) ul. Jagiellońska 1, (open Tues–Sat 11.00–13.00, and an hour before performances). A small display on the history of the Old Theatre (*Stary Teatr*).

Wawel:

- **Castle (Royal Chambers, Royal Treasury and Armoury, Exhibition of Oriental Art)** (open Tues, Fri 09.30–16.30, Wed–Thur 09.30–15.30, Sat 09.30–15.00, Sun 10.00–15.00). The highlight is a collection of magnificent 16C Brussels tapestries.
- **Cathedral** (open Mon–Sat 09.00–17.30, Sun 12.15–17.30, summer; Mon–Sat 09.00–15.00, Sun 12.15–15.00, winter). The highlights are the Renaissance Zygmunt Chapel and the tombs of Polish monarchs. Fine views over Kraków from the Zygmunt Tower.
- **Cathedral Museum** (open Mon–Sat 09.00–17.30, Sun 12.15–17.30, summer; Mon–Sat 09.00–15.00, Sun 12.15–15.00, winter). A collection of items from the Cathedral Treasury.
- **'Lost Wawel'** (open Mon, Wed, Thur 09.30–15.30, Fri 09.30–16.30, Sat 09.30–15.00, Sun 10.00–15.00). An archaeological exhibition showing the vestiges of the earliest stone church in Kraków, the pre-Romanesque Rotunda of St Mary.

Churches

Due to the increasing number of thefts, churches have more stringent opening times than a few years ago. Famous and historic churches are open all day, but less important ones may be accessible only during mass or at the visiting times indicated outside. It is not considered polite to wander about a church during mass and those who do may get some stern looks or be asked to leave. There is a Catholic mass in English on Sundays at 10.30 at the Church of St Giles (see p. 117).

Shopping

Opening hours Most shops are open Mon–Fri 10.00–18.00, Sat 10.00–14.00, and are closed all day on Sundays. However, there are 24-hour off-licences, food shops and pharmacies (see below). Most supermarkets have Sunday opening. Banks are usually open Mon–Fri 08.00–18.00, and sometimes on Saturday mornings. Many supermarkets now accept major credit cards, as do high-street outlets selling clothes, jewellery, etc. (but not food). At weekends you can pick up groceries and miscellaneous items at outdoor markets, usually for a lower price than in regular shops. Bakeries (*piekarnie*) and patisseries (*cukiernie*) open early and are a good place to buy cheap and delicious food for breakfast.

Antiques

Special licences are required to export antiques or any goods produced before 1945. For information on how to apply, see p. 12. There are scores of antique shops in the Old Town, particularly in the streets north and south of the Market Square.

The reputable *Desa* chain has salons at ul. Floriańska 13 (open Mon–Fri 11.00–18.00, Sat 10.00–14.00), ul. Grodzka 8 (open Mon–Fri 10.00–18.00,

Sat 11.00–14.00), ul. Stolarska 17 (open 11.00–18.00, Sat 11.00–14.00, ul. Mikołajska 10 and ul. Sławkowska 4, where you can often pick up items at bargain prices.

Other good places for browsing include: *Galeria Hetmańska*, Rynek Główny 17 (in the passageway; open Mon–Fri 11.00–19.00; Sat 11.00–15.00), which mostly deals in art; *Salon Dzieł Sztuki i Antyków*, ul. Szewska 27 (open Mon–Fri 10.00–14.00, 15.00–19.00; *Antyki. Dom Aukcyjny*, ul. Jagiellońska 6a (open Mon–Fri 10.00–20.00, Sat and Sun 10.00–15.00); and *Antyki*, ul. Jagiellońska 5 (open Mon–Fri 10.00–17.00, Sat 10.00–13.00).

Books

The *Hetmańska*, Rynek Główny 17 (open Mon–Sat 09.00–21.00, Sun 11.00–21.00), which occupies the ground floor of the Hetman House (see p. 98), probably has the best selection of English books, especially photograph albums and fiction.

The nearby *Odeon-Hetmańska*, Rynek Główny 5 (open daily 09.00–23.00) has some foreign language publications as well as art albums, children books, local guides, posters and postcards, and a good selection of maps and atlases in the basement.

Also on the Market Square is the *Suszczyński i S-ka*, Rynek Główny 23 (open Mon–Fri 09.00–19.00, Sat 10.00–16.00, Sun 11.00–15.00), dealing mainly in school textbooks, but with an upstairs section (separate entrance) devoted to academic foreign-language publications. The shop next door (No. 25) sells foreign-langauge newspapers. A good place for music books and scores is the *Kurant*, Rynek Główny 36 (open Mon–Fri 09.00–19.00, Sat 10.00–15.00), where you can also pick up CDs, cassettes and videos.

Pegasus, ul. Dunajewskiego 1 (open Mon–Fri 10.00–19.00, Sat 10.00–16.00), has a wide range of textbooks and a small English section.

Interbook, ul. Karmelicka 27 (open Mon—Fri 10.00–18.00, Sat 10.00–15.00), specialises in English-language teaching and is a good place to buy dictionaries.

Znak, ul. Sławkowska 1 (open Mon–Fri 10.00–18.00, Sat 10.00–14.00), associated with the high-brow journal of the same name, is the best place for books on philosophy, history, art and religion, but the small English section has only paperback fiction.

Ossolineum, ul. Sławkowska 17, is a respected academic bookshop, with a good science section but surprisingly few foreign-language publications.

For books on Jewish culture and history, try the *Jarden*, ul. Szeroka 2 (open Mon–Fri 10.00–18.00, Sat and Sun 11.00–18.00) in the district of Kazimierz.

Second-hand books

Shops called *antykwariaty* specialise in second-hand and antique books. Bear in mind, however, that a special licence is required to export any book published before 1945. Applicants should contact the Centre for the Protection of Cultural Goods (*Ośrodek Ochrony Dóbr Kultury*) at the National Library (*Biblioteka Narodowa*) in Warsaw, al. Niepodległości 213, ☎ (022) 608 2999). The procedure takes around two weeks and permission may not be granted if the book is of special value and the National Library doesn't own a copy. While many foreign visitors ignore the licence regulations and take old books abroad with them, in the letter of the law this is considered smuggling and you should expect no mercy from Polish customs if you're caught.

All the shops listed are located in the Old Town. The *Antykwariat Księgarski*, ul. Bracka 6 (open Mon–Fri 10.00–19.00, Sat 10.00–15.00) has books in Polish, English, French and German, as well as albums, dictionaries and maps. A good place for old postcards and photographs is the *Krakowski Antykwariat Naukowy*, ul. Św. Tomasza 8.

Two other shops worth trying are the *Antykwariat Naukowy*, ul. Floriańska 15 (1st floor; open Mon–Fri 10.00–18.00, Sat 10.00–14.00) and the *Antykwariat Księgarski*, under the arcades on ul. Stolarska (open Mon–Fri 10.00–18.00.

The *Antykwariat Księgarski*, ul. Św. Jana 3 (open Mon–Fri 09.00–17.00, Sat 10.00–13.30), is a typical second-hand bookshop, with lots of newer (post-1945) books, thematically arranged.

Rara Avis, ul. Szpitalna 7 (open Mon–Fri 10.00–18.00, Sat 10.00–14.00; first floor), offers a wide selection of second-hand and antique books (also in English) as well as paintings, graphic art, woodcuts, dictionaries and maps.

Bibliofil, ul. Szpitalna 19 (open Mon–Fri 10.00–18.00, Sat 10.00–14.00), specialises in encyclopaedias, dictionaries, art and literature, and has both new and second-hand books.

Folk art and craft

The *Cepelia* chain, established in 1949, deals in various types of folk art: wood sculpture, ceramics, embroidery, paper products, as well as tapestries designed and produced by traditional techniques. There is a branch at ul. Karmelicka 23.

The Cloth Hall (*Sukiennice*, open Mon–Fri 10.00–18.00, Sat and Sun 11.00–15.00), very popular among tourists, is the classic place for hand-made goods, particularly amber jewellery, wood sculpture, embroidery and pottery, though you could probably find the same products for half the price in Zakopane or other provincial towns.

Confusingly, there is a shop called *Sukiennice* at ul. Bracka 11 (open Mon–Fri 10.00–19.00, Sat 10.00–15.00), which also deals in folk art, but has no connection with the Cloth Hall on the Market Square.

Other places to try include the shops under the arcades (*Kramy Dominikańskie*) on ul. Stolarska, and *Milenium: Galeria Sztuki Ludowej*, Rynek Główny 17 (in the passageway; open Mon–Sat 10.00–20.00, Sun 11.00–20.00).

Galeria Osobliwości, ul. Sławkowska 16 (open Mon–Fri 11.00–19.30) is good for wood sculpture, jewellery and curiosities.

Calik, Rynek Główny 7, 1st floor (open Mon–Fri 10.00–19.00, Sat 10.00–17.00, Sun 10.00–15.00) specialises in wonderful Christmas decorations in a multitude of designs.

Souvenirs

Amber products (necklaces, brooches, rings etc.) are typically Polish and by Western standards still relatively cheap. A good place to browse is ul. Floriańska, where there are many reputable jewellers' (*jubiler*), though you could also try the shops listed under *Folk art and craft*.

Other places selling gifts and souvenirs include *Brama*, pl. Wszystkich Świętych 9 (open Mon–Sat 10.00–20.00, Sun 11.00–19.00), good for glass and ceramics; *Luka*, ul. Gołębia 3 (open Mon–Fri 11.00–19.00), and *Porfirion: Fabryka Prezentów* (Gift Factory), ul. Św. Tomasza 26 (open Mon–Fri 09.00–19.00, Sat 09.00–15.00).

Contemporary Polish art

The *Starmach Gallery*, run by the art historian Andrzej Starmach, is without doubt one of the best galleries of contemporary art in Poland. It concentrates on the work of the 'Kraków Group' (see p. 103), the foremost current in Polish art since the war, but is also eager to exhibit the work of young artists active today. One branch of the gallery is located on the Market Square (Rynek Główny 45, open Mon–Fri 11.00–18.00, Sat 11.00–14.00). Far more impressive, though, is the main building in the district of Podgórze (ul. Węgierska 5, open Mon–Fri 11.00–18.00), whose ultra-modern interiors incorporate the façade of a synagogue destroyed during the Second World War.

The *Potocka* at pl. Sikorskiego 10 (open Tues–Thur 16.00–18.00) is less commercially-oriented, but displays work in a variety of media and is an excellent place to check out the latest developments in Polish art. You can visit the gallery outside normal hours by prior arrangement (☎ 421-0278). The owner—Maria Anna Potocka—also plans to open an Artists' Museum in Pieskowa Skała castle near Kraków (see p. 173).

Equally good is the *Zderzak* at ul. Floriańska 3 (open Tues–Sat 12.00–17.00), established in the early 1980s as the first 'underground' (independent) gallery in communist Poland, where artists out of favour with the state could exhibit their work. Run by the artist Marta Tarabuła, it participates in major Western art fairs, such as 'Art Forum' in Berlin, 'Messe' in Frankfurt-am-Main, and 'ARKO' in Madrid, one of very few Polish galleries to do so. Again, the emphasis is on young artists and a variety of media—photograms, installations, etc.

The best place for graphic art is the *Jan Fejkiel* gallery on ul. Grodzka 25 (open Mon–Fri 11.00–19.00, Sat 11.00–16.00), which exhibits work by Polish and foreign artists.

For more traditional Polish painting, you could try the *Grotta Nobile* (Rynek Główny 33, Open Tues–Fri 11.00–18.00, Sat 11.00–14.00), which has strong links with the Academy of Fine Arts (see p. 107).

The *Rostworowski* gallery (ul. Św. Jana 20; open Mon–Fri 11.00–18.00, Sat 11.00–19.00), run by the sculptor Dominik Rostworowski, exhibits the work of young local artists, with an emphasis on classical media. On the same street you could visit the gallery of the cartoonist Andrzej Mleczko (ul. Św. Jana 14; open Mon–Fri 11.00–17.00, Sat 10.00–14.00), whose satirical sketches—available in postcard and poster form—stand out for their bold, zany, and sometimes vulgar humour.

Clothes and shoes

Despite the multitude of outlets, Kraków is not a good place to shop for clothes and shoes. If you're used to designer shops and Western-style chain stores, you may be disappointed. As a rule, clothes shops are small, understocked, and not very customer-friendly. Prices vary depending on the brand names, but generally they are comparable to Western prices. On average you should expect to pay from 100 to 500 PLN for a single garment. The best streets to explore are ul. Grodzka and ul. Floriańska, both of which have everything from smart boutiques to inexpensive outlets. Most clothes shops open on weekdays at 10.00 or 11.00, closing at 18.00 or 19.00; on Saturdays they close earlier, usually at 15.00 or 16.00.

Ul. Floriańska: no. 7. *Pabia* (*Pierre Cardin*), men's and women's clothes; expensive; no. 12. *Mon Image* (*Jus d'Orange, Morgan*), young fashion; no. 15. *Benetton*, young fashion; no. 18. *Paradise* sells designer labels: *Escada, Boss, Ungaro, Joop!, Kenzo*, men's and women's clothes; expensive; no. 31. *Troll*, young fashion, inexpensive; no. 14. *Vero Moda*, women's clothes; no. 32. *Sunset Suits*, men's clothes.

Ul. Grodzka: *Sunset Suits* (no. 16), men's clothes; *Jenner* (no. 13), men's and women's clothes; *Troll* (no. 38), young fashion, inexpensive; *Paradise* (no. 5), men's and women's clothes, expensive; *De Mehlem* (no. 43), leather goods (bags, purses, wallets, etc.); *Vistula* (no. 46; also at ul. Szpitalna 3) men's clothes; *Venezia* (no. 48), women's clothes; *Leo Lazzi* (no. 62), women's clothes; expensive.

Other popular stores include: *Deni Cler* at ul. Św. Jana 2, women's clothes; expensive; *Simple* at ul. Dominikańska 3/1, women's wear; *Jackpot & Cottonfield*, at Rynek Główny 38, men's and women's clothes; and *Miasto Kobiet* at ul. Jagiellońska 9, rather pricy but very stylish women's clothes.

For shoes, try *Olivier* at ul. Szewska 9 or *Zebra*, either at ul. Floriańska 3, or Rynek Główny 7. The best shops for children's clothes are *Ulmax* at ul. Wiślna 9 and *Oban & Obani* at ul. Gołębia 3.

Department stores

There are two department stores (*domy towarowe*) located very close to the Market Square: *Galeria Centrum*, ul. Św. Anny 2 (open Mon–Fri 09.00–20.00, Sat 09.00–19.00, Sun 10.00–16.00) and *Elefant*, ul. Podwale 6–7 (open Mon–Fri 10.00–19.00, Sat 10.00–15.00). Both are good for cosmetics, fabrics, cheap clothes and shoes.

Slightly further afield are *Herbewo*, al. Słowackiego 64 (by the Nowy Kleparz market), with a *Vision Express* optician on the ground floor, and *Jubilat*, al. Krasińskiego 1/3 (by the Dębnicki Bridge, open Mon–Fri 09.00–20.00, Sat 09.00–18.00, Sun 10.00–15.00), which also sells food (24 hours) and photographic equipment.

Speciality food shops

Delicatessens (*delikatesy*) are the best place to buy Polish vodka and liqueurs (see *Eating and Drinking*), as they stock rarer brands not usually available in other shops. There are two good delicatessens on the Market Square at nos 6 and 34. The small shop at no. 7 sells alcohol as well as perfumes and tobacco, and stays open late on Saturdays and Sundays. Another option is *Baryleczka* at ul. Szczepańska 9, just off the Market Square. If you want to buy a bottle of **Polish vodka** as a gift, bear in the mind that there is no duty free at Balice airport.

The best places to buy **wine** are *In Vino Veritas* (ul. Łobzowska 26), and *Skład Win Pod Niedźwiedzią Łapą*, which has branches at ul. Św. Tomasza 25a and ul Pijarska 11, the latter staying open until midnight. French and Italian wines can be bought at *Pod Aniołami* (ul. Grodzka 35), which also sells **highland cheeses** and traditional Polish sausage.

Pożegnanie z Afryką (Out of Africa) at ul. Św. Tomasza 21 has an excellent selection of **coffee** from around the world (see, also, *Cafés*). Another branch has just opened at ul. Floriańska 15. The *Palarnia Kawy* at ul. Karmelicka 17 (in the courtyard) sells its own blends of coffee and has a good choice of black, green and fruit flavoured teas.

Supermarkets and convenience stores

Supermarkets have the best choice of food and drink, but none are located in the city centre. In town, *spożywcze* shops sell basic groceries, opening early on weekdays, at 06.00 or 07.00, and closing at 18.00 or 19.00. There are a few in the vicinity of the Market Square, including two on ul. Szpitalna: *Witaminka* (no. 11) and *Maria* (no. 30), and two on ul. Floriańska: no. 6, in the courtyard, and no. 50, near *McDonald's*. *Dominik* on pl. Dominikański operates longer hours and is conveniently open at weekends (Mon–Fri 06.00–22.00, Sat 6.00–19.00, Sun 10.00–18.00).

Kraków has experienced a recent boom in supermarket shopping. All the supermarkets listed below are located outside the city centre. You can take the bus, but they are best reached by car or taxi—the minimal cost far outweighs the time and effort of going by public transport. Three major French chains have opened branches here:

Carrefour, ul. Zakopiańska 62 (open Mon–Sat 09.00–21.00, Sun 10.00–19.00; bus no. 119, tram nos 8, 19, 22, 23), also good for clothes.

Geant, ul. Bora Komorowskiego 37 (open Mon–Sat 09.00–21.00, Sun 09.00–18.00; bus nos 159, 129, 139, 152), also good for cosmetics.

Hit, ul. Wielicka 259 (open Mon–Sat 08.00–21.00, Sun 09.00–18.00; bus nos 103, 173, 502, tram nos 3, 9, 13, 23), has the best selection of food.

You could also try: *Alkauf*, ul. Witosa 7 (open Mon–Fri 09.00–21.00, Sat 08.00–20.00, Sun 09.00–16.00; bus nos 124, 179), credit/debit cards not accepted.

Billa, ul. Mackiewicza 17 (open Mon–Fri 09.00–21.00, Sat 08.00–20.00, Sun 09.00–16.00; bus nos 114, 115, 164), credit/debit cards not accepted.

Krakchemia, ul. Pilotów 6 (open Mon–Sat 08.00–22.00, Sun 10.00–18.00; bus nos 124, 152, 184, 501, 502, 511.

There are a number of **24hr shops** selling food and alcohol. The closest one to the Market Square is *Delikatesy A & C* (ul. Starowiślna 1, opposite the main post office). The others are all well outside the Old Town: *Kristin*, ul. Krakowska 22, *ABJ-POL*, ul. Kazimierza Wielkiego 117, *Delicje-delikatesy*, Rynek Kleparski 5, *Hean*, ul. Królewska 49, and *Jubilat*, al. Krasińskiego 1/3 (by the Dębnicki Bridge).

Outdoor markets

The most popular market is the *Stary Kleparz*, just off ul. Basztowa, where you can buy cheap fruit and vegetables, as well as wild mushrooms (fresh or dried), nuts and berries. A short way up ul. Długa is the similar *Nowy Kleparz* market (corner of al. Słowackiego), which specialises in wicker baskets. The *Hala Targowa*, situated by the viaduct on ul. Grzegórzecka, sells mainly fruit and vegetables, but also has an antique and book fair on Sunday mornings. For cheap clothes and miscellaneous items, the best place is the *Tandeta* at ul. Krzywda 1, near Kraków-Płaszów station (open Tues–Sun 06.00–15.00). There is also a Sunday morning **flea market** on pl. Nowy (see p. 144) in the district of Kazimierz, as well as fruit and vegetable stalls on other days.

Music shops

In general, music shops in Kraków are not well stocked with foreign titles and anything new is usually snapped up in a matter of days, sometimes hours. On the positive side, CDs and cassettes are significantly cheaper than in the UK and most Western countries—you should expect to pay around 55–60 PLN for a single item.

The best shop is *Music Corner*, which has branches at ul. Św. Jana 18 (good for Jazz), ul. Sienna 9 and Rynek Główny 12 (good for classical and Polish pop music). It also stocks collectors' items and obscure labels.

Rock Serwis, ul. Szpitalna 7 (open 10.00–19.00, Sat 10.00–15.00), is a small shop with friendly staff and reasonable prices.

KB Music, ul. Stolarska 1 (open Mon–Sat 11.00–20.00, Sat 11.00–16.00), specialises in German/Dutch Gothic and industrial music.

Mag Magic, ul. Floriańska 28 (open Mon–Sat 09.00–21.00, Sun 10.00–18.00), is fairly large for Kraków but has inflated prices and unhelpful staff.

The *Hetmańska* bookshop (see *Bookshops*) also has a small music section in the passageway off the Market Square.

For classical music you could try *Musica Antiqua* at ul. Senacka 6 (open Mon–Fri 11.00–19.00, Sat 11.00–16.00)—the choice is pretty small, but this is about the best you'll find.

Kurant, Rynek Główny 36 (open Mon–Fri 09.00–19.00, Sat 10.00–15.00), has music books and scores, but the CDs and cassettes are overpriced.

Classical music and scores are also available from the *Polskie Wydawnictwo Muzyczne* (al. Krasińskiego 11a), a state-run publishing house.

For the lowest prices in town you could check out the market (*giełda pod Elbudem*) on ul. Wadowicka, open on Saturday and Sunday mornings. In addition to music, you can buy computer software, videos, and various electronic goods. Be warned, however, that much of the merchandise is pirated (which probably explains the low prices). The police ritually raid the place and make a few arrests, but no one really seems to care—the traders simply pay their fines and return the following week.

Posters

There is a long tradition of poster art in Poland, which had its heyday in the 1960s. Some of the best designs of recent decades can be purchased at the *Galeria Plakatu* (Poster Gallery), under the arcades on ul. Stolarska (open Mon–Fri 11.00–17.00, Sat 11.00–14.00). The shop also frames posters for an additional charge.

Photographic equipment

There are numerous shops selling film and photographic equipment, including *Kodak Express*, Rynek Główny 46 (open Mon–Fri 09.00–20.00, Sat 09.00–15.00), which also does express developing, *Big-Fox*, ul. Grodzka 51, with a good selection of cameras and lenses, *Agfa*, ul. Szpitalna 3, and *Foto Expert*, ul. Karmelicka 13.

Religious artefacts

Two good places for religious books, posters and paintings are *Dewocjonalia*, Mały Rynek 9 (open Mon–Fri 10.00–18.00, Sat 10.00–14.00) and *Księgarnia Archidiecezjalna*, ul. Straszewskiego 2 (corner of ul. Podzamcze, open Mon–Fri 09.00–17.00, Sat 10.00–14.00). The latter also has CDs, tapes and videos of papal sermons from around the world.

Arkos at pl. Mariacki 5 (open Mon–Fri 10.00–18.00, Sat 10.00–14.00) has fabrics for liturgical vestments, candles and other paraphernalia.

Stationery

Renesans, ul. Szewska 7 (open Mon–Fri 09.00–20.00) and *Elipsan*, ul. Grodzka 1 (open Mon–Fri 10.00–19.00, Sat 10.00–15.00) sell envelopes, notebooks, pens and much else.

Ulmax, ul. Wiślna 9 (open Mon–Fri 10.00–18.00, Sat 09.00–14.00) and *Redis*, ul. Św. Tomasza 33 (open Mon–Fri 09.00–19.00, Sat 10.00–14.00), sell toys in addition to stationery.

Sport

Football

Massive investment by the *Telefonica* company in the 1990s has seen Wisła Kraków FC rise from the doldrums to the dizzy heights of the Polish premier league. However, the club is yet to make its mark in European competition, an aim hampered by sub-standard domestic opposition. Crowd violence has also been a problem. In 1998, during a UEFA cup match against Parma of the Italian league, the midfielder Dino Baggio was struck by a knife thrown from the crowd. The incident led to Wisła being banned from European competition for a year, and even became the subject of a successful television play—*A Knife in the Head of Dino Baggio*.

Tickets for Wisła games can be bought directly at the ground (ul. Reymonta 22), but membership cards are in force. These can be arranged at the *Hotel Forum* (see *Where to stay*), but you could also try to talk your way in by showing your passport and feigning ignorance. Matches takes place on Fridays, Saturdays or Sundays (check the local press for details). The stadium itself is a shabby 1950s affair, with roofless terracing and no facilities to speak of, though a major renovation project is planned. Rather depressingly, the home fans have a habit of brandishing Union Jack banners with 'Chelsea hooligans' or other edifying phrases scrawled across them. That said, since the Dino Baggio incident there has been a strong police presence at all matches and you are unlikely to encounter any violence. Just keep a low(ish) profile and don't cheer the away team. The two other Kraków clubs are Cracovia FC (second division in 1999/00), who play at ul. Kałuży next to the *Cracovia* hotel, and Hutnik FC (third division), who play at ul. Ptaszyckiego in Nowa Huta (see p. 151). Not for the purist.

Skiing

The best place to go is the resort of Zakopane in the Tatra Mountains (see *Days Out from Kraków*).

Tennis

The *Centrum Tenisowe* at ul. Na Błoniach 1 (between two football pitches at the end of the Błonia common) has good clay and artificial grass courts with floodlights. Very popular, so book well in advance (☎ 425 2998). Open 07.00–midnight. The club also has two clay courts nearby at ul. Kasztelańska (open 07.00–dusk, summer only).

KKS Olsza at ul. Siedleckiego 7 (☎ 421 1069) has both indoor (06.00–23.00) and open-air (08.00–dusk) courts. Prior booking is essential if you want to play in the evening or on a weekend.

You could also try *Nadwiślan* at ul. Koletek 20 (close to Wawel Castle). Open 8.00–20.00, summer only (☎ 422 2122). Some hotels (e.g. the *Continental* and the *Piast*) have their own tennis courts.

Cycling

A number of pleasant cycling trips can be made in the environs of Kraków. Generally, the best area to explore lies to the south and east of the Błonia common, and includes Salwator and the Kościuszko Mound (see p. 158), Wola

Justowska (see p. 162), and the Wolski Forest (see p. 160). You could also make a longer trip to the Benedictine Abbey at Tyniec (see p. 163), beginning in Dębniki on the south side of the Vistula. Bikes can be rented from the *Żaczek* student dormitory (see *Where to Stay*) at the edge of the Błonia. Cycling in the city centre can be hazardous due to the lack of segregated bicycle lanes and aggressive driving. Take special care at all times. Riding two abreast is illegal.

Fitness clubs
Euro Fitness Club, ul. Biskupia 18 (☎ 633 0113). Gym and aerobics classes (open Mon–Fri 08.00–22.00, Sat 09.00–19.00, Sun 09.00–16.00).
Active Sport, ul. Westerplatte 15/16 (☎ 422 9566).
Inside the *Dom Turysty Hotel*, Solarium, sauna, and gym (open Mon–Fri 8.00–22.00, Sat and Sun 09.00–18.00).
Hades, ul. Krowoderska 5 (☎ 422 2198). Women-only gym.
Sport Luka, ul. Makowskiego 1 (☎/fax 637 4725, mobile 0602 250 165). Aerobics (water and traditional), weight training, massage, solarium, swimming and tennis.
Relax Body Club, ul. Mogilska 70 (☎ 411 0360). Huge gym and solarium.

Horse riding
Owing to the long Polish tradition of horse breeding, there are numerous riding clubs and stables in the vicinity of Kraków. The following can all be reached by bus no. 152 from the *Cracovia* hotel:
Decjusz. Stadnina Koni, al. Kasztanowa 1 (☎ 425 2421), in the western suburb of Wola Justowska (see p. 162).
Krakowski Klub Jazdy Konnej, ul. Niezapominajek 1 (☎ 425 2548), in the suburb of Chełm.
Klub Turystyki Konnej, ul. Kosmowskiej 1 (☎ 425 1237), in the suburb of Olszanica.

If you are prepared to travel out of Kraków, the choice is much greater. Ask at tourist information offices and travel agents for details. Riding holidays can be booked in the UK or US through Orbis and other tour operators.

Swimming
There is no shortage of swimming pools in Kraków, but in many cases, hygiene standards leave a lot to be desired.

However, the *Forum* and *Continental* (see *Where to Stay*) are a safe bet. Both have their own indoor pools (open 10.00–22.00) with extra facilities like saunas and solariums, which may be used by non-guests for an extra charge.

The *Korona*, ul. Kalwaryjska 9 (open Mon–Fri 6.30–20.45, Sat 09.30–20.00, Sun 09.30–17.00), is a much larger indoor pool, also with extra facilities, but the building itself is pretty grim.

Two reasonable outdoor pools are the *Cracovia* on al. 3 Maja, which faces the Błonia common, and the *Wisła* on ul. Reymonta, near the Wisła football stadium.

If you prefer more natural surroundings, the artificial lake at Kryspinów, 10km west of Kraków (bus nos 209, 239, 249 from the city centre), might be a good option. In summer the shores tend to get very crowded with day-trippers, so be sure to come early in the day. The water is clean and there are facilities for windsurfing and other water sports. The main beaches, where there are food and refreshment stands, tend to get the most crowded, but there are plenty of secluded coves further around the lake. You may be charged a small entrance fee.

Polish language

Many Poles have a talent (an extra gene, say some) for foreign languages and are usually open and responsive to foreigners—particularly those who make an attempt, no matter how hopeless, at speaking Polish. However, English is by now the most widely-spoken foreign language in Kraków, and certainly the first language of tourism. EFL teaching is a booming industry, and younger people will usually have at least a smattering of English; the linguistic abilities of some may even put native speakers to shame. German ranks second on the list on account of the city's proximity to Austria and its historic links with that country. Until the onslaught of English, French was the main foreign language of the intellectual elites, but nowadays it is restricted to the fifty-something generation. Knowledge of Russian is not as useful as one might expect: while many Poles understand this language, they will not admit to speaking it.

Polish belongs to the West Slavonic group of languages (along with Czech, Slovak and Wendish). It is a challenging prospect, particularly for the Anglo-Saxon tongue, and has been ranked by linguists among the ten most difficult languages in the world. However, many Polish words are derived from Latin roots (much more than in, say, Russian), so elements of Polish will be familiar to English-speakers.

A native English speaker faced with the task of learning even the very rudiments of Polish is confronted by two obstacles: inflexion and pronunciation. The long, uninterrupted strings of consonants, like *wzbronione* (forbidden), or *szczególnie* (in particular) are rather daunting. Due to the numerous 'hissing' phonemes, like *cz* or *sz*, Polish sounds harsh and lispy. Sometimes, the specific way in which you hiss may make all the difference, as in *proszę* (thank you) and *prosię* (pig), which to foreigners tend to sound alike. On the positive side, the stress nearly always falls on the penultimate syllable of a word.

Some of the special sound effects are spelt with characters not found in other languages, causing headaches to Polish users of word-processors and e-mail. In addition to accented letters (ń, ó, ż), there are nasalised versions of *a* and *e*, spelt with a hook similar to the cedilla (ą and ę), a character called *z dot accent* (ż), and *l* with a stroke (ł), pronounced somewhat like *w* in *well*.

Poles often despair when faced with the sixteen tenses of English. In Polish there are fortunately only three—past, present and future—so verbs present less of a problem. Likewise, Polish vocabulary is not as vast as English. Many words, especially the new ones, are taken from English, as well as from German, French or Russian.

Polish is a heavily inflected language, with nouns and adjectives, in particular, taking many forms. There are seven cases, two numbers and three genders, and an adjective qualifying a noun must agree with the latter in all three respects. Prepositions determine the case endings of nouns. What with the many irregularities, archaisms and diminutives (sometimes several variants per word are in use), Polish has a rather steep learning curve.

Word order is very flexible in Polish and this often causes problems for foreigners, as case endings are sometimes identical. Masculine nouns, for instance, have the same ending in the nominative and accusative. Thus, the sentence 'Iran zaatakował Irak' will usually mean 'Iran attacked Iraq' but it could equally mean 'Iraq attacked Iran'—you have to guess from the context.

Pronunciation
Vowels

a	'u' as in 'fun'		i	'ee' as in 'seem'
ą	'ong' as in 'song', but more nasalised; for most intents and purposes can be pronounced as 'om' or 'on'		o	'o' as in 'dot'
			ó	'u' as in 'rule'
			u	identical to 'ó'
e	'e' as in 'lemon'		y	'i' as in 'simple'
ę	'en' as in 'send', but more nasalised; at the end of a word pronounced like 'e'			

Consonants

b	at the end of a word pronounced like 'p'		n	'n' as in 'next'
			ń	soft 'n', as in the 'gn' of 'cognac'
c	'ts' as in 'bits'			
ć	'ch' as in 'cheap'		p	'p' as in 'port'
d	at the end of a word pronounced like 't'		r	never soft, always rolled
			s	's' as in 'sing'
f	'f' as in 'free'		ś	'sh' as in 'shirt'
g	always hard, as in 'get'; at the end of a word pronounced like 'k'		t	't' as in 'talk'
			w	'v' as in 'vest'; at the end of a word pronounced like 'f'
h	'ch' as in Scottish 'loch'			
l	'l' as in 'lamp'		z	'z' as in 'zebra'
ł	'w' as in 'water'		ż	as in the French 'j' of 'jour'
m	'm' as in 'man'		ź	'z' as in 'seizure'

Letter combinations

ci	pronounced 'ch-ee'		ni	soft 'n', identical to 'ń'
cz	similar to 'ć' but harder		rz	identical to 'ż'
dz	'ds' as in 'friends'; at the end of a word pronounced 'ts' as in 'cats'		si	pronounced 'sh-ee' not 'see'
			sz	similar to 'ś' but harder
dż	as in the French 'j' of 'jour' with a 'd' before it		szcz	'sh-ch' as in 'English Channel'
			zi	pronounced 'zh-ee'
dź	as in the soft 'd' of 'during'; at the end of a word pronounced 'ch'			

Useful words and phrases ~ the basics

pan	pan	sir; formal 'you', equivalent to the French 'vous' and the German 'Sie'
pani	pa-nee	madam; formal 'you', same as above
ty	ti	informal 'you', equivalent to the French 'tu' or the German 'du'
dzień dobry	jen-dob-ri	good morning; good afternoon
dobry wieczór	do-bri wye-chor	good evening

do widzenia	do-vee-dzen-ya	goodbye
dobranoc	do-bra-notz	goodnight
cześć	cheshch	informal greeting; means either 'hi' or 'bye'
dziękuję	jen-ku-yeh	thank you
przepraszam	pshe-pra-sham	excuse me; I'm sorry
proszę	pro-she	please; you're welcome

Questions and answers

czy	chi	forms a question, eg '*Czy tutaj?*', 'here?'
czy mówi Pan/ pani po angielsku/ francusku/ niemiecku?	chi moovee pan/ pan-yee po an-gyel-skoo/ fran-tzooz-koo/ nye-myetz-koo	do you speak English/French/ German?
nie rozumiem	nye roh-zoo-myem	I don't understand
nie mowię po polsku	nye moo-vye poh polskoo	I don't speak Polish
kiedy	kye-di	when
o której godzinie?	oh ktoo-ray goh-jee-nye	at what time?
gdzie	gje	where
gdzie jest toaleta	gje yest toh-a-leh-tah	where is the toilet?
gdzie mogę kupić...?	gje mogeh koo-peech...?	where can I buy...?
ile	ee-leh	how much? how many?
ile kosztuje?	ee-leh kosh-too-yeh	how much does it cost?
którędy (do)...?	ktoo-ren-di	which way (to)...?
jak długo	yak dwoo-go	how long?
ten/ta/to		this one
tamten/tamta/ tamto		that one
dobrze	dob-zhe	fine; OK
czy ma pan/ pani...?	chi ma pan/ pan-nyee	do you have...?
nie ma	nye mah	there isn't any; there is no...
jestem	jes-tem	I am ...
brytyjczykiem (m) brytyjką (f)	bri-tee-chik-yem/ bri-tee-kong/	British
amerykaninem (m) amerykanką	amerika-nyee-nem/ ameri-kan-kong	American
po angielsku	poh an-gyel-skoo	in English
chwileczkę; moment	hfee-lech-keh	one moment; wait a moment
tak		yes
nie	nye	no
tu	too	here
tam		there

wczoraj	fchoh-ray	yesterday
dzisiaj	jee-shay	today
jutro	yoo-troh	tomorrow
rano	rah-no	in the morning
w południe	fpoh-wood-nye	at noon
wieczorem	vye-choh-rem	in the evening
prosto	proh-stoh	straight ahead
na/w prawo	nah/v pra-woh	to the right
na/w lewo	nah/v levoh	to the left
moja żona	moh-ya zho-nah	my wife
mój mąż	muy monsh	my husband

Expressing wishes

Chciałbym (used by a man) or	h-chow-bim/	I would like ...
chciałabym (a woman)	h-chowa-bim	
Poproszę o...	poh-proshe	I'll have.. (when ordering food etc)
Proszę o kartę/ jadłospis/ menu	poh-prosze oh karteh yad-wo-spees/ menu	could I have the menu, please
Proszę o rachunek	proshe oh ra-hoo-nek	could I have the bill, please
Proszę o bilet do ...	proshe oh bee-let doh	could I have a ticket to... please
Czy mogę...?	chee mo-geh	may I...?

Emergencies

wypadek	vi-pah-dek	accident
lekarz	le-kazh	doctor
pogotowie	poh-goh-toh-vye	ambulance
szpital	shpee-tal	hospital
ambasada	am-bah-sah-dah	embassy
policja	poh-lee-tzya	police
na pomoc!/ pomocy!	nah poh-motz!/ po-mo-tzi!	help!

Numbers

jeden	yeh-den	one
dwa	dva	two
trzy	tshi	three
cztery	chte-ri	four
pięć	pyench	five
sześć	sheshch	six
siedem	shye-dem	seven
osiem	o-shyem	eight
dziewięć	djye-vyench	nine
dziesięć	djye-shench	ten
jedenaście	ye-de-nash-cheh	eleven
dwanaście	dva-nash-cheh	twelve

trzynaście	tshi-nash-cheh	thirteen
czternaście	chter-nash-cheh	fourteen
piętnaście	pyet-nash-cheh	fifteen
szesnaście	shes-nash-cheh	sixteen
siedemnaście	shye-dem-nash-cheh	seventeen
osiemnaście	o-shyem-nash-cheh	eighteen
dziewiętnaście	jeh-vyent-nash-cheh	nineteen
dwadzieścia	dva-jesh-cha	twenty
dwadzieścia jeden	dva-jesh-cha yeden	twenty one
dwadzieścia dwa	dva-jesh-cha dva	twenty two
trzydzieści	tshi-jesh-chee	thirty
czterdzieści	chter-jesh-chee	forty
pięćdziesiąt	pyen-jesh-ont	fifty
sześćdziesiąt	shesh-jesh-ont	sixty
sto	stoh	one hundred
dwieście	dvyesh-cheh	two hundred
trzysta	tshi-stah	three hundred
czterysta	chteri-sta	four hundred
pięćset	pyen-set	five hundred
sześćset	shesh-set	six hundred
siedemset	shye-dem-set	seven hundred
tysiąc	ti-shontz	one thousand
dwa tysiące	dva ti-shon-tzeh	two thousand
trzy tysiące	tshi ti-shon-tzeh	three thousand
cztery tysiące	chte-ri ti-shon-tzeh	four thousand
pięć tysięcy	pyench ti-shen-tzi	five thousand
sześć tysięcy	sheshch ti-shen-tzi	six thousand
milion	mee-lee-on	million
miliard	mee-lee-ard	billion (a thousand million)

Getting around

bilet	bee-let	ticket
bilet powrotny	bee-let po-vrot-ni	return ticket
pierwsza/druga klasa	pyerf-sha/drooga klasa	first/second class
miejscówka	myay-stzoovka	seat reservation
kuszetki	koo-shet-kee	couchettes
miejsca sypialne	myay-stza si-pyal-ne	sleepers
samochód/auto	sam-o-hood/ow-toh	car
autobus	ow-toh-boos	bus
pociąg	po-chong	train
dworzec kolejowy	dvo-zhetz	train station
dworzec autobusowy	dvo-zhetz ow-toh-boo-soh-vi	bus station
peron	pe-ron	platform
kasa	kasa	ticket-office/cash desk
przechowalnia bagażu	pshe-ho-val-nya ba-gah-zhoo	left luggage

taksówka	tak-soof-ka	taxi
samolot	sa-moh-lot	aeroplane
lotnisko	lot-nee-skoh	airport
przyjazdy/ przyloty	pshi-yaz-di/ pshi-loh-ti	arrivals
odjazdy/odloty	od-yaz-di/od-loh-ti	departures
poczta	poch-tah	post office
objazd	ob-yazd	diversion
stacja benzynowa	statz-ya ben-zi-novah	petrol station
benzyna	ben-zi-nah	petrol
olej napędowy	oley na-pen-dovi	diesel oil
olej silnikowy	oley sheel-nee-kovi	engine oil
woda	voda	water

Signs

wejście	vay-shcheh	entrance
wyjście	vee-shcheh	exit
otwarte	ot-var-teh	open
zamknięte/ nieczynne	zam-knyen-teh/ nye-chin-neh	closed/out of order
awaria	a-var-ryah	not in service
przerwa	psher-vah	break
toaleta	toh-a-leh-tah	toilet; men's marked with a triangle, ladies' with a circle
samoobsługa	samoh-ob-swooga	self-service
płatny	pwat-ni	paid, e.g., paid car park, cloak-room etc.
parking	par-keeng	car park
szatnia	shat-nya	cloak-room
(wstęp) wolny	(fstemp) vol-ni	free (entry)
koncert	kon-tzert	concert
wystawa	vi-stah-vah	exhibition
pokoje/noclegi	poh-koh-yeh/ notz-leh-gee	rooms (to let)
kantor	kan-tor	exchange office
remont	reh-mont	renovation in progress
baczność/uwaga	bach-noshch/ oo-vah-gah	caution; danger

Sightseeing

muzeum	moo-zeh-oom	museum
kościół	kosh-chool	church
katedra	kah-teh-drah	cathedral
kaplica	kah-plee-tza	chapel
klasztor	klash-tor	monastery
galeria	gah-leh-ree-yah	gallery
teatr	teh-atr	theatre
dom	dom	house

pałac	pah-watz	palace
zamek	za-mek	castle
wieża	vye-zha	tower
dworek	dvo-rek	manor house
przewodnik	pshe-vod-neek	guide
wycieczka	vi-chech-kah	excursion
piwnice	pee-vnee-tzeh	cellars
skansen	skansen	open-air museum
kino	kee-noh	cinema

Geographical

droga	droh-gah	road
most	most	bridge
miasto	myas-toh	town, city
rynek	ri-nek	market square
stare miasto	stah-reh myas-toh	old town
ratusz	rah-toosh	town hall
cmentarz	tzmen-tash	cemetery
las/puszcza	las/poosh-chah	forest/(primeval) forest
góra	goo-rah	hill; mountain
kopiec	koh-pyetz	mound
wzgórze	vzgoo-zheh	hill
szczyt	shchit	summit
skała	skah-wah	rock; cliff
rzeka	zhe-kah	river
jezioro	yeh-zho-roh	lake
kopalnia	koh-pal-nyah	mine
ogród	o-grood	gardens
dolina	doh-li-nah	valley
województwo	vo-yeh-vootz-tvoh	voivodship; county
granica	grah-nee-tza	national border
państwowa	pan-stvo-vah	
zdrój	zdrooy	spa
ziemia	zhye-mya	land, region

Additional Information

Public holidays

1 January (New Year's Day)
Easter Monday (March/April)
1 May (Labour Day)
3 May (Constitution Day)
Corpus Christi (May/June)

15 August (Feast of the Assumption)
1 November (All Saints' Day)
11 November (National Independence Day)
25 December (Christmas Day)
26 December (St Stephen's Day)

Tourist information offices in Kraków

The quality of tourist offices varies, but most will at least sell information brochures, guide books, catalogues, maps and plans. In the better offices, you can get information about local places of interest, guides, travel agency services, transport, restaurants, accommodation, sports equipment rental, and cultural events. Nowadays, the staff will often speak English and/or other foreign languages. Hotel receptions may also be a good source of information.

• *Orbis*, also known abroad as *Polorbis*, is a major national tourist organisation specialising in travel (leisure and business) for individuals and groups. Orbis offices are convenient for buying domestic and international rail and coach tickets as you can avoid the queues at the station. The company also sells airline and ferry tickets and there is an American Express desk at the office in Rynek Główny (see below).

Privatised in the 1990s, the company runs a national chain of reliable, high standard hotels. Reservations can be made at any Orbis office, or at the **Orbis website** (www.orbis.pl). Staff will provide you with information about guided tours and excursions, equipment hire, car rental, guides, cultural and sporting events etc.

Holidays can be booked direct through Orbis offices abroad (see below), which also supply a good selection of general information about Poland.

Orbis **offices in the Old Town**: Rynek Główny 41, ☎ 422 4035, fax 422 2885 (open Mon–Fri 08.00–18.00, Sat 08.30–15.00); pl. Szczepański 2, ☎ 422 3044, fax 422 6147 (open Mon–Fri 10.00–18.00, Sat 10.00–14.00). Other Orbis offices, providing most of the above services can be found at the *Cracovia Hotel*, al. Focha 1, ☎ 4219 880, fax 422 498 and *Hotel Forum*, ul. Konopnickiej 28, ☎ 266 4730, fax 266 3130.

• The *PTTK* (Polish Tourist Association) office at ul. Westerplatte 15 deals mainly in hostel accommodation, countryside trips and outdoor pursuits.

• *Tourist Information Centre* (*Centrum Informacji Turystycznej*), Rynek Główny 1/3 (Cloth Hall), ☎ 421 7706, or ☎ 421 3051 (open Mon–Fri 09.00–18.00, Sat 09.00–13.00). Information about hotels, cultural events, excursions and insurance. The office sells tickets for Cracow Tours—various guided tours around Kraków and its environs, including Zakopane, Auschwitz and the historic salt mine in Wieliczka (Cracow Tours tickets can also bought at Orbis, Intercrac and most hotels). In the same building is the *Dexter Travel* office (a member of IATA and ASTA), where you can buy airline tickets.

• *Tourist Information*, ul. Floriańska 37, ☎ 9319 (open Mon–Sat 08.00–18.00, Sun 08.00–15.00) organises trips to Wieliczka and Auschwitz and sells international coach tickets.

• *Intercrac Travel Agency*, Rynek Główny 14, ☎/fax 421 9858 (open Mon–Fri 08.30–16.00) offers services for groups and individuals: hotel reservations, excursions and local sightseeing, coach and car rental.

• *Tourist Information Centre* (*Centrum Informacji Turystycznej*), ul. Pawia 8, ☎ 422 0471, or ☎ 422 6091 (open Mon–Fri 8.00–18.00, Sat 09.00–13.00. In the same building is the *Waweltur* office, ☎ 422 1921 (open Mon–Fri 08.00–20.00, Sat 08.00–14.00), which can arrange accommodation in private lodgings.

• *Almatur*, ul. Grodzka 2 (just off the Market Square), ☎ 422 4668, or ☎/fax 428 4520 (open Mon–Fri 09.00–18.00, Sat 10.30–14.30). Airline tickets, domestic (*Polski Express*) and international coach tickets. As the main student travel bureau it issues ISIC, ITIC and GO25 cards and offers cheap holidays and accommodation for young people in Poland and abroad.

• *Jan-Pol Travel Agency*, ul. Westerplatte 15/16 (inside the *Dom Turysty Hotel*), ☎ 421 4206 or ☎ 421 4106, fax 421 2726. Services for groups and individuals: hotel reservations, local sightseeing tours, air, coach and train tickets.

• *Jordan*, ul. Sławkowska 12, ☎ 422 2033 (open Mon–Fri 10.00–18.00); ul. Pawia 12, ☎ 422 1996 (open Mon–Fri 08.30–18.00); ul. Długa 9, ☎ 421 2125 (open Mon–Fri 09.00–18.00, Sat 09.00–15.00). Coach services to Austria, Italy, Hungary, France and Holland. Package tours and excursions. The office on ul. Długa is a TUI agent and sells airline tickets; the office on ul. Pawia organises trips to Zakopane, offers guides and coach rental.

• *Gromada*, pl. Szczepański 8, ☎ 422 3745, ☎/fax 422 6150 (open Mon–Fri 09.00–17.30, Sat 10.00–14.00). Package holidays in Poland and abroad (specialises in spa holidays), airline tickets, hotel reservations (the company has its own chain of hotels), and car rental.

• *Juventur*, ul. Sławkowska 1, ☎ 422 2437 (open Mon–Fri 10.00–18.00, Sat 10.00–14.00).

Visiting the rest of Poland

By air

LOT Polish Airlines (ul. Basztowa 15, ☎ 422 4215; open Mon–Fri 08.00–19.00, Sat 08.00–15.00; ☎ 952 or 953 for 24 hour reservations and enquiries) operates daily **domestic flights** to Warsaw, but there are no direct services to other Polish cities. To fly from Kraków to Gdańsk, Poznań, Wrocław, Szczecin or Rzeszów, you will need to catch an onward flight from Warsaw. Tickets may be bought at *LOT* and *Orbis* offices, from travel agents, or directly at the airport. You may get discounts on weekend or night travel.

Tickets for **international flights** are best bought from travel agents (see below), which offer the lowest prices, or directly from airlines. *British Airways* is at ul. Św. Tomasza 25 (☎ 422 8621, ☎ 422 8645; open Mon–Fri 09.00–17.00); *Swissair* at ul. Krakowska 41 (☎ 429 1877, fax 429 2354; open Mon–Fri 08.30–17.00); and *Austrian Airlines* at ul. Krakowska 41, 1st floor (☎ 429 6666, fax 429 2006; open Mon–Fri, 09.00–17.00).

By train

Kraków is an ideal base for visiting other fascinating places in Central Europe. There are daytime **Eurocity** trains to Berlin (9hrs) and Budapest (9hrs), with convenient connecting trains to many other German and Hungarian cities. Two of the most popular destinations are Prague (8hrs 30mins) and Vienna (8hrs), both serviced by direct, overnight trains. You can also make longer journeys (departures from Kraków Płaszów station) to Odessa (24hrs 30mins) and Kiev (21hrs 30mins, via Lviv) in the Ukraine, and Bucharest (23hrs) in Romania.

In general, trains are an efficient and reliable means of transport. There are regular daily services from Kraków to many Polish cities, including: Warsaw (2hrs 30mins), Wrocław (4hrs), Poznań (5hrs 30mins), Łódź (3hrs 30mins) Lublin (4hrs), Gdańsk (6hrs 30mins) and Szczecin (10hrs 30mins) (these are fully described in *Blue Guide Poland*). Four categories of train run on domestic lines: *Intercity*, *Expres* (express), *Pospieszny* (fast), and *Osobowy* (local). **Intercity** trains, and their international counterpart—Eurocity, have clean, modern carriages, proper restaurant cars, and six seats per compartment in first and second class. **Express** trains travel at the same speed as Intercity services but sometimes stop at more stations, so journey times are slightly longer. There are eight seats per compartment in second class. Eurocity/Intercity and express trains carry compulsory seat reservations (denoted by the letter R in a box). **'Fast'** trains, stopping at larger stations, hardly live up to their name and are often dirty and overcrowded. **Local** trains stop at almost every station and should be avoided except for very short journeys.

Polish Rail (**PKP**) has a good website (www.pkp.com.pl) with up-to-date timetables and information on all train services in Poland. At the station, international tickets are sold at the *kasa zagraniczna* (window nos 22 and 23, open 24hrs). Tickets for domestic and international trains can also be bought at Orbis offices and certain travel agents. First class tickets (*pierwsza klasa*) are 50 per cent more expensive than second class (*druga klasa*); a return ticket (*bilet powrotny*) is usually twice as expensive as a single (*bilet w jedną stronę*). If you want a non-smoking compartment, ask for *dla niepalących*. On domestic trains, tickets may be bought from the guard for a small additional charge—you should inform him as soon as you board. At the time of writing, a second class Intercity return from Kraków to Warsaw was 80 PLN ($US20).

Most long distance trains have couchette cars (*kuszetki*) with six beds in each compartment, and/or sleepers (*sypianly*) with three beds in second class and two in first. Be careful not to confuse departure boards (*odjazdy*, yellow-coloured) with arrivals boards (*przyjazdy*, white-coloured). The boards show the times as well as the platform (*peron*) and track (*tor*) numbers of departing and arriving trains. The types of train are denoted by the following symbols: Eurocity—EC; Intercity—IC; Express—Ex; Fast—Posp., marked in red; Local—Osob., marked in black.

By bus/coach

The state bus company (**PKS**) operates **local** (black), **semi-fast** (green) **fast** (red) and **express** (red—Ex) services on regional and national routes. When visiting places near Kraków it is often faster and more convenient to travel by bus (see *Days Out*). Tickets should be bought beforehand at the main bus station or from a travel agent. You can also buy your ticket from the driver if there are free seats available. On popular and long distance routes it is always advisable to book in advance. The departure boards at the station indicate the final destinations (*kierunek*) and routes (*przez*) of buses. The place you want to go to will not necessarily be listed as a final destination, so you may have to check the *przez* column also.

PKS does run some international services, but there are scores of companies offering coach trips to Western Europe and the UK, so it is best to shop around. Sometimes international coaches depart from the stop by ul. Bosacka behind the railway station—be sure to check with your travel agent before you leave.

Travel agents

In recent years Poland has experienced a boom in package holidays, and there are a number of travel agents specialising in this, such as:

• *Jagiellonia*, a TUI and Neckermann agent, situated just off the Market Square at ul. Wiślna 2 (☎ 422 0345, fax 422 7793; open Mon–Fri 08.00–18.00, Sat 09.00–14.00), also a good place to buy air, ferry and bus tickets.

- *Scan Holiday* at ul. Karmelicka 12 (☎ 422 9631, fax 423 0344; open Mon–Fri 09.00–19.00, Sat 10.00–15.00), which offers last minute deals to popular foreign resorts.
- *City Center Travel Club* at ul. Sienna 9 (☎ 422 4188; open Mon–Fri 08.00–18.00, Sat 09.00–13.00), a Neckermann and TUI agent.
- *Dana Air Travel* at ul. Szpitalna 40 (☎ 422 7500, fax 422 5097; open Mon–Fri 08.00–18.00, Sat 09.00–14.00), another Neckermann and TUI agent.
- *Ving* at ul. Szewska 2 (☎ 429 6130, fax 429 6328; open Mon–Fri 10.00–20.00, Sat & Sun 10.00–15.00).

The best place to buy ferry tickets is *Fregata Travel* at ul. Szpitalna 32 (☎ 422 4144, fax 421 1290; open Mon–Fri 08.00–18.00, Sat 09.00–14.00).

Crime and personal safety
Street crime in Poland has risen dramatically in recent years, but Kraków is still a lot safer than many Western cities and certainly safer than Warsaw. Two areas to be wary of at night are Nowa Huta and the vicinity of the main railway station. Valuables are best left at the hotel reception (ask for a receipt), or in a left luggage locker at the station. Beware of pickpockets on crowded buses and trams and in shops and outdoor markets. The Polish police are often castigated for taking far too long to arrive at crime scenes and doing little to help the victims. The language barrier may also be a problem. Cases of theft and attack should be immediately reported to a police station (see below). There is no compulsion on foreigners to carry passports with them, but it is always wise to carry some form of identity and a contact address in case of accidents. Polish police (blue uniforms) carry guns and can stop and search anyone behaving suspiciously. There are also black-uniformed municipal (traffic) police (*straż miejska*), with far more limited powers.

Emergency telephone numbers
Ambulance ☎ 999   Police ☎ 997
Fire brigade ☎ 998

Central police stations
Komisariat I Kraków Stare Miasto, ul. Szeroka 35, ☎ 610 7711.
Komisariat III Kraków-Dworzec Główny (main railway station), ul. Lubicz 10b, ☎ 610 7811.
Komenda Rejonowa Kraków Centrum, ul. Batorego 25, ☎ 610 7115.
Komenda Wojewódzka, ul. Mogilska 109, ☎ 610 4444.
There is also a police station on the Market Square, near the Town Hall Tower.

If you lose your **passport** you should contact your embassy to get a temporary one issued. US citizens can do this at their consulate in Kraków (ul. Stolarska 9, ☎ 429 6655, fax 421 8292), but UK, Australian and Canadian citizens will have to make arrangements at their respective embassies in Warsaw. There is a British Honorary Consulate in Kraków at ul. Św. Anny 9 (☎ 421 7030, fax 422 4264), but they do not issue passports. You should always report the loss of a passport to the police.

The Kraków District Office (*Urząd Rejonowy*) has a section dealing with **lost property** at al. Słowackiego 20, ☎ 616 9289. For property lost on public transport, contact the Municipal Transport Authority (MPK): *Biuro Znalezionych Rzeczy,* ul. Sławka 10, ☎ 655 4300 (open 06.30–16.00). Don't hold out much hope.

If you need urgent **medical treatment** you should go to the emergency room (*ostry dyżur*) at one of the city's hospitals. As these operate a rota system, first call the emergency ambulance number (☎ 999) to find out which hospitals are receiving emergency patients that day. If you need an ambulance (*pogotowie ratunkowe*), you can also call the public service at ul. Św. Łazarza 14 (☎ 422 3600, ☎ 422 2999) or *Falck*, a private organisation (ul. Racławicka 26, ☎ 96 75).

Useful websites
www.polhotels.com details on hotels, reservations, prices
www.pkp.com.pl tickets and timetables for Polish railways
www.karnet.krakow2000.pl lists special events planned for 2000 and beyond
www.inyourpocket.com to find out what's on in Krakow (website for *Kraków in Your Pocket*)

Newspapers
The most popular daily is the left-liberal *Gazeta Wyborcza*, set up in 1989 to help with Solidarity's election campaign and today edited by the ex-dissident, Adam Michnik. Other national dailies include *Rzeczpospolita*, focusing on business and government affairs, and *Życie*, which has broadly Christian-Democratic sympathies. Best-known of the weeklies are *Wprost*, a sort of Polish *Newsweek*, *Polityka*, a post-communist mouthpiece, and *Tygodnik Powszechny*, a liberal Catholic journal based in Kraków. The best English-language publication is *The Warsaw Voice* (available in Kraków), which has national coverage of politics, business, arts and culture. Western newspapers can be bought at larger hotels (especially the *Orbis* chain) and from certain kiosks (eg at the corner of ul. Sienna and ul. Stolarska, and in the main hall at the railway station); they are at least a day late and always overpriced.

The two most popular local newspapers are *Dziennik Polski* and *Gazeta Krakowska*, but for listings and advertisements it is best to look in the Kraków section of *Gazeta Wyborcza*, especially the Friday edition, which has comprehensive information on events over the coming weekend. For cultural listings, you can also check one of the English-language information brochures published in Kraków (see *Entertainment*).

Laundry
Dry cleaners (*pralnie*) offer normal and express cleaning, but laundrettes with self-service washing machines are virtually unknown. As in left luggage offices, you will have to specify the value of the item(s) you leave. **Betty Clean Pralnia Ekologiczna**, at ul. Zwierzyniecka 6, ul. Długa 17 and ul. Wielopole 28, will dry-clean your clothes within 24hrs (normal) or 3hrs (express). Many hotels have their own laundry services. Students can get their washing done at the Piast Dormitory (*Dom Studencki Piast*), ul. Piastowska 47 (☎ 637 4933).

Toilets
Public toilets are scarce and rarely clean. It is always better to use the facilities in hotels or restaurants. A charge of 1 PLN is standard. Toilets are sometimes marked with symbols: men's with a triangle, women's with a circle.

Cloakrooms

Cloakrooms are often compulsory in restaurants, theatres and museums. The attendant will expect payment of 1 PLN or more.

Time zone

Poland lies within the Central European Time Zone, i.e. GMT plus one hour in winter and GMT plus two hours in summer (last Sunday in March to last Sunday in October).

Electric current

Poland uses standard European two-pin 220V adapters. If you are bringing electrical equipment from the UK, you will need to use a three-to-two-pin adapter (available from electrical shops and airports).

BACKGROUND INFORMATION

Kraków's history and culture

By Paweł Pencakowski

In the centre of Kraków's Old Town, a bugle signal (*hejnał*) is sounded on the hour, day and night, from the taller tower of St Mary's church. The call ends abruptly, mid-way through the melody.

According to legend, during a Tartar (Mongol) invasion in the 13C, the night watchman sounded his bugle to warn the city's inhabitants of impending attack. Halfway through the call, his neck was pierced by a Tartar arrow, but in raising the alarm the dutiful watchman saved the city from destruction. Today, to commemorate the event, the melody is played from the Signal Tower of St Mary's by a fireman from the city's fire brigade. The tower is topped with a magnificent late Gothic spire and, together with the melody, remains one of the city's most enduring symbols.

Since 1927, the midday bugle signal from the tower of St Mary's has been broadcast on national public radio. In this way, Kraków—the former capital of Poland and today its cultural capital—reminds the world of its thousand-year history, traditions, culture, art and architecture.

Kraków in the Middle Ages

The lands of the upper Vistula were inhabited by Slavs from at least the 5C. Christianity came some 500 years later, during a period of Czech rule. It is from this period that the earliest written record of Kraków appears, in the travelogue of Ibrahim ibn Yaqub, a Jewish merchant from Cordova, who visited the region in 960–65. The merchant writes of the city of 'Karako,' an important trading centre on the Vistula river, three weeks' journey from Prague.

The Polish **Piast dynasty** asserted itself in Kraków in the late 10C, after the first Piast prince—Mieszko I (d. 992)—had converted to Christianity. During the reign of Bolesław the Brave (992–1025), a bishopric was founded. Over the centuries, the bishops, from Poppon (1000–08) to Karol Wojtyła (1963–78, currently Pope John Paul II) and Franciszek Macharski (1978–), have made a strong contribution to the history and culture of the city. An important role was also played by the cathedral chapter, whose coat of arms—the Three Crowns—is today visible above the gateways of numerous palaces and houses, for instance on ul. Kanonicza (see p. 114).

At the beginning of the 11C, Kraków became the capital of the Polish kingdom, a function it would retain until 1595. The city was located at the crossroads of major trade routes: the east–west route from Byzantium and Kievan Rus' to Silesia, Germany, France, Italy, Austria, Hungary and Bohemia, and the north–south route to Mazovia, Prussia, Lithuania, Scandinavia, the duchies of northern Rus', and Moscow. Consequently, Kraków's multinational character began to take shape very early on. Settlers included Jews, Germans, Czechs, Hungarians, Italians, Flemish, Scots, and others.

In the early Middle Ages, Kraków consisted of a fortified royal and ecclesiastical seat on Wawel hill, a settlement known as Okół (see p. 106), defended, from the 7C–8C, by earth and wood ramparts, and several other open settlements. The 11C city had around twenty stone churches. The most important of these arose on Wawel hill: the Church of St Mary, a rotunda with four apses; the 'first' cathedral, dedicated to Christ the Saviour and St Wacław (Wenceslaus); and the aisled Church of St Gereon, which had a transept and a chancel with a vaulted crypt, its columns decorated with knot-like ornamentation. Other monuments built on the hill during the 11C included the 'room on 24 posts' (the hall of the royal *palatium*), two more apsed rotundas, and a aisleless, rectangular church. Construction was not restricted to Wawel, as shown by the oldest parts of the Skałka Church (see p. 146), St Adalbert's (see p. 93), St Andrew's (see p. 113), and others.

Significantly, with the adoption of Christianity, Polish culture became tied to that of the Latin West, and from the 10C onwards the development of art reflected and converged with European trends. It is not surprising, therefore, that today in Cracovian churches we find pre-Romanesque and Romanesque sculpture, and in church treasuries—early examples of goldwork, reliquaries, and 10C–11C codices richly illustrated with miniatures, initially imported from Germany, France and Italy, and later made by local craftsmen, too. The most valuable reliquary is the spear of St Maurice, which Emperor Otto III presented to Bolesław the Brave in 1000 at the Congress of Gniezno, and which now rests in the Cathedral Museum (see p. 126).

In the 11C, the Polish Kingdom and its capital, Kraków, suffered two major crises. The first was a period of internal anarchy caused by the Czech invasion of 1038, which saw the Piasts lose control over much of their territory. During the reconstruction effort, a Benedictine abbey was founded at Tyniec (see p. 163), a few miles up the Vistula. The second crisis involved a now infamous struggle for power between King Bolesław the Bold (1040–81) and the Bishop of Kraków, Stanisław Szczepanowski (see p. 146). Bolesław murdered the Bishop and was forced to flee the country in 1079. This marked the beginning of a period of feudal disintegration, which intensified after 1138 when Bolesław the Wrymouth (1102–38) divided the Polish lands among his sons, thus ushering in two centuries of wars and sibling rivalry on a grand scale. Throughout these 'dark ages', Kraków remained the nominal capital, but thanks only to the primacy of tradition.

The 12C was the heyday of **Romanesque architecture** in Kraków. It coincided with the introduction of a new building material—ashlar stone—which harmonised with the increasing complexity of ground plans and variety of building types. The greatest Romanesque building in Kraków was the 'second' cathedral, raised by the Piast princes. Today, its only surviving remnants are the aisled Crypt of St Leonard (see p. 122), the lower parts of the towers flanking the crypt, and a few fragments in the cellars of the 'third', Gothic cathedral. A new church was built in the district of Salwator, on the site of a pre-Romanesque rotunda (see p. 158), and several pre-Romanesque churches were remodelled, among them the Church of St Adalbert (see p. 93). At the beginning of the 13C, the aisled Church of St Andrew (see p. 113), originally built for the Benedictines, received transepts, vaults, and westwork. It has retained its Romanesque character to this day, and remains one of the most beautiful early Medieval buildings in the city. Late Romanesque fragments are also preserved in the foundations of St Mary's Church on the Market Square (see p. 93), and in the refectory (1222) of the Dominican Monastery, which was redesigned in the 15C.

Despite the feudal disintegration of Poland, the destruction caused by repeated **Tartar invasions** (1241, 1259–60 and 1287), and the internecine struggles of the Piast princes, Kraków continued to develop during the 13C: there was steady growth in trade and construction; the city gained its first taste of municipal government; the arts and crafts flourished. Much of this was spurred by the influx of newcomers from the West and by the establishment of salt mines in the nearby towns of Bochnia and Wieliczka (see p. 168). These were the first industrial plants in Poland, over the centuries generating vast revenues for Kraków's rulers. The mine in Wieliczka has survived to this day as a unique and fascinating example of pre-modern engineering.

In 1257, Bolesław the Chaste (1243–79) endowed Kraków with a new and lasting **royal charter**. Under its terms, a new town was laid out north of the original settlement of Okół. It consisted of a grand market square (see p. 89), the largest in contemporary Europe, at the centre of a regular grid of streets leaving it at right angles, and a smaller, auxiliary market square (see p. 103). The entire grid was divided into lots, on which houses, palaces, churches and public institutions were later built.

The architecture of the 13C was a mixture of Romanesque forms—simple plans, heavy proportions, and rounded windows—and early Gothic ones, such as cross-rib vaults, pointed arches and tracery. Brick building gained impetus with the arrival of new monastic orders from Western Europe. The Cistercians settled in Mogiła in 1222, raising their abbey church of St Wenceslaus (see p. 154). They were soon joined by the Dominicans (1222) and Franciscans (1237), both of whom began construction of their churches on the old market square, now called pl. Wszystkich Świętych (see p. 109). These buildings were given striking ceramic decoration, as shown by the beautiful moulded brick frieze in the chancel of the Dominican Church. Items of metalwork began to appear in Cracovian churches, too: the huge fonts standing in the vestibule of St Mary's (see p. 93), liturgical vessels and reliquaries (St Andrew's), and the solid gold diadems of Bolesław the Chaste and Kunegunda (?), which were joined and made into a cross in the 15C (now in the Cathedral Treasury). The earliest examples of stained glass—made for the Dominicans and currently in the National Museum—also date from the 13C.

The development of Latin literature in the 13C owed much to the monastic orders, who produced treatises and hagiographies, bringing intellectual ideas from western Christendom to Kraków. Wincenty of Kielce, for instance, wrote the *Life of St Stanisław* (see p. 146) as well as the words of the prayer-hymn *Gaude Mater Polonia*, which would become the anthem of the Kraków Academy (see p. 130). The Franciscans composed the melody to the Marian prayer-hymn *Bogurodzica* (Mother of God), the Polish text of which dates from as early as the 10C–11C. Other important figures included the bishops Wincenty Kadłubek—author of the erudite *Polish Chronicle*—and Iwo Odrowąż, a church reformer and graduate of the Sorbonne.

In 1298, the new town was fortified with a 'modern' ring of stone walls, approximately 3.5km in length, interspersed with several gates and forty towers. As military technology changed, the fortifications were strengthened and their aesthetic appearance improved to underscore the city's growing status. In parallel, efforts were taken to bolster the municipal infrastructure with a system of moats and aqueducts.

The Piast prince **Władysław the Short** (1306–33), who for nearly a quarter of a century had fought for the unification of the Polish lands, was crowned King of Poland in Wawel Cathedral in 1320, thus ending almost two hundred years of feudal division. In a climate of economic prosperity and political stability, and with the arrival of masons from Germany, Bohemia, and particularly Alsace, architectural projects on an unprecedented scale could be realised. Soon after the coronation, work began on the 'third', Gothic cathedral on Wawel hill, followed in 1340 by the chancel of St Mary's Church (see p. 97).

The pre-eminent ruler of the 14C was **Kazimierz the Great** (1333–70), the last of the Piasts to rule Poland, who proved an outstanding patron of architecture, culture, art and learning. Two years after acceding the throne, he founded the new town of Kazimierz (see p. 140), named after himself, just south of Kraków, and raised a Gothic castle on Wawel hill. Kazimierz had its own fortifications and parish church of Corpus Christi (see p. 144). Following a ruling by the royal court in 1495, it became home to Kraków's Jewish community, which was resettled in the east part of the new town. Synagogues, publishing houses and a cemetery appeared. Generation after generation of Jews lived in Kazimierz right up until the Second World War, when the entire community was wiped out by the Nazis.

In the mid-14C, Kraków was an averaged-sized European city with a cosmopolitan population of around 15,000. Traditional links with the Hanseatic League (which Kraków joined in the 1360s) and cities like Nürnberg were maintained. The guilds prospered, their number rising steadily from 13 in 1399 to 29 a century later. Kraków's importance was confirmed in 1364, when it was chosen as the venue for a conference of European monarchs. The guests, who included Emperor Charles IV and Louis, King of Hungary, attended a lavish banquet hosted by Mikołaj Wierzynek (see p. 98), a wealthy patrician and royal adviser.

King Kazimierz's finest achievement was the establishment of the Kraków Academy (later the Jagiellonian University; see p. 130) in 1364, whose purpose was to train a corps of lawyers, civil servants and diplomats. Initially, there were three faculties, with a fourth—theology—being added in 1400, after Queen Jadwiga d'Anjou (1385–99) had endowed the Academy with most of her vast fortune. Colleges and student lodgings, headed by the Gothic Collegium Maius (see p. 130) and Collegium Iuridicum (see p. 114), sprang up all over the city. Cracovians could truly take pride in their *Alma Mater Cracoviensis*.

Several great monuments of **Gothic architecture** arose in the 14C. The 'third' (present) cathedral on Wawel, erected in 1320–64, was the first building to use the specifically Cracovian pillar-and-buttress system. Of similar design were the main bodies of the great municipal churches: St Mary's (see p. 93) in Kraków and Corpus Christi (see p. 144) and St Catherine's (see p. 145) in Kazimierz. Their slender chapel-type chancels are the quintessence of Cracovian Gothic.

Another important building to go up in the 14C was the Town Hall (see p. 92), whose Gothic tower, decorated with stone facing, still dominates the Market Square. All the other medieval public buildings on the square, with the exception of the Cloth Hall, were dismantled in the 19C... but not entirely: as in other old cities, Kraków rose steadily in height over the centuries, as rubble was levelled, building materials brought in, and new paving laid. The present surface of the square is between 2.5 and 4m above the original (from 1257). Thanks to this, the cellars and ground floors of numerous medieval buildings have been preserved underground.

In the 14C, the first Gothic **royal tombs** appeared in Wawel Cathedral: those of Władysław the Short (after 1333) and Kazimierz the Great (after 1370), the latter carved in Hungarian red marble. The monarchs are shown in death, as supine figures resting on a sarcophagus, at the sides of which are figures of mourners. In Kazimierz the Great's tomb, the mourners are members of the Royal Council, shown discussing the crisis of state brought about by the heirless death of the king. Another royal tomb, carved in red marble by an anonymous Florentine artist from the circle of Ghiberti and Donatello, was added to the Cathedral in c1420. It was commissioned by Władysław Jagiełło (1386–1434), the Grand Duke of Lithuania, who became King of Poland after his marriage to Queen Jadwiga in 1385, thus beginning the **Jagiellon dynasty** (1386–1572).

Altar and devotional sculpture in the 14C was influenced by trends in France, Bohemia and Silesia. Examples include the so-called Crucifix of St Jadwiga from c1380 (see p. 123) and the numerous wooden and stone sculptures of the Virgin representing the International Gothic, or 'Beautiful' style. Monumental painting is best represented by the stained glass in the chancel of St Mary's, preserved in three of the apse windows (from c1360, 1380 and 1400). The monumental murals recently discovered in the Augustinian cloister (see p. 146) date from c1430; those in the Franciscan monastery, notably *Christ in the Vine Press*, *St Francis Receiving the Stigmata* and *Annunciation*, are slightly later. Also visible on the walls of the Franciscan cloister are fading Gothic portraits of Cracovian bishops. The monks won the right to collect such images in the mid-13C. Their bishops' gallery provides a potted history of Cracovian painting from Gothic to modern times.

Late Gothic and Renaissance

By the second half of the 15C, Kraków had evolved into a major Central European city. The University and royal court, cathedral chapter and monastic orders, as well as the bourgeois elite and aristocracy, provided most of the cultural impetus of the period. It was here that Jan Długosz, a canon at the Cathedral and tutor to the children of Kazimierz the Jagiellon (1444–92), wrote his seminal *Chronicles of the Glorious Kingdom of Poland*—a key source document for Polish history in the Middle Ages. Towards the end of the century Italian Humanism arrived in Kraków, headed by the great Florentine scholar **Filippo Buonaccorsi** (alias 'Callimachus'; d. 1496). **Nicholas Copernicus** (see p. 132), the Kraków Academy's most famous graduate, overturned medieval cosmology by proving that the earth revolves around the sun, and not vice-versa. With the characteristic versatility of a Renaissance Man, Copernicus wrote treatises on many subjects, including astrology and economics. He co-founded the principle that bad money drives good money out of circulation—popularly known as Gresham's Law. Accompanying these epistemological breakthroughs was a revolution in book production: in 1473 the first printed document appeared in Kraków, predating the beginnings of printing in England by three years.

From around the mid-15C, when the construction projects begun during the reign of Kazimierz the Great were nearing completion, attention was turned to smaller buildings, simpler in composition but with more striking decoration such as stone facing, and to various additions: vestibules, chapels, stepped gables and monastery wings. The best examples are the south porch of St Catherine's Church in Kazimierz (see p. 145), the stone decoration of the Cathedral's chapter house and 'Jagiellonian chapels' (Holy Cross and Holy Trinity), and the pinnacled gables of the Corpus Christi Church (see p. 144). Generally, cross-rib vaults gave way to the star and net variety.

In 1478, the taller north tower of St Mary's (see p. 93) was given a steep Gothic spire and a decade later the fine open-work Chapel of Gethsemane was added to the Church of St Barbara (see p. 97). Collegium Maius (see p. 130) was remodelled in 1493, receiving superb cloisters and bay windows. From the mid-15C onwards the city walls were raised and strengthened, and new foregates erected, such as the Barbican in 1499 (see p. 106). Also from this period dates the oldest preserved example of wooden architecture in the city: the parish church of St Bartholomew (see p. 155), built in 1466 by the royal carpenter Maciej Mączka.

Painting and sculpture achieved a high standard, both strongly influenced by 15C realist art from the Netherlands and southern Germany. The exception, testifying to the aesthetic pluralism of the age, are the Byzantine-style murals (c 1470) in the Cathedral's Chapel of the Holy Cross.

In the last quarter of the 15C, a number of beautiful painted and sculpted **altars** were produced in Kraków, the finest being the retables of the Holy Trinity and Our Lady of Sorrows (both now in the Cathedral's Holy Cross Chapel), and the high altars in the Augustinian and Dominican churches, depicting Passion scenes (now in the National Museum). From the early 16C dates the *Behem Codex*, a book recording the privileges and statutes of Kraków and its guilds (now in the Jagiellonian Library), richly illustrated with miniatures.

A separate place in Cracovian art is occupied by the high altar of St Mary's Church on the Market Square (see p. 96)—a massive limewood polypytch with folding wings, made by the German sculptor **Veit Stoss**. The main scene, in the centre panel, shows the *Dormition of the Virgin*, with the *Life of Jesus and Mary* in the wings. Stoss came to Kraków from Nürnberg in 1477 and worked in the city for the next twenty years. Apart from the high altar—remarkable for its meticulous detail, lively colours and sweep of vision—he also left to posterity the marble tomb of Kazimierz the Jagiellon in the Cathedral (see p. 126), considered to be one of the finest medieval sepulchral monuments, the huge stone crucifix in St Mary's (see p. 96), outstanding for its perfect representation of human anatomy, and other works.

The artistic links between Kraków and the lands of southern Germany were particularly strong during the first half of the 16C. Numerous German painters were active in Kraków. Wealthy burghers imported altars, bronze memorial tablets, and goldwork from German cities; **Zygmunt the Old** (1506–48) commissioned Hans Dürer (brother of Albrecht) and others to make the beautiful silver altarpiece for the Zygmunt Chapel in the Cathedral. Yet, ultimately, it was Italian artists and sculptors who set the tone of Cracovian art and architecture in the 16C. The trend was strengthened by Bona Sforza, the Milanese wife of Zygmunt the Old, who brought with her to Wawel a vast retinue of Italian courtiers and physicians, poets and writers, musicians and cooks. Under the

Jagiellons, Kraków experienced its golden age. The list of outstanding writers, scholars, and artists of the period is too long to enumerate, but special mention should be made of Jan Kochanowski (1530–84), perhaps the greatest Slav poet prior to the early 19C.

In political matters, too, Kraków rose to the centre stage. On 10 April 1525, in a grand ceremony on the Market Square, Albrecht Hohenzollern (1490–1568), the Grand Master of the Teutonic Knights, swore an historic oath of fealty to Zygmunt the Old. The Knights were a medieval religious-cum-military order with whom Poland had long struggled for control over the Baltic, and through this act of feudal tribute they formally recognised Polish dominance in the region. The event, which came to be known as the '**Prussian Homage**', was later immortalised on canvas by the painter Jan Matejko (see p. 92). It is also commemorated by a slab set into the stone paving of the Market Square.

The first Italian artist to make a name in Kraków was **Francesco Fiorentino**, who sculpted the beautiful sandstone arch containing the tomb of King Jan Olbracht (1492–1501) in the Cathedral (see p. 123), and decorated the new royal castle on Wawel hill (see p. 127). This sumptuous residence was begun in 1503 and completed in 1536. The three-tiered arcades surrounding the castle courtyard are an interesting synthesis of 'Italian fashion' and domestic traditions and needs. Fiorentino was aided in his task by Cracovian and German artists, among them the sculptor Sebastian Tauerbach, who designed the extraordinary coffered ceiling— decorated with carved wooden heads—in the castle's Audience Hall (see p. 128).

The most important Italian artist of the period was another Florentine, **Bartolomeo Berrecci**, who designed the sepulchral chapel of the last Jagiellons, known as the Zygmunt Chapel. Berrecci was educated in the circle of Michelangelo and arrived in Kraków in 1517. His Zygmunt Chapel was dubbed 'the jewel of the Italian Renaissance north of the Alps'. It is a monument of outstanding beauty, emanating Florentine harmony, with the architectonic composition of each wall based on the form of a triumphal arch. In the main recesses are royal tombs, altars and stalls, with figures of saints and seers filling the medallions and niches; the pilasters and plinths are covered in grotesque forms in bas-relief.

The Zygmunt Chapel and the somewhat more modest Chapel of Bishop Tomicki (see p. 125) were the first examples of a new building type, later widely used: that of the domed sepulchral chapel on a central plan. There also appeared Florentine-inspired sculpture and a new type of ornamentation—the grotesque. All these novelties emanated the ideas of the Italian Renaissance: humanism, neoplatonism, and a reverence for antiquity.

Berrecci and his compatriots 'monopolised' the production of sepulchral monuments, memorial tablets, stonework and, in time, construction too, as evidenced by the Decius Villa (see p. 162) in the suburb of Wola Justowska. Older buildings were also modernised, notably the Cloth Hall (see p. 90) on the Market Square, which was given a sumptuous parapet wall (the 'Polish Parapet'). This type of lively cresting in place of traditional battlements was used in several public buildings (the town halls in Kraków and Kazimierz), houses, monasteries, presbyteries, and even the Old Synagogue in Kazimierz (see p. 141).

To this day, Cracovian churches are filled with the reclining figures of kings, knights and bishops, resting on tombs, whose composition, following the Zygmunt Chapel, is based on the triumphal arch. Such designs were not accidental: death signified a gateway to eternal life and a triumphant return to God. Preserved in St Mary's Church (by the rood) is a Renaissance canopied altar designed by the Paduan architect and sculptor, Giovanni il Mosca. Murals by the Cistercian monk Stanisław Samostrzelnik, the best Polish painter of the early 16C, adorn the transept and chancel walls of the Cistercian Abbey in Mogiła (see p. 154); royal prayer books decorated by Samostrzelnik can be seen in London's British Museum. To this day, Poland's most famous bell—the 'Zygmunt'—hangs in the Cathedral's Zygmunt Tower (see p. 120). The bell is sounded on major church and state holidays, its resounding D-sharp audible several kilometres away.

The Wawel tapestries (see p. 127) constitute the most magnificent, uniform collection of Renaissance art in Kraków. Commissioned in Brussels by the last Jagiellon monarch Zygmunt August, himself a great patron and collector of art, the tapestries were intended for the royal chambers of Wawel Castle. They were designed by Michiel van Coxcie and Willem Tons, and painstakingly woven from 1555 onwards, with seemingly no amount wool, silk or gold- and silver thread spared. The tapestries fall into three basic groups: figurative—depicting Biblical scenes (Adam and Eve, Story of Noah, Tower of Babel), the so-called verdures, with images of plants and animals, and finally the grotesque tapestries, each bearing the cipher of Zygmunt August.

The Counter-Reformation

In the second half of the 16C, **Mannerism** emerged in Cracovian art. Its main features—complexity, richness of ornamentation and *horror vacui*—were discernible in the work of the new generation of architects and sculptors. The leading figures were the Pole, Jan Michałowicz of Urzędów, and the Italian, **Santi Gucci** from Florence. Both men fused Italian forms, by then well-known in Kraków, with ornamentation characteristic of Flemish art. In c1600, the Venetian Tomaso Dolabella arrived in the city. He worked as court painter until 1650, specialising in monumental historical and religious scenes, in which elements of Venetian Mannerism were gradually displaced by Cracovian and Polish ones. Other notable artists included the Silesian Marcin Kober, who painted a now famous portrait of Stefan Bathory (1576–86), Prince of Transylvania and King of Poland, showing the monarch dressed in Polish-Hungarian costume, consisting of a nobleman's red robe, yellow boots and fur cap. The painting became a model for portraits of kings and noblemen in the 17C–18C, establishing a current known to art historians as Sarmatian portraiture (see p. 137).

From the mid-16C onwards, the **Counter-Reformation** dominated Polish affairs. The Jesuits were brought into Kraków in 1582, with the aim of stamping out the Reformation and reinvigorating the Church of Rome. They raised the Church of SS Peter and Paul (see p. 112), an outstanding early Baroque work based on the Gesù in Rome. At the same time, the Renaissance royal castle on Wawel hill was remodelled with the addition of impressive corner towers and staircases. In Bielany, near Kraków, the austere Camaldolite Order raised their magnificent monastery on a remote wooded hill (see p. 160), while in the city the Dominican Church received new chapels, funded by the Myszkowskis, Zbaraskis and Lubomirskis (see p. 109). All this construction displayed a certain severity and grandeur—what was later known as the 'Vasa style', a version of early Roman Baroque. The style gained currency during the reign of King Zygmunt III (1587–1632), the first Polish monarch of the Swedish Vasa line.

The 17C saw the development of huge columned altars, decorated with sculptures and paintings. Of similar proportions and character were the new stalls, confessionals and organ lofts. Black marble was introduced as a new building material, and was used in small-scale architectural projects, memorial tablets, portals etc. This also had a certain symbolic meaning, black being the colour of death.

The fear of, and fascination with, death was characteristic of the Counter-Reformation, and of the mid-17C, when Poland was ravaged by war and plagues. The notion of a valiant death appealed to the ancestral pride and vanity of the nobility and magnates, whose chief preoccupation was to build monuments to their eternal glory. These ideas were reflected in the reconstruction of the city after the so-called **Swedish Deluge** (1655–57), when the invading army of Charles Gustav laid siege to Kraków, wreaking widescale destruction. In the Bernardine Church at the foot of Wawel Castle, for instance, there is an oil painting depicting the *Dance of Death* (see p. 148), in which members of the four estates are invited to take part. The inevitability of death and the desire for earthly glory are two themes which emanate from the Baroque sepulchral chapels, tombs, and memorial tablets of the period. There are good examples in the Cathedral, SS Peter and Paul's, and several other churches.

The architecture, art, and religious culture of 17C–18C Kraków remained under the steady influence of Rome. This had its disadvantages: theatricalism pervaded art and liturgy; masses, funerals, coronations, the ingress of bishops, and processions marking various occasions became pompous in the extreme; sermons, poetry and literature—increasingly obscure and macaronic. However, because Kraków was an important centre of religious life, several outstanding architectural monuments appeared. In the years 1689–1703, the new collegiate church of St Anne was built for the University. It was designed by the Dutchman Tylman van Gameren, with stuccoes by the Italian, Baldassare Fontana and murals by the Swede, Karl Dankwart. This 'international work' is an exceptionally pure example of Roman Baroque and remains the most important monument funded by the University in its 600-year history. Mention should also be made of the somewhat later churches built for the various monastic orders active in Kraków: the Discalced Carmelite Nuns (see p. 151), Piarists (see p. 138), Missionary Fathers (see p. 149), Paulines (see p. 146) and Trinitarians (see p. 145). Painting and sculpture tried hard to keep up with the rapid development of architecture, but a shortage of local talent meant that artists from Warsaw, Silesia, Moravia, and further afield, were often employed. The same was true of crafts: the magnificent silver coffin containing the ashes of St Stanisław (see p. 121) was made by Pieter van der Rennen from Gdańsk.

The late 18C and the Age of Partitions

The final thirty years of the 18C brought far-reaching political changes. After the **First Partition of Poland** (1772), when one third of the country was annexed by Russia, Austria and Prussia, Kraków suddenly found itself in the outlying provinces of a diminished Polish state. The Vistula river marked the border between Kraków and the Austrian Empire. A new Austrian town (the present-day district of Podgórze) soon emerged on the south side of the river, taking over much of the city's trade and accelerating her economic decline. Despite these misfortunes, however, the Enlightenment managed to reach Kraków. Its effects were primarily felt in schools and colleges, thanks to the progressive policies of the National Education Commission, the first Department of Education in Europe. New University buildings went up, among them the neo-classical Observatory (1788) in the Botanical Gardens (see p. 151). A few palaces in the city, notably the Potockis' on the Market Square and the Wodzickis' on ul. Św Jana, received impressive new façades and interiors.

In the spring of 1794, a **national uprising** broke out against Russia and Prussia. It was led by Tadeusz Kościuszko, a hero of the American War of Independence, who made a rousing call to arms on Kraków's Market Square (today commemorated by a slab set into the stone paving). An entire cross-section of the population joined in the struggle: nobility and peasantry, bourgeoisie and army, Catholic clergy and Jews. But despite this show of solidarity, the insurrectionaries were eventually defeated. In 1795, under the **Third Partition**, Russia, Prussia and Austria divided among themselves the remaining territory of Poland, which disappeared from the map of Europe for the next 123 years. The Kościuszko Uprising passed into patriotic mythology; to this day it is rooted in the national consciousness of Poles.

After 1795, under **Austrian rule**, Kraków fell into provincial obscurity. Change for the better came at the **Congress of Vienna** in 1815, when the peacemakers decreed Kraków a mini-republic, with its own, relatively liberal constitution, under the direct supervision of the three Imperial powers. Though it lasted barely thirty years, the **Republic of Kraków** (1815–1846) proved vastly important for the survival of Polish culture. Polish remained the language of instruction in schools and universities, and the city had its own native administration. Poles from the partitioned lands—aristocrats and artists, scholars and politicians, conspirators and insurrectionaries—flocked to the city, which lived on as a small pocket of freedom. The effect of this was a growing interest in Polish affairs, in the country's history and monuments, especially Wawel—the ultimate symbol of Polish statehood. Instead of royalty, it was national heroes who were laid to rest in the Cathedral. The Austrians turned a blind eye to the ceremonial funerals of Józef Poniatowski (1817) and Tadeusz Kościuszko (1818), both famous military leaders who had fought the Imperial powers. The city even raised a mound in honour of Kościuszko in 1820–23, modelled on the prehistoric mounds of Krakus and Wanda. (To this day it offers one of the best panoramas of the city).

One of the most eminent Cracovians of the period was **Piotr Michałowski** (1800–55), Poland's greatest Romantic painter, best known for his vivid representations of battle scenes and striking portraits of peasants. Sculptures by Bertel Thorvaldsen and the followers of Antonio Canova began to appear in the city's churches. In 1844 the Warsaw–Vienna railway line was extended to Kraków. A new station was built, and day trips to the spa in nearby Krzeszowice soon became fashionable. By the mid-century, the population had grown to around 40,000.

Inevitably, Kraków became a focal point of the increasingly vigorous claims for national independence. When a local uprising was crushed in 1846, the Republic was formally dissolved and annexed to Austria. The next twenty years were the most repressive period of Austrian rule in the city. Economic decline was exacerbated by two natural disasters: famine and a typhoid epidemic in 1848, followed by a massive fire in 1850 which destroyed much of the Old Town, including the Dominican and Franciscan churches. During the reconstruction effort, the Austrians decided to transform Kraków into a massive fortress. Wawel Castle was used as an army barracks, and by the 1870s a double ring of fortifications known as *Festung Krakau* had been completed.

Kraków's fortunes were to turn again in 1867, when the constitution of the new Austro–Hungarian Empire gave Galicia (i.e. the Austrian Partition) wide-ranging autonomy. The Germanisation policies of the previous two decades, particularly in the civil service and academia, went into reverse. Galicia enjoyed a level of cultural freedom that was the envy of Poles fleeing Czarist autocracy and Prussian absolutism. It was even dubbed the Polish Athens, or the Polish Piedmont, in anticipation of the role the city would play in rebirth of the Fatherland.

Kraków's cultural development was marked by two distinct trends: Historicism (the main artistic and intellectual current of the 19C) and Modernism (also known, depending on the language, as 'Young Poland', 'Art Nouveau', 'Secession', or the 'New Style'). Both these trends played a major role not only in the history of Kraków, but in the history of Poland, too.

Until the turn of the 19C, **Historicism** was dominant. Its protagonists, chiefly based at the University and Academy of Sciences and Letters, enjoyed wide public respect and produced work of the highest quality. As a result of their efforts, the city acquired new buildings designed in an eclectic spirit or conforming to one of the traditional styles. Examples include the Słowacki Theatre (see p. 139), based on the Paris Opéra, the University's Collegium Novum (see p. 133), and the headquarters of the School (later Academy) of Fine Arts (see p. 107); even the huge pump station supplying water to the city was an outstanding achievement of neo-Romanesque architecture. New buildings shaped the appearance of the city centre, and because they recalled Polish and European architecture of times past, also added to its unique atmosphere.

Historical painting was the vogue at the Academy of Fine Arts, the country's leading art school. Its chief representative was **Jan Matejko**, an ardent patriot, who did for painting what the great Romantic bards (Adam Mickiewicz, Juliusz Słowacki, Zygmunt Krasiński) had done for poetry. His huge canvases (see p. 92) are much more than illustrations of important events from Polish history: they are examples of historiosophical painting, in which past events are not just presented, but also evaluated, in the hope of prompting the captive nation into action. Like his contemporaries, Matejko was deeply involved in the restoration of Kraków's historic buildings. He participated in the renovation of the Cloth Hall, which was transformed into a branch of the National Museum (see p. 91), and designed and executed a series of superb murals for St Mary's (see p. 94). Concern for the fate of historic monuments served as a unifying, integrating force among Cracovians and, in so far as it was possible, among Poles, too. An important role was played by the National Museum, which amassed collections of Polish art, as well as art from other countries and cultures. Of special significance was the donation made by the Czartotyski family (see p. 138), which included works by Leonardo, Raphael and Rembrandt, as well as national memorabilia, military accessories, and collections of ancient and medieval art.

The generation of Jan Matejko's students was educated during the **Young Poland** (Modernist) period. Ivory-towered professors were now eclipsed by Kraków's artistic *bohème*, which took delight in ridiculing all forms of authority.

It was this new elite that raised art to a level unseen in Kraków for at least two centuries. The plays of **Stanisław Wyspiański** (see p. 116), as well as his murals and stained-glass designs (see p. 110), achieved an unsurpassed excellence. Artists at the Academy turned their attention to Parisian post-Impressionism and European neo-Romanticism, which, fused with their own suffering, nostalgia and yearning for freedom, bore fruit in a number of exceptionally refined works. But while the formal virtuosity of this output is beyond doubt, its meaning, from today's perspective, is obscure and hermetic, not least for the foreigner. The same is true of theatre, literature, and especially poetry, all of which flourished in the last quarter of the 19C. It was during this period that an important collection of Japanese woodcuts was donated to the city by the writer and explorer Feliks Jasieński (1861–1929), nicknamed 'Manggha' (see p. 149).

In the years 1906–11, the Austrian army gave the fortress area back to the city, thus allowing urban development to proceed beyond the ring of fortifications. A programme to transform Kraków into a garden city was begun. The municipal infrastructure was modernised and new districts emerged, accompanied by a spate of Modernist construction, the best examples of which are found on pl. Szczepański. Impressive, too, are the Secessionist interiors of the *Jama Michalika Café* on ul. Floriańska (see p. 105). Generally, the early 20C was a favourable period for artists, writers and original thinkers of all sorts, but these were the twilight years of Kraków's *bohème*, and the **First World War** signalled its definitive end.

Kraków from 1918 to 1945

The war years were relatively kind to Kraków: no fighting took place within its borders, and once the Austro–Hungarian Empire had finally disintegrated, it was the first Polish city to be free. On 31 October 1918 German and Austrian military units were disarmed, and Cracovians spontaneously began to tear down the Imperial emblem from barracks and public buildings around the city. At midday the Polish flag was hoisted above the Town Hall Tower, and the famous 'Zygmunt' bell rang out from Wawel Cathedral. The dream of generations had finally come to fruition. Yet few present at that joyful moment could have predicted that their hard-won independence would last for only 20 years.

In 1918, Kraków numbered around 180,000 inhabitants. Between the wars the city developed slowly, hindered by the world economic crisis of 1929–33. Its position as the leading centre of the arts and sciences in Poland was undermined by Warsaw, which was once again designated as the capital of the new Polish state, and as a result attracted the best minds and talents in the country. However, several important institutions—the National Museum (see p. 156), Jagiellonian Library (see p. 156), and Academy of Mining and Metallurgy (see p. 156) among them—had new headquarters and branches built in Kraków. Many notable writers and actors left the city, but theatrical and literary circles continued to function, with various currents represented, while educational institutions nurtured a whole new generation of artists and scholars. In 1939, a young man from Wadowice called Karol Wojtyła began a degree in Polish literature at the University.

Kraków surrendered to the invading German army in 1939 without a fight, and consequently avoided the mass bombing and destruction that befell Warsaw. In October, it was designated as the seat of the *General Gouvernement*. Segregation of the city began almost immediately. The best districts in the west were reserved for Germans. Poles were expelled to the poorer, Jewish districts of Kazimierz and Stradom, the Jewish community to labour camps in Germany or, after 1941, to the new ghetto in Podgórze across the river. Before the **Second World War**, a fifth of Kraków's 250,000 inhabitants were Jews, but as few as 1,000 managed to survive it. Mass exterminations began in 1942 with the first transports of Jews to concentration camps at Płaszów in Podgórze, and at Auschwitz–Birkenau, 50km east of Kraków. Repression was also stepped up against the Polish population, particularly the intelligentsia—priests, teachers, lawyers, doctors; as early as 1939, 184 Jagiellonian University professors had been deported to Sachsenhausen. Many priceless works of art were looted: Veit Stoss's altarpiece in St Mary's, paintings from the Czartoryski collection, books and documents from the Jagiellonian Library and private archives. The Nazis removed from the city all monuments to Polish national figures, Mickiewicz and Kościuszko among them. To underscore the death of Polish culture, the rooms of Wawel Castle were converted into the offices of the Governor, Hans Frank. But in spite of the hardships and extreme risk, cultural life in the city refused to die: the University carried on underground teaching; school lessons were organised; secret performances of Polish plays and Polish music were held. As nowhere else in occupied Europe, an entire 'underground state' was in operation in Poland, with its own courts, publishing houses, cultural and educational institutions, and an armed resistance. The penalty for any kind of independent activity was death, but people were undeterred: the reward, they believed, would be freedom and independence.

At the end of the war, again, Kraków escaped destruction. Like its buildings, the city's pre-war social structure (minus the entire Jewish population) survived the war years. There were new settlers from Lwów (Lviv), though, which Stalin incorporated into the Socialist Republic of Ukraine, as well as from other lost territories in the east. Kraków was slowly returning to normal life. Teaching began at the University, looted works of art were repatriated, prisoners returned home from Nazi and Soviet camps. Reconstruction of the country got under way. The problem was that the new communist authorities had their own plans for postwar Poland.

Kraków under Communism (1945–89)

For Kraków, the **communist period** spelled disaster. With the erection in the 1950s of a huge iron and steel works (see p. 154), serviced by a model 'workers' town', on the periphery of the city, pollution levels soared. Buildings in the historic city centre began to turn a blackish-grey and fall into disrepair, while lack of funds meant not enough could be done in the way of renovation. At institutions of higher education, the intake of students from proletarian and peasant backgrounds was vastly increased to undermine the dominance of 'reactionary' professors. Marxist-Leninist methodology found its way into all branches of learning, with the 'unsurpassed achievements of Soviet science' setting the example for all to follow. Socialist Realism was decreed the new official doctrine, to which art and architecture had to adhere. The University's theological faculty was closed down, and a ban was imposed on the construction of new churches.

Yet Kraków managed to survive these dark years, and ultimately the proletarianising zeal of the communist authorities backfired. The academic establishment proved it could be neither bribed nor frightened into submission.

Intellectual circles consolidated around the Catholic journal *Tygodnik Powszechny* and the *Znak* publishing house. After the death of Stalin, and the 'thaw' of 1956, Socialist Realism was scrapped and cultural activity underwent a revival. Tadeusz Kantor's *Cricot 2 Theatre* (see p. 115), the *Piwnica pod Baranami Cabaret* (see p. 99), the music of Krzysztof Penderecki, and Andrzej Wajda's (see p. 150) film and theatre productions, all showed that much could still be done in the face of adversity.

Every few years, social discontent erupted onto the streets. In 1961, in the 'socialist' district of Nowa Huta, demonstrators demanded freedom of conscience and the right to build churches. In the revolutionary year of 1968, students revolted against state censorship and the stifling of culture. And during the heady days of 1980–81, the Lenin steelworks (see p. 154) became a bastion of Solidarity, the first and only independent mass movement in the communist bloc.

Kraków grew rapidly during the post-war period. To accommodate an expanding population (750,000 in 1989) vast, dehumanising housing estates, of universally poor quality, were hastily built around the city suburbs. Concomitantly, the number and variety of schools and institutions of higher education increased: once again Kraków became a leading centre of the arts and sciences. Theatre flourished and excellent literary works appeared, such as the poems of Nobel prize-winner Wisława Szymborska. At best, the authorities were indifferent to cultural initiatives and for the most part were suspicious of them. But this did not stop the International Graphic Art Biennale (now Triennale), the International Short Film Festival, and several other events and festivals from earning a permanent place in the city's cultural calendar. Life, as they say, went on, despite the dourness and inertia of the system.

The election of Kraków's Metropolitan-Archbishop Karol Wojtyła to the Papacy on 16 October 1978 was a momentous event for the Polish nation, and for Cracovians in particular. Once again the 'Zygmunt' bell was sounded from the tower of Wawel. The popular feeling was that better times were approaching. John Paul II made his first visit to Poland in June 1979, on the occasion of the 900th anniversary of the death of Bishop Stanisław (see p. 146). The Pope's open-air mass held on the Błonia common was the largest gathering in the history of the city, attended by over a million believers. In those unforgettable days, people suddenly regained a sense of pride and dignity, for the first time becoming aware of their collective power. There is no doubt that the Pope's visit played a major role in the birth of the Solidarity movement in 1980. And despite the attempted destruction of the movement during the gloomy days of Martial Law (1981–83), it was Solidarity which triumphed a decade later (1989), when the physical and metaphorical walls separating East from West came tumbling down.

Further reading

History and general background

Abramsky, Chimen, Jachimczyk, Maciej and Polonsky Anthony (eds). *The Jews in Poland* (Blackwell, Oxford, 1986).

Acherson, Neal. *The Struggles for Poland* (Pan, London 1988).

Bauman, Janina. *Winter in the Morning* (Virago, London, 1986).

Garton Ash, Timothy. *The Polish Revolution: Solidarity 1980–82* (Jonathan Cape, London, 1983).

Davies, Norman. *God's Playground: A History of Poland* (2 vols) (Clarendon Press, Oxford).

Davies, Norman. *Heart of Europe: A Short History of Poland* (Oxford University Press, Oxford, 1984).

Wat, Aleksander. *My Century. The Odyssey of a Polish Intellectual* (University of California Press, Berkeley, 1988).

Zamoyski, Adam. *The Polish Way: A Thousand-year History of the Poles and their Culture* (John Murray, London, 1987).

Art and architecture

Chrzanowski, Tadeusz. *The Wonders of Poland* (Kluszczyński, Kraków, 1998).

Chruścicki, Tadeusz and Stolot, Franciszek. *Museums of Cracow* (Arkady, Warsaw, 1994).

Crossley, Paul. *Architecture in the Reign of Casimir the Great* (Kraków 1984).

Krzysztofowicz-Kozakowska, Stefania. *Polish Art Nouveau* (Kluszczyński, Kraków, 1999).

Ostrowski, Jan. K. *Cracow* (International Cultural Centre, Kraków, 1992).

Ostrowski, Jan. K. *Masters of Polish Painting* (Kluszczyński, Kraków, 1999).

Literature

Hoffman, Eva. *Lost in Translation: A Life in a New Language* (Viking Penguin, 1990).

Kantor, Tadeusz. *Journeys Through Space: Essays and Manifestos: 1944–90* (University of California Press, 1993).

Kantor, Tadeusz. *Wielopole, Wielopole* (Marion Boyars, 1990; re-issue edition).

Keneally, Thomas. *Schindler's Ark* (Hodder & Stoughton, London, 1982).

Lem, Stanisław. *Solaris* (Faber & Faber, 1970).

Lem, Stanisław. *The Cyberiad: Fables for the Cybernetic Age* (Secker and Warburg, 1975).

Lem, Stanisław. *The Star Diaries* (Avon, USA, 1977).

Lem, Stanisław. *Memoirs Found in a Bathtub* (Harcourt Brace, 1986).

Mrożek, Sławomir. *Tango: A Play in Three Acts* (Grove, USA, 1968).

Mrożek, Sławomir. *Six Plays* (Jonathan Cape, London, 1968).

Mrożek, Sławomir. *The Emigrants* (Samuel French, London, 1984).

Szymborska, Wisława. *Sounds, Feelings, Thoughts: Seventy Poems.* (Princeton University Press, USA, 1981).

Szymborska, Wisława. *People on a Bridge* (Forest Books, London, 1990).

THE GUIDE

Walks around the Old Town

1 • The Market Square

Much of your time in Kraków will be spent in and around the **Market Square**, located at the centre of the city's historic Old Town. The square, or *Rynek* (from the German, 'Ring') is the largest medieval market square in Europe (200m by 200m). In the Middle Ages, it was the commercial and administrative centre of the city, the venue for ceremonies and parades, public meetings and executions. From the late 15C, it was where the magnates put up their grand palaces to be closer to the royal court on Wawel. Today, in summer, children feed the swarms of pigeons, the flower-sellers open their stalls, and the cafés move their chairs and tables outdoors, providing an excellent vantage point from which to admire the ancient buildings—the Cloth Hall, Town Hall Tower, Church of St Mary—or just watch the crowds.

The history of the Market Square begins in 1257, when Bolesław the Chaste (1243–79) endowed Kraków with a municipal charter based on Magdeburg law. A new market square was laid out at the centre of a regular grid of streets. The plan was symmetrical, though in some places concessions had to be made to accommodate extant buildings, such as the churches of St Mary and St Adalbert. Likewise, the existing street plan had to be taken into account: ul. Grodzka, for example, the old thoroughfare running south towards Wawel Castle, broke the rule that streets should enter the square at right angles. With urban expansion limited by the town walls, the *Rynek* was soon crammed with a maze of stalls and municipal buildings: a Gothic town hall; Renaissance granary; large weighing house; foundry; pillory; and cloth hall. Over the centuries, the Gothic appearance of the Market Square gradually changed: the narrow medieval buildings around the periphery were demolished or combined to form new houses and palaces. Bare Gothic brick gave way to plaster; storeys and decorative parapets were added, and buttresses were often used to bolster the frailer buildings. A major transformation took place during Austrian rule in the 19C, when the stalls and the old buildings, except the Cloth Hall and the Town Hall tower, were demolished to make way for a broad open space lined with trees. The façades on the houses one sees today generally date from this period. Most are Neo-classical, often concealing older elements: beam-framed ceilings, numerous portals (15C–18C), painted decoration and stuccoes (16C–19C). Restoration work carried out during the communist period was generally shoddy and often controversial. In the 1960s, for instance, the original limestone cobbles on the floor of the square were replaced with smooth paving stones, very slippery when wet with rain. Since 1989, however, the city authorities have taken far more care in planning the appearance of the square. The three main buildings—St Mary's, the Cloth Hall and Town Hall Tower—have all had major facelifts, and the end result is truly impressive.

The ceremonial functions of the Market Square began in 1320. That year, for the first time, the city burghers paid official tribute to the new monarch: on the day after his coronation, Władysław the Short (1306–33) was presented with the golden keys to the city and 1000 ducats. From the 14C onwards, royal coronations and burials were preceded by grand parades along the Royal Way (see p. 104), from the Floriańska Gate to Wawel Castle. Some medieval ceremonies have survived to the present day. In June, the spectacular **Corpus Christi procession**, attended by vast crowds, begins at Wawel Cathedral and ends with an army of monks and nuns kneeling in prayer on the Market Square. In the following week, you might catch a glimpse of Lajkonik, a horseman dressed in a costume designed by the early 20C painter and playwright, Stanisław Wyspiański (see p. 116), and meant to represent a Tartar chieftain. The **Lajkonik parade** sets out from the Premonstratensian Convent in Salwator (see p. 158) and proceeds to the Market Square. In December, the *Rynek* is the venue for a competition of *szopki*, or Christmas cribs, which are put on display around the statue of Adam Mickiewicz (see below).

The Cloth Hall

The middle of the *Rynek* is occupied by one of Kraków's best known and best loved architectural monuments, the **Cloth Hall, or *Sukiennice*. Rectangular in shape, and measuring almost 100m in length, the Cloth Hall was the medieval city's main centre of trading, surrounded on all sides by a labyrinth of market stalls. Nowadays, the building's mercantile traditions are sustained by a covered market offering a variety of souvenirs, folk art, handicraft and leather goods; everything from carved chess sets and amber brooches to Stalin dolls with miniature Yeltsins inside. After visiting the stalls you could stop in at the *Noworolski* café under the east arcade, which has opulent, turn-of-the-century decor. The upper floors of the Cloth Hall house a Gallery of Polish Painting (see below), where some of the best art in the country can be seen.

Market Square showing St Mary's church and the Cloth Hall

History of the Cloth Hall

The earliest fragments of the Cloth Hall date from the 13C, when Bolesław the Chaste promised to provide stalls for the cloth traders under the terms of the city's charter. A Gothic edifice was raised in the second half of the 14C, only to be gutted by a huge fire in 1555. The rebuilding of the Cloth Hall was entrusted to one of the best architects of the Polish Renaissance, **Santi Gucci** (though some historians attribute the work to Gucci's brother, Matteo), who gave the building a new Mannerist form in 1556–60, crowning it with a decorative parapet wall. The 'Polish Parapet', as it later came to be known, took the form of a lively cresting in place of the traditional battlements, with a sunken roof as additional protection against fire. Gucci's version, consisting of a blind-arcade frieze with volute crowning, is the earliest example of its kind. His too are the grotesque masks on the parapet, their faces contorted with pain or convulsed in satanic laughter. Inside, the Cloth Hall was given a massive vault with lunettes, while the Paduan architect, **Giovanni il Mosca**, added columned loggias, reached by stairs, to the external lower sections (north and south ends).

Originally, the Cloth Hall was hemmed in on all sides by stalls, demolished in the 19C to make way for the massive central projections you see today. **Tomasz Pryliński**, the architect in charge of the reconstruction project, skilfully masked the bare hall façades with neo-Gothic arcades (1875–79), allowing entry to the stores within. The capitals on some of the columns were adorned with sculptures designed by Jan Matejko, who also supplied the new carved wooden stalls. In 1883, a National Museum was opened exhibiting works donated by local artists, a trend established by Henryk Siemiradzki, who presented his huge *Torches of Nero* for public display in 1879.

For an overview of Polish art in the 19C, there is no better place than the *Cloth Hall Gallery (open Tues, Wed, Fri–Sun 10.00–16.00, Thur 10.00–18.00), entered from the east arcade. The earliest works are late 18C portraits and depictions of battle scenes by Marcello Bacciarelli, Michał Stachowicz, and others. Romantic painting is represented by Wojciech Korneli Stattler (1800–75)—whose enormous *Maccabees* allegorises of the fate of partitioned Poland—and Piotr Michałowski (1800–55), an artist preoccupied with Napoleonic themes, as revealed in *The Charge at Somosierra*. The best late 19C works include Józef Chełmoński's (1849–1914) evocative impressions of the Polish countryside in *Foursome*, *Forest Road*, and *Storm*, and Jacek Malczewski's (1854–1929) moving scenes of *Christmas Eve in Siberia* and *The Death of Ellenai*. Polish Impressionism comes to the fore in the winter landscapes and hunting scenes of Julian Fałat (1853–1929), Leon Wyczółkowski's (1852–1936) *A Game of Croquet*, and Władysław Podkowiński's (1866–95) once controversial *Ecstasy*, which explores the mythological theme of a woman in the dual role of demon and innocent victim. The most popular exhibits are the huge 'patriotic' paintings by Jan Matejko—*The Prussian Homage*, *Kościuszko at Racławice* and *Wernyhora the Seer*.

Jan Matejko

The 19C was a golden age for Polish painting, much of which became tied to the struggle for national independence, and it was in the works of Jan Matejko (1838–1893)—the greatest Polish exponent of historical painting—that art which aimed to serve the nation reached its apogee. Matejko's *oeuvre* constitutes a monumental cycle of scenes from Polish history, a vision so evocative that it has become deeply rooted in the national consciousness: even today, Poles view their national history through his eyes.

For Matejko there were more important issues than formal perfection: he called art a weapon of the struggling nation, and his paintings went far beyond simple illustration. He tried to depict not isolated events but entire sequences of causes and effects, in the hope of inspiring the nation to analyse its own historical situation and take an active part in shaping Poland's future. By the age of 24, Matejko had already produced one of his best paintings—*Stańczyk*, in which historical narrative is mixed with a strong ideological message: Stańczyk, the court jester of King Zygmunt the Old (1506–48), is portrayed as a pensive, embittered sage who has foreseen the loss of Poland's independence. In *The Sermon of Piotr Skarga* (1865) and *Rejtan* (1867), which won him European fame and two gold medals at the Parisian Salon, Matejko again castigated those responsible for Poland's downfall.

Soon to be regarded by his contemporaries as the spiritual leader of the Polish nation, it was Matejko's commitment to this role that caused him to shift the emphasis to issues that could unite the Poles. Instead of examining the roots of national disaster, his later works concentrated on the triumphant episodes of Polish history: *The Union of Lublin* (1869), *Bathory at Pskov* (1872), *The Battle of Grunwald* (1878), *The Prussian Homage* (1882), *Sobieski at the Battle of Vienna* (1883) and, finally, *Kościuszko at Racławice* (1888). It was in this mature phase that Matejko's dynamic, almost Baroque style—full of larger-than-life figures and garish colours—crystallised.

Aside from history and Baroque art, an important source of inspiration for Matejko was the work of the medieval sculptor Veit Stoss, and in particular the high altar of St Mary's Church (see p. 96). In 1889–91, Matejko designed and executed superb murals for the nave and chancel of St Mary's—today restored to their original splendour. Throughout his life he also painted numerous portraits of aristocrats and political figures, often in dignified, defiant poses, as if to stress that they (read: the Poles) were destined for freedom.

The imposing *Town Hall Tower (70m, 50cm off vertical)* in the southwest part of the *Rynek* is all that now remains of Kraków's 14C Town Hall, demolished in 1817 after falling into a state of disrepair.

Begun at the beginning of the 14C, the Town Hall was originally a long one-storey building running from east to west, with stepped gables on its shorter sides. It served a variety of purposes, housing the City Council and judiciary, a storehouse, and down below in the cellars, an alehouse, torture chambers and prison. The adjoining tower, with its steep Gothic spire modelled on St Mary's across the square, accommodated the municipal treasury and chapel.

The tower is mainly brick, with Gothic stone fluting. The upper sections of the building suffered extensive damage during a fire in 1680. During reconstruction a new crowning in the form of a Baroque double-lantern was added. Another fire in the 18C destroyed the Nürnberg clock and oriel windows. The latter were rebuilt in the 1960s, but the end result outraged many conservators as inauthentic.

The Town Hall Tower is now a branch of the **Historical Museum of Kraków** (open Wed–Fri, Sat–Sun 09.00–16.00, summer only), entered via the stairs on the north side of the building. More interesting than the display (history of the city authorities) is the interior itself, which has some fine Gothic masonry. Inscribed on the stone facing in the former ground floor Treasury are a dozen or so stonemason's marks dating from 1444 when the tower was reconstructed. Upstairs you will find the chambers of the City Council, and on the third floor a series of rooms, former prison cells, offering a fine view over the city. The cellars, reached by a separate entrance, house a tiny theatre with an adjoining bar—the *Ratuszowa* (see *Late-night bars and clubs*).

Southwest of the Cloth Hall stands **St Adalbert's church**, a modest, domed building on a square plan. Built in the 11C, it is in fact one of the oldest surviving examples of Romanesque architecture in the city, pre-dating the Market Square. As successive layers of paving were added to the square, so the church began to sink—almost 3m over the centuries. St Adalbert's has now been restored right down to its foundations.

Small Romanesque windows with slanting jambs are preserved in the lower sections. Adjacent to the north is a sacristy (1711), and to the south, a chapel (1778). Underneath the church are cellars housing a small but worthwhile branch of the **Archaeological Museum** (open Mon–Sat 12.00–16.00, May–Sept) devoted to the life of St Adalbert, the first martyr of the Polish Catholic Church. In the late 10C, the Czech-born Adalbert was sent on a fatal mission to convert the heathen Prussians to Christianity. He was later canonised and his remains bought from the Prussians and enshrined in the town of Gniezno in western Poland, where they remain to this day.

Walking north to St Mary's church you will pass the **Monument to Adam Mickiewicz**, the greatest Polish poet of the Romantic period. Teodor Rygier designed the piece in bronze in 1898. It stands on a solid granite plinth decorated with allegorical figures symbolising Patriotism, Learning, Poetry and Valour. Destroyed by the Nazis in 1940, the monument was rebuilt and placed in its present spot in 1955—the hundredth anniversary of the poet's death. Today it serves as a meeting point, popularly known as *'pod Adasiem'*—'by Adam'.

The Church of St Mary

When viewed from afar, the city's skyline is dominated by the ****Church of St Mary**, revered by many as Poland's finest architectural monument, surpassing even Wawel Cathedral. St Mary's is the quintessential Cracovian church; it is also one of the city's oldest, pre-dating the *Rynek* around it by almost half a century.

History of St Mary's Church

Discoveries of Romanesque foundations suggest that a stone basilica, probably destroyed during a Tartar invasion, existed at this spot as early as 1222. After the arrival that year of the Dominicans, who took over the church of the Holy Trinity on pl. Wszystkich Świętych (see p. 108), St Mary's became Kraków's parish church. In the 1290s a low brick hall went up on the same site, preserving from the Romanesque structure only the bases of the columns separating the nave from the aisles. A chancel, sponsored by Mikołaj Wierzynek (see p. 98), followed in 1355–65, and finally a Gothic brick basilica with transept was raised in the last three decades of the 14C, under the supervision of the German builder Nicolaus Wernher from Prague. Because its contemporary—Wawel Cathedral—was the royal and episcopal church of Kraków, St Mary's saw little of the royal and ecclesiastical patronage that was lavished on its rival. Instead it was financed by wealthy burgher families, whose memorials still adorn the walls and chapels.

The lowest sections of the giant twin towers of St Mary's are remnants of the 13C Gothic hall church. The shorter south tower (late 14C) was set aside for the belfry and has five bells, the largest—the 'Half-Zygmunt', in reference to the greater bell on Wawel—cast in 1438. It is topped with a Renaissance spire. The taller north tower reached its present height of over 80m in 1477, when Mathias Heringk gave it a steep Gothic spire adorned at its base with a wreath of eight turrets topped by smaller spires. A gilded crown was later mounted on the spire. In the Middle Ages the tower was manned by the city watch: in times of danger the bugler at the top would give the signal to close the city gates. Today, this tradition is maintained by a fireman, who sounds the bugle signal on the hour (see p.73).

The somewhat severe **façade** of St Mary's is enlivened by stone detailing and a decorative pattern of different coloured brick. Tall thin panels and Gothic windows rise up the towers, between which nestles a huge pointed arch window with fine tracery, its lower section concealed by the west **Porch** (1). Rich thematic sculptures (1360–65) decorate the supports of the moulding and the keystones of the window frames around the external chancel wall. The strong buttresses are finished with pinnacles above the chapels, nave and aisles.

Interior (open Mon–Sat 12.00–18.00, Sun 14.00–18.00) Enter St Mary's through the porch, its outer doors decorated with the sculpted heads of church dignitaries and apostles. Two chapels adjoin the **Vestibule** (2): to the right, the **Chapel of the Virgin of Częstochowa** (3), its altar containing a copy of the famed Black Madonna (see *Glossary*), and usually crowded with believers kneeling before the Holy Sacrament; to the left, the more sombre **Chapel of St Anthony** (4), where prisoners awaiting execution would be held. The altar here dates from the 18C.

The **nave**, 28m high and four bays long, is separated from the aisles by huge piers. Especially fine is the Gothic cross-rib vault, its clarity contrasting with the Baroque opulence of the altars below. In the distance you will see a giant crucifix (c 1520) high on the rood beam, and beyond it, in the chancel, Veit Stoss's celebrated high altar. The 19C murals covering the walls are by Jan Matejko, who included, among the plant motifs, guild emblems and royal crests. Either side of

ST MARY'S

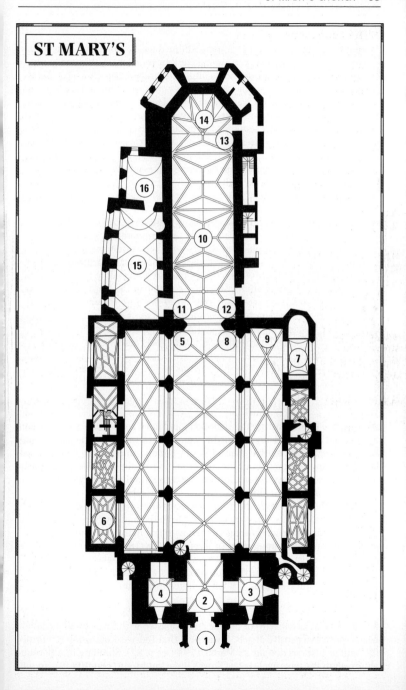

The High Altar

Stoss began the piece in 1477 and continued for 12 years. He achieved a work of true genius, a superb example of European late Gothic, today coveted as one of Poland's greatest cultural treasures. The altar cost 2808 florins to construct, roughly equal to the entire city budget for one year. During the Second World War it was removed to Germany by the Nazis, and eventually retrieved from the cellars of Nürnberg castle. After extensive conservation, the altar was restored to its original place in the church in 1957.

The proportions of the altar are huge: even 'closed' it commands the whole church, its lavish gilding in striking contrast to the chancel's sombre surroundings. The main scene in the *corpus* represents the ***Dormition of the Virgin***. Huge (up to 2.85m high), three-dimensional figures of the apostles support the fainting Mary. The figures, in their dramatic poses, reveal the artist's astonishing eye for detail: not a single muscle contour, expression or facial blemish seem to have escaped Stoss's attention. Above the apostles, still in the main *corpus*, is a scene of the ***Assumption***; dotted around that, sculpted figures of people from Stoss's own surroundings—knights, students, merchants and artisans—all carved with equal meticulousness and sensitivity. On the hinged wings of the *corpus* are six scenes in flat relief: (left, top to bottom) ***Annunciation, Nativity, Adoration of the Magi***; (right, top to bottom) ***Resurrection, Ascension, Descent of the Holy Ghost***. The scene in the altar crowning depicts the ***Coronation of the Virgin***, flanked by the patrons of Poland—SS Stanisław and Adalbert; below the main *corpus* is a predella panel with the genealogical tree of Jesus and Mary. When closed, the wings of the altar reveal a further twelve scenes in low-relief from the ***Life of Jesus and Mary***. The mood of the entire work is enhanced by the opalescent light filtering in through the medieval stained glass windows in the apse behind.

the entrance to the nave are the aldermen's and town councillors' pews, covered by canopies from the 16C, and further on, adjacent to the middle pillars, early Baroque pews. Black marble altars (18C), by Bażanka and Placidi, adorn the pillars separating the nave from the aisles; many contain valuable paintings by such masters as the Venetian Giovanni Battista Pittoni, whose best piece—the *Annunciation*—is in an altar (5) to the left of the rood screen.

Between the buttresses in the north and south aisles are six chapels (1435–46) with late Gothic vaults. They are closed off from the nave by Baroque gates and marble portals. The chapels are decorated with fine murals by some of Poland's greatest painters, including those of Józef Mehoffer (1869–1946) in the Chapel of John the Baptist (6), an artist best known for his stained-glass designs, murals and portraits of women, and those of Włodzimierz Tetmajer (1862–1923) in the Chapel of St John Nepomuk (7), who painted marvellously colourful scenes of village life.

Moving to the right of the chancel arch, notice Giovanni il Mosca's Renaissance tabernacle (8) of marble and alabaster, with three small medallion heads above two pensive angels. It was here that Tadeusz Kościuszko reaffirmed the oath of insurrection on 25 March 1794 (see p. 82). Standing in a Baroque altar next to the tabernacle is Veit Stoss's huge sandstone *crucifix (9), an outstanding example of 15C stone sculpture, with Christ represented in 'heroic' style against a background of Jerusalem.

The **chancel** (10) is as long and tall as the nave, but, unlike it, has a truly Gothic slimness of proportion. In 1442, the stonemason Czipser put up the present vault of four-pointed stars. Then, in the late 19C, Jan Matejko covered the vault and walls with murals depicting angels playing musical instruments and holding banners with verses of the Litany of Loreto. The upper sections of the walls sport a painted frieze with royal and ecclesiastical coats of arms, emblems of the various city guilds, and other heraldic motifs. Notice, to the right and left as you enter the chancel, the raised Mannerist tombstones of the celebrated Montelupi (11) and Cellari (12) families, depicted as a group of bronze effigies. These, like the Renaissance bronze tablet to Peter Salomon (d. 1506) at the east end of the chancel (13), originate from Vischer's Nürnberg workshop and are among the best sculptural monuments in the church. Running down the sides of the chancel are late Mannerist stalls (1632) with reliefs by Fabian Möller, a magnificent example of local woodcarving from the first half of the 17C.

Dominating the east wall of the chancel is Veit Stoss's ****High Altar** (14), a massive limewood polyptych (13m by 11m) with folding wings.

Completed in 1370–1400, and attributed to the mysterious Michael, '*vitraetor de Cracovia*' (glass-maker of Kraków), the windows behind the altar are stylistically linked to the French Gothic school of stained glass. Each window consists of three columns, containing on average 40 scenes from the Old and New Testaments.

The door in the north wall of the chancel leads to the **sacristy** (15), its ceiling decorated with 18C murals depicting the triumph of the Christian faith. Behind it is the **Treasury** (16) (c 1600), with a rich collection of liturgical vessels (14C–18C), including late Gothic chalices and embroidered chasubles.

Leaving St Mary's from the south side of the chancel you emerge onto the tiny **St Mary's Square** (pl. Mariacki), formerly the parish graveyard, with the Church of St Barbara at its southern end. The 'pigeon fountain' in the middle of the square is surmounted with a bronze figure of a schoolboy—a modern copy of one of the figures from Veit Stoss's altar.

The **Church of St Barbara** began its existence as a cemetery chapel in 1338. It was later remodelled by the Jesuits, who built their college (today facing the Small Market Square) adjacent to its chancel. Of the original Gothic elements, only two were left intact: the west gable and the small Chapel of Gethsemane to the left of the main entrance (facing St Mary's Square). The chapel, containing stone figures of Jesus and three apostles (1488–1516) from Veit Stoss's workshop, is one of the best of its kind in the city. The interior of St Barbara's underwent significant alterations during the Baroque period. By far the finest work is a late Gothic *Pietà* (c 1400) by an anonymous medieval sculptor known only as the 'Master of Beautiful Madonnas', which rests in a niche in the north aisle.

The modern appearance of **Hippolitus House** at no. 3 (corner of ul. Szpitalna) belies the 16C origins of the building. In the vestibule are Gothic, Renaissance, and Baroque portals. Some of the rooms have beam-framed ceilings, with rich stuccowork and murals by Baldassare Fontana. Go through into the narrow courtyard to see the restored 17C wooden galleries resting on a

Tuscan column. The building is a branch of the **Historical Museum** (open Wed, Fri–Sun 09.00–15.30, Thur 11.00–18.00), currently hosting temporary exhibitions, though a permanent display of 19C interiors is planned.

Houses on the Market Square

Between St Mary's Square and ul. Grodzka (east side)

The huge, three-storeyed **Grey House** at no. 6 (corner of ul. Sienna) dates from the 14C. It later became the town residence of the powerful Zborowski family, after whom it is sometimes still called. Murals by Józef Mehoffer adorn the Gothic vaults in the ground floor delicatessen.

The **Italian House** at no. 7 was, from the 16C, the residence of the wealthy Italian family of Montelupi. The first Polish postal service was established here in 1558, when a stagecoach set off bound for Venice. The event is commemorated by the plaque beside the Mannerist portal. The mock stagecoach by the house (summer only) is actually a post office selling stamps and postcards.

The 15C **Lizard House**, further on at no. 8, is named after a late Gothic bas-relief of two entwined lizards above the entrance (original in the National Museum). The ground floor is occupied by the *Pod Jaszczurami* student club, which has a raucous Friday night disco and frequent jazz and rock concerts (the passageway is a convenient short-cut through to the Small Market Square).

Between ul. Grodzka and ul. Wiślna (south side)

The **Morsztynowski House** at no. 16 and part of the adjoining Hetman House were combined to form one building after restoration work in 1975–79 and today house the *Wierzynek Restaurant*. The restaurant's culinary traditions stretch back to 1364, when Kraków was chosen as the venue for a Congress of Monarchs, attended by Emperor Charles IV, Louis, King of Hungary, and other illustrious figures. Once the official ceremonies had finished, the guests were treated to a lavish banquet hosted by Mikołaj Wierzynek, a wealthy patrician and royal advisor, who served the revellers lark pie, roast peacock, bear paws baked in honey, and other specialities of the day. After the Second World War, a restaurant was opened in Wierzynek's house, soon acquiring the reputation of Poland's finest eating establishment. It was here that communist officials would engage in idle banter with visiting foreign dignitaries, seeking to impress them with the great achievements of the People's Republic: vodka and pickled dill cucumbers. But the *Wierzynek* has failed to keep up with the times and the cooking and service have long since been surpassed by other restaurants in the city. The management is trying to remedy the crisis, but so far little has been achieved. That said, the restaurant still merits a visit, if only to see the plush first floor rooms with beamed ceilings and the huge 19C canvas depicting the historic feast of 1364.

The 14C **Hetman House** at no. 17 was formerly the residence of the king's field commanders (hetmans), hence the stone heraldic emblems above the entrance and high up on the façade. One of the ground floor rooms, presently occupied by the *Hetmańska* bookshop, has well-preserved Gothic ribbed vaulting (c 1380), recalling the eastern areas of the Cathedral, with carved stone bosses, two of which depict Kazimierz the Great and his sister, Queen Jadwiga of Hungary. Another bookshop upstairs (entrance from the passage) has a miniature Gothic stone arch and, embedded in the wall, a stove decked out in Baroque tiles that were found during restoration work in the 1980s. The cellars of Hetman House are occupied by the *Da Pietro* Italian restaurant (see p. 35).

Over the centuries, the 16C **Zbaraski Palace** at no. 20 (corner of ul. Bracka) was successively owned by many of Poland's great noble families. The Flemish architect van Pecne remodelled the three wings in the early 17C, adding a tiny, late Renaissance arcaded courtyard with loggias. The building acquired its present Neo-classical appearance after major renovation and alteration work in 1777–83. Nationalised after the Second World War, the palace was repossessed in the 1990s by its former owner, Count Potocki of Tulczyn. The Goethe Institute, which frequently organises German-language films, plays, and other cultural events around the city, is based here.

Stone boss depicting Kazimierz the Great, Hetman House

Between ul. Św. Anny and ul. Szczepańska (west side)

The Potocki Palace at no. 27, better known as the **'Rams' Palace** (*Pałac Pod Baranami*), was created in the 16C when Justus Decius, secretary to King Zygmunt the Old, purchased two Gothic buildings at this spot and transformed them into his town residence. After numerous alterations—a new façade was added in the 18C—the palace was given its present architectural form in 1874. The ground floor rooms off the inner courtyard have 15C Gothic ribbed vaulting, while upstairs the interiors are mainly Neo-classical. The name 'Rams' Palace' probably derives from the fact that there was originally an inn here, with rams for sale in its courtyard. Three stone ram heads can be seen on the façade just below the balcony. The Potockis owned the palace from 1822 until expulsion by the Nazi authorities, recovering it again in 1990.

After 1945 the Rams' Palace began a new life as a Community Centre, comprising reading rooms, music studios, a library and cinema. In 1956, in the cellars off the courtyard, a group of actors, artists and musicians established what came to be known as the **Piwnica Pod Baranami Cabaret**. The *spiritus movens* of this new initiative was Piotr Skrzynecki, under whose shrewd and wonderfully eccentric stewardship the cabaret acquired a legendary status. The shows, which offered a seductive mix of music, poetry, politics and wit, enjoyed huge popularity, establishing the names of some of Poland's top performers and musicians, Zygmunt Konieczny, Ewa Demarczyk, Zbigniew Preisner and Grzegorz Turnau among them. The cabaret officially closed in 1996 following Skrzynecki's death, but it has now been revived (see *Cabaret* for details). Unfortunately, though, the current line-up fails to meet the standards of excellence demanded by Skrzynecki, and the satirical humour—wickedly funny during the cabaret's 1970s heyday—seems comparatively tame in these post-communist times. On

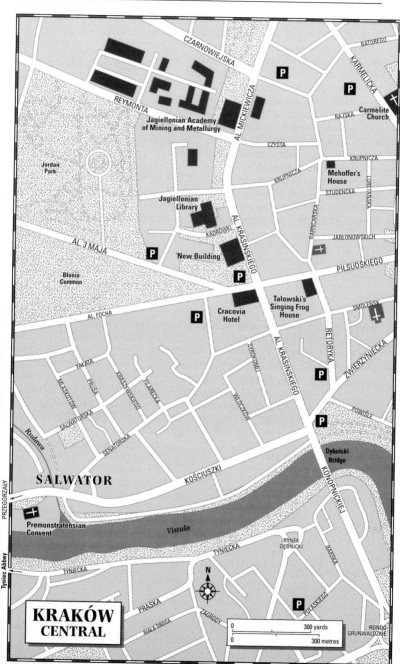

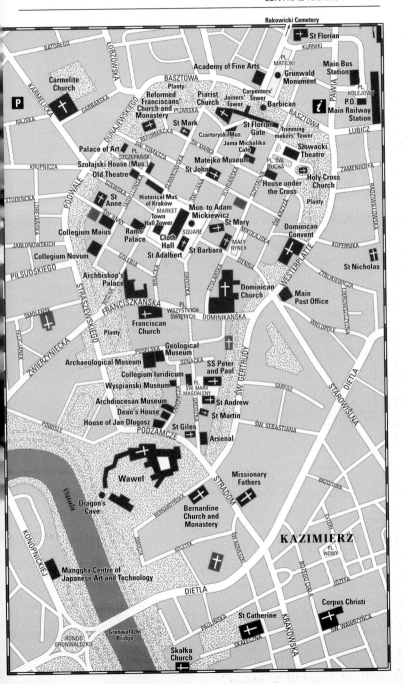

the positive side, the reliance on visual gags and music makes the show readily accessible to foreigners. You can visit the rooms where the cabaret is held (turn right at the bottom of the stairs). The wall decoration, designed by the performers and associates of the cabaret, still captures the special mood of the place.

The **Spiski Palace** at no. 34 was bought in 1592–98 by the wealthy magnate Stanisław Lubomirski (see p. 174), who turned it into a palatial residence. Later architectural accretions somewhat ruined the original Baroque façade. The first floor of the building is now occupied by the exclusive *Tetmajerowska* restaurant, one of the best and most expensive in the city. Its Tetmajer Room, which the artist decorated in 1891, has a frieze depicting the grotto of the infamous black magician, Twardowski, and three banquets: the patricians', nobles', and court.

The legend of Twardowski

Twardowski, a figure familiar to every Polish child, is largely the product of 19C Romantic fable, but his prototype may well have been a real alchemist-cum-astrologer in the service of King Zygmunt August. Twardowski reputedly signed a pact with the Devil, in return for which he was able to perform such amazing feats as balance an enormous boulder on its tip, create a lake during a single night, or fashion a whip out of sand. Under the terms of the pact, the Devil could only take Twardowski's soul from Rome. Unable to entice him to Italy, he built a tavern in the village of Sucha Beskidska near Kraków, which he called 'Rome', and thus trapped the unsuspecting magician. The Holy Virgin took pity on Twardowski and saved him from the torments of Hell—he lives on the moon, and is usually portrayed astride the crescent.

The **Krzysztofory Palace** at no. 35 is so-called after a figure of St Christopher (1380) which adorned the façade until the 18C (presently in the Historical Museum—see below). In 1848, it became the headquarters of the revolutionary National Government of Kraków, pledged to the expulsion of the Austrian occupiers. Inside you can visit a branch of the **Historical Museum of Kraków** (open Thur 11.00–18.00, Wed and Fri–Sun 09.00–15.30), with a display of medieval documents and seals, weaponry, chests, furniture, a copy of the 1257 municipal charter, mayoral rings and sceptres, and the renowned *Srebrny Kur* (silver cockerel)—a symbol of the medieval rifle guilds, endowed by King Zygmunt August in 1565. The two best rooms, with stuccoes by Baldassare Fontana, are on the first floor overlooking the *Rynek*. Upstairs on the second floor is an exhibition of clocks.

The vestibule entered from ul. Szczepańska 2 gives access to a courtyard with a columned loggia. Just before it on the right is a door leading down to the *Krzysztofory* art gallery, which shot to fame in the 1930s when it became the headquarters of the 'Kraków Group' (see below). Kantor's avant-garde Cricot 2 Theatre (see p. 115) put on a number of performances here in the 1960s and 70s. The gallery puts on temporary exhibitions and some of the art is displayed in the adjoining café. On Friday nights it doubles as a techno disco.

The Kraków Group (Grupa Krakowska)

Founded by Maria Jarema, Jonasz Stern and other students of the Academy of Fine Arts, the Kraków Group emerged in the 1930s as informal circle of people interested in abstract art and left-wing politics. After a lull enforced by the Second World War, it re-emerged in 1957, to be joined by such figures as Tadeusz Brzozowski and Tadeusz Kantor. The Group was novel in a number of ways. Most importantly, it was the first, independent (i.e. not state-sponsored) artistic initiative of the post-war era, which until 1956 had been dominated by hermetic and suffocating dogma of Socialist Realism. In contrast to the official art establishment, the Kraków Group was receptive to world developments in art, pioneering the first 'happenings', installations and video shows in Poland.

Though many of the founders are now dead, the Kraków Group continues to exist. Its long-time director, Józef Chrobak, puts on retrospective exhibitions and displays the work of younger members at the Krzysztofory, the Group's official headquarters. The output of the Kraków Group is also shown in two commercial galleries: the Starmach (Tadeusz Brzozowski, Tadeusz Kantor, Jonasz Stern, Maria Jarema, Jerzy Nowosielski; see p. 53) and the Zderzak (Jadwiga Maziarska, Jerzy Joniak, Adam Tarabuła; see p. 54).

Between ul. Sławkowska and ul. Floriańska (north side)

Opposite the Wodzicki Palace stands the 14C **Pear House** (ul. Szczepańska 1). Two first floor rooms house the Journalists' Club bar and restaurant; a third, usually closed, has fine stucco decoration by Baldassare Fontana (c 1700) concealing Gothic rib vaults and the remnants of Renaissance murals. Its walls are decked out in 17C Dutch tiles.

The **Eagle House** at no. 45 was where one of the first city apothecaries was established in 1625. High up on the Gothic red brick façade is an ornamental stone eagle. Renaissance coffered ceilings have been preserved on the first floor and part of the ground floor.

Small Market Square (Mały Rynek)

The covered passageway next to St Barbara's church will bring you onto the Small Market Square. Some of the houses around it date back as early as the 14C. Those on the east side used to be fronted with *przedproża*, or raised platforms covering partly sunken cellars, but today only a section of stone terrace remains. The west side is dominated by the back of St Barbara's church and the adjacent **Jesuit College** (no. 8), which once rivalled the Jagiellonian University as the city's most prestigious seat of learning. In the late 18C, the first clinical hospital in Poland was established here. From the inner courtyard there is a back entrance to St Barbara's.

2 • North of the Market Square ~ ul. Floriańska

This walk takes you north of the Market Square along ul. Floriańska, one of the Old Town's showpiece streets. Over the centuries it was bought up by Kraków's wealthiest burgher families, who transformed the original Gothic houses—from which a number of fine portals and façades have survived—into impressive town residences, today occupied by jeweller's shops, galleries and boutiques. Despite the crowds of shoppers, ul. Floriańska manages to preserve a unique and captivating charm. As you walk up it, look back at the lofty towers of St Mary's for a classic picture-postcard image of the city. The north end of the street is closed by the St Florian Gate, or *Porta Gloriae* (see below), which marks the beginning of the 'Royal Way', a route leading south through the city to Wawel hill, traditionally taken by Polish monarchs on coronation day. At royal funerals, the cortège would assemble in the district of Kleparz to the north of the gate and proceed along the same route to bury the deceased in the Cathedral. It was also through the St Florian Gate that invading armies, such as the Swedes in 1655, made their victorious entry into the Royal City.

The **Ethiopian House** at no. 1—alarmingly translated by some local guidebooks as 'The House Under the Negroes'—once belonged to an apothecary known as *Sub Aethiopibus* and is so-called on account of the plaster relief on the façade of two Ethiopians holding a basket of fruit.

The upper floors of the adjacent **Ciechanowski House** (no. 3) contain rich interior decoration from the second half of the 18C, including murals by Michał Stachowicz, stucco work and a splendid marble fireplace. The rooms are presently occu-

View of St Mary's from ul. Floriańska

pied by the Polish Chamber of Foreign Trade. Down in the Gothic cellars you could visit the excellent *Zderzak* gallery (open Tues–Sat 12.00–17.00), established in the early 1980s as the first 'underground' (independent) gallery in communist Poland, where artists out of favour with the state could exhibit their work. It is now commercially run and displays the work of young artists using a variety of media. Also in the basement is one of Kraków's best jazz clubs—*U Muniaka*—where you can hear trad jazz concerts on Fridays and Saturdays at 21.30.

Crossing ul. Św. Tomasza, notice the 16C building at no. 13, one of the best on the street. It is known as the **Kmita Palace** after a former owner, the magnate and Palatine of Kraków, Piotr Kmita. The façade has Renaissance window frames and is topped by a Neo-classical attic with scenes in relief. Inside are two antique shops belonging to the *DESA* chain (open Mon–Fri 11.00–18.00, Sat 11.00–14.00), the upstairs one contained in an impressive room with Renaissance murals, wooden beamed ceilings, and an original column of 1508.

The **Rose Hotel** (*Hotel Pod Różą*) at no. 14 was originally known as the *Hôtel de Russie* in begrudging honour of Czar Alexander I, who stopped here in 1805. It received its present name when the restaurant of the *White Rose Hotel* was moved here from ul. Stradom (see p. 149). The event gave rise to confusion, notably an apocryphal story that Balzac had stayed here in 1850—as the plaque on the wall suggests—when in fact he had stayed at the hotel on ul. Stradom. The building dates from the 16C, though only a fine Renaissance portal (c 1550) has survived the numerous later alterations. The Latin inscription reads: 'May this house stand until the ant drinks the waters of the oceans and the tortoise travels the earth'. For a meal in elegant surroundings, try the *Pod Różą* restaurant inside the hotel, or the equally good *Amarone* at the back. The latter's entrance is on ul. Św. Tomasza and faces the *Loch Camelot* café, a great place to browse foreign newspapers (available to guests) over a morning coffee.

With over 150,000 exhibits, the **Museum of Pharmacy** at no. 25 is the largest of its kind in Europe (open Tues 15.00–19.00, Wed–Fri 11.00–14.00; entry for group tours, by prior arrangement; ☎ 421 9279). The display traces the history of Polish pharmacy from medieval times until the present day. The highlight is a reconstruction of an old dispensary in the basement.

No. 41 is the house where Jan Matejko (1838–93; see p. 92), the greatest exponent of Polish historical painting, lived and worked. Twenty years before his death, Matejko himself remodelled the façade of this 16C house in neo-Baroque style and built a new studio on the third floor. Inside is a small **Matejko Museum** (open Tues–Thur, Sat–Sun 10.00–15.30, Fri 10.00–18.00; for group tours, ☎ 422 5926) with original 19C interiors and memorabilia, including cartoons of the murals he executed for St Mary's, and religious art from Matejko's personal collection.

Two doors down (no. 45) is the renowned **Jama Michalika** café. In the early years of the 20C, it was a mecca for the Cracovian *bohème*, especially members of the modernist 'Young Poland' movement (see p. 83). Artists, poets and literati would meet here to enjoy provincialism being ridiculed by the satirical *Green Balloon* literary cabaret (1905–12). The best sketches were penned by Tadeusz Boy-Żeleński, a writer also known for his excellent translations of French literature into Polish (his version of Proust's *A la recherche du temps perdu* remains unsurpassed to this day). In a separate show, Karol Frycz's puppets would lampoon ivory-towered professors, Austrian bureaucrats and petit-bourgeois mores in a sort of fin-de-siècle *Spitting Image*. Frycz, a talented set designer, also did the lavish Art Nouveau interior (1910), much of which has been preserved. Nowadays, Jama Michalika tends to attract an elderly, tea-drinking Sunday clientele, though efforts have been made to reinvigorate the traditions of the puppet theatre, with a popular show being staged on Saturday nights (see *Cabaret*).

The ***St Florian Gate** and the Furriers' Tower above it were

St Florian Gate

constructed in 1298–1307 as part of the city's fortifications. In the 15C a brick upper storey with machicolations and a steep roof were added, the Gothic crowning being replaced with a Baroque one in 1656. At night, or in times of danger, the gate-keeper would lower the heavy portcullis, remnants of which are visible at the corners of the gate. Notice the 18C bas-relief of St Florian above the south entrance, and on the opposite (north) side a stone coat of arms bearing the Piast eagle, designed by Jan Matejko. The classical altar, with a painting of the Virgin, was placed inside the gate in 1835.

To the west and east of the gate are fragments of the city's medieval fortifications, consisting of a section of wall with three towers linked by a guards' gallery: the **Carpenters' Tower**, integrated into the corpus of the two-storey former Arsenal (which now houses part of the Czartoryski Museum; see p. 138); the **Joiners' Tower**; and the semi-circular **Trimming-makers' Tower**, decked out in zigzags of glazed brick. By the gate is a street gallery where works by aspiring artists and students are put on display in spring to late autumn.

Town fortifications

Once Kraków had received its municipal charter in 1257, work commenced on fortifying the medieval city. A ring of stone walls was begun in the late 13C, initially stopping short of the castle in order to emphasise the independence of the town from its monarch. However, after an unsuccessful revolt led by the predominantly German burgher community in 1311, this privilege was revoked and the fortifications were extended to the settlement of Okół and Wawel hill. (As punishment for the rebels, the prince ordered the execution of all those who could not correctly pronounce the Polish words for 'lentils', 'wheel', 'grind' and 'mill'!). Today, the only extant 13C remnants are found by ul. Św. Sebastiana (uncovered in 1989), in the Franciscan and Dominican monasteries, and here, in the St Florian Gate and parts of its adjoining walls.

With the rise of new military technology in the 15C, the fortifications were strengthened and improved. A new, outer ring consisting of a low wall preceded by a moat was begun in 1404. Foregates, like the Barbican (see below), were erected beyond the moat to provide further protection. Responsibility for repelling enemy attack lay solely with the burghers, with each guild having its own tower and section of wall to defend. By the 18C the defensive system had risen to formidable proportions: 3.4km of walls, 10m high, in places 2.5m thick, interspersed with eight gates and 46 towers. In 1806 the Austrian authorities decided to tear down the fortifications. However, following protests headed by professors at the Jagiellonian University, a small section of wall and the St Florian Gate were preserved as a lasting showpiece.

Passing through the St Florian Gate you emerge onto the *Planty*, a ring of parks created in the 1810s to replace the dismantled city walls and moat. Facing you is the late Gothic ****Barbican** (open Mon–Fri 09.00–12.45, 13.15–18.00, Sat–Sun 09.00–17.00),

The Barbican

Built in 1498–99, when Kraków was subject to Ottoman threat, this turreted and machicolated circle of reddish brick arose as a remarkable piece of military technology. Its purpose was to defend the St Florian Gate, to which it was connected by a covered passageway allowing supplies and ammunition to be swiftly replenished at all times. With an upper gallery, machicolation, and 130 loopholes on four levels, it was virtually impregnable to enemy attack until siege techniques changed. Today the Barbican endures as a unique example of late medieval defensive architecture. In the summer months, plays and concerts are occasionally staged inside.

Visible beyond the Barbican on **pl. Matejki** (Matejko Square) is the rather grim-looking **Grunwald Monument**. It commemorates the victory of the Polish and Lithuanian armies against the Teutonic Knights in what was one of the greatest and bloodiest battles of the Middle Ages (1410; an event described by the writer Henryk Sienkiewicz in his novel *The Teutonic Knights*). Funded by the pianist and inter-war statesman Ignacy Paderewski, the monument was erected in 1910 to mark the quincentenary of the battle. During the Second World War the Nazis destroyed it for its 'anti-German' connotations. The monument was eventually reconstructed in 1975 and combined with the Tomb of the Unknown Soldier. Nowadays, it serves as an assembly point for skinheads and right-wing groups before going on demonstrations. Their standard ritual on National Independence Day (11 November) and Constitution Day (3 May) is to throw eggs at public officials (i.e. 'national traitors') and generally to disrupt the laying of wreaths of flowers by the tomb.

Facing the monument, at the corner of pl. Matejki and ul. Basztowa, is the neo-Renaissance **Academy of Fine Arts** (1880), which experienced its heyday in the late 19C and early 20C (see p. 83). Among its professors were many of Poland's top artists—Matejko (see p. 92), Wyspiański (see p. 116), Mehoffer, Wyczółkowski, Fałat. Later generations of graduates included such figures as Tadeusz Kantor (see p. 115) and Andrzej Wajda (see p. 150).

The far end of pl. Matejki is dominated by the Baroque twin-towers of **St Florian's Church**, once owned by the University and where many of its former professors are buried. The medieval origins of St Florian's are no longer discernible, but preserved is a fine early 16C altarpiece attributed to Hans Suess von Kulmbach. The altarpiece, funded by the Boner family, originally stood in the family's chapel in St Mary's church. St Florian's also boasts a magnificent treasury (inaccessible) containing reliquaries, chalices, monstrances and other items amassed over the centuries. The surrounding district of Kleparz was for a period also known as Florencja, after the church's patron.

3 • South of the Market Square ~ ul. Grodzka

The Royal Way (see Walk 2) continues along **ul. Grodzka**, one of Kraków's oldest streets, which exits from the southeast corner of the Market Square. On this walk you visit four of Kraków's finest churches: the Dominican and Franciscan, either side of pl. Wszystkich Świętych, St Andrew's and SS Peter and Paul, further down ul. Grodzka. All are well worth a visit. Like ul. Floriańska, ul. Grodzka, with its cobbled paving and pastel-coloured buildings, is one of the city's showpiece streets. The short first stretch, between the Market Square and pl. Dominikański, was broadened after the great fire of 1850 to give it a more august appearance. There are no signature buildings here, though you could drop in to the *Krew i Róża* restaurant inside the *Rezydent* Hotel (no. 9), which serves good traditional food in a stylish cellar (see *Restaurants*).

The Dominican Church
Turn left at the first intersection for the *Dominican Church (Basilica of the Holy Trinity). It stands on **pl. Dominikański**, a small square that was once the heart of the medieval city.

The Dominicans were brought to Kraków from Bologna in 1222 by Bishop Iwo Odrowąż, who endowed them with the parish church of the Holy Trinity on this spot. Soon, a new Gothic church went up on the south side of the existing cloister, preserving only the refectory from its Romanesque predecessor. Consecrated in 1249, it had a long, simple hall design, with a square ended chancel. Alterations and enlargements followed in the late 14C and 15C, when the church attained its present form of an aisled basilica.

Viewed from outside, the church is immediately striking for its east and west gables, adorned with spikes and panels. The slender Gothic body is flanked by sumptuous chapels from later periods, clearly visible on both sides. Around the external chancel wall runs a moulded brick frieze marking the height of the original 13C church.

Interior You enter through the neo-Gothic vestibule, beyond which is a splendid medieval doorway abounding in carved stone leaves. The interior, cold and empty, had to be thoroughly rebuilt after 1850, which resulted in much arid detail, particularly in the neo-Gothic altars.

By far the greatest attraction are the **chapels**, beginning with the **Zbaraski**

Chapel at the west end of the north aisle. Designed by Constantino Tencalla in 1629–33, it conforms to the model established by the Zygmunt Chapel in Wawel Cathedral (see p. 125): that of a domed sepulchral chapel on a central plan, here containing the tombs of the last Zbaraskis, the brothers Jerzy and Krzysztof. The chapel of St Hyacinth, the oldest, and perhaps best chapel, is reached via the white marble staircase further along the north aisle. Originally built in 1581, it contains stuccoes (c 1700) by Baldassare Fontana, particularly impressive around the inside of the dome, and the Baroque sarcophagus of St Hyacinth, the first abbot of the monastery. The painted decoration is by the Venetian Tomaso Dolabella (c 1570–1650).

In the **chancel**, at the east end of the north wall, you should not miss Veit Stoss's exquisite bronze tablet (c 1500) to **Filippo Buonaccorsi** ('Callimachus'; d. 1496), a great Humanist scholar and the Florentine mentor to King Kazimierz the Jagiellon's (d. 1492) children.

From the south aisle you can enter the **Our Lady of the Rosary Chapel** (1685–88), which backs on to ul. Poselska. Almost a church in itself, it was built as a votive for King Jan Sobieski's (1674–96) victory at Vienna. The highlight is a miraculous image of the *Virgin*, which was copied from the Basilica of Santa Maria Maggiore in Rome.

Close by is the **Myszkowski Chapel**, a somewhat pompous Renaissance mausoleum (1603–16) attributed to the Santi Gucci (see p. 91) workshop. Again modelled on the Zygmunt Chapel, it has an eight-sided coffered dome, around the inside of which is a gallery of busts representing members of the Myszkowski family. The external walls, of rusticated sandstone, bear a cartouche with the founding tablet. Another Renaissance mausoleum—the Lubomirski Chapel—has painted decoration from the same period and stands at the west end of the south aisle.

The Lubomirski Chapel

Generations of Lubomirskis are commemorated here. When a member of the clan died in the 1950s, there were fears that the communist authorities would not allow his memorial tablet to be placed in the chapel (on account of the family's aristocratic origins). However, in a masterly pre-emptive strike, the Dominicans sent a letter of protest to the city council, arguing *against* Lubomirski's proposed inclusion in the family tomb. They knew full well that the hostile bureaucrats would do the exactly the opposite of what the Church wanted. The clever plan worked: the protest was dismissed and Lubomirski's tablet was allowed to appear in the chapel alongside those of his ancestors.

Adjoining the church to the north are impressive Gothic **cloisters** (enter from the north aisle or from ul. Stolarska 12) with a refectory (after 1225), chapter house (c 1250), remnants of medieval murals, and many paintings. Embedded into the walls are over 150 tombs and memorial tablets.

Pl. Wszystkich Świętych (All Saints Square), to the west of the Dominican church, is dominated by the 16C Wielkopolski Palace, currently the offices of the city authorities. In front of it stands Ksawery Dunikowski's **statue of Józef Dietl** (1938), a former Mayor of Kraków (1866–74).

The Franciscan Church

The chancel of the *Franciscan Church backs onto the square to the right of the Wielkopolski Palace. You may sometimes enter through the monastery cloisters. If not, walk around to the west entrance.

The Friars of St Francis arrived in Kraków from Prague in 1237. The construction of their church was the initiative of Bolesław the Chaste (1243–79), who, along with his sister, the Blessed Salomea, was laid to rest in one of the chapels. The cruciform plan of the first Gothic brick church was somewhat altered in 1401–36, when the nave and chancel were lengthened, and the huge Corpus Christi Chapel, in the form of an aisle, added. Major changes carried out in 1850–1912 gave the interior its present neo-Gothic appearance. The monastery (south), with its two cloister gardens, was begun in the 14C, but like the church suffered extensive damage during the fire of 1850 and had to be reconstructed (1900–12).

The best view of the early Gothic church is from ul. Bracka, where the large ogival windows and triangular gable with an arcaded moulded-brick frieze are revealed. The main reason for visiting the interior is to see the **murals and stained glass** executed by Stanisław Wyspiański (see p. 116) at the turn of the last century. The finest of the murals—a composition of floral and heraldic motifs, geometric patterns and religious scenes—are found in the chancel and transepts. Equally impressive is the stained glass rising up above the musicians' choir (west), a *tour de force* of modern religious art. The monumental scene, with its flowing shapes and striking colours, depicts *God the Father in the Act of Creation*, the treatment of the figure being inspired by Michelangelo's *Moses*. There is more stained glass in the chancel, with a scene of St Francis, the church's patron, and the Blessed Salomea, whose tomb lies in a chapel adjoining the north transept.

Like the chancel, the cloisters, entered from the south transept, have mostly kept their 15C Gothic vaults. Along the walls are fine **murals** from the same period—notably *Christ in the Vine Press, St Francis receiving the Stigmata* and *Annunciation*—now in desperate need of restoration. Better still is the Gallery of Cracovian Bishops, a series of some 30 portraits, including one of Bishop Piotr Tomicki painted by the best Polish artist of the early 16C, Stanisław Samostrzelnik, a Cistercian monk from the monastery at Mogiła (see p. 154).

Leave by the west exit. Facing the green at the back is the vast 16C **Archbishop's Palace** (ul. Franciszkańska 3), a three-winged building with an irregular courtyard, whose present Baroque design dates mainly from 1642–47. Like so many other buildings, the palace suffered badly during the great fire of 1850, when most of its treasures were lost. The palace is famous for being the former residence (1964–78) of **Cardinal Karol Wojtyła**, later Pope John Paul II, whose monument stands in the courtyard.

John Paul II

John Paul II (Karol Wojtyła), regarded by many Poles as the world's leading moral authority and one of the greatest figures of the 20C, was born in 1920 in the town of Wadowice, 40km west of Kraków. A keen actor and poet in his youth, Wojtyła moved to Kraków to study theology and literature at the Jagiellionian University, and it was through these early experiences that he forged a strong emotional attachment to the city. During the Second World War he worked as a labourer for the Solvay soda plant, hewing limestone at the quarry in Zakrzówek. Wojtyła's ecumenical career began in 1949, when he was appointed vicar of St Florian's church (see p. 108), thereafter rising up through the ranks of the Cracovian clergy. He won major recognition for his prominent role in the work of the Second Vatican Council. After being appointed Metropolitan-Archbishop of Kraków in 1967, he took up residence here at the Archbishop's Palace.

The election of Cardinal Karol Wojtyła to the papacy in 1978 had far more than just a religious significance. His first visit to Poland in 1979 caused a major breakthrough in the collective consciousness of Poles, precipitating the rise of the Solidarity movement. Millions attended the Pope's open-air masses on the Błonia common (see p. 156) and in other Polish cities. Above all, these vast gatherings demonstrated that the power of the state was not unlimited, and that its authority could sometimes be defied. Communist leaderships all over Europe were rightly fearful of the national ferment in Poland. According to some historians, the attempted assassination of the Pope in 1981 by a Turkish gunman was masterminded and funded by the Soviet KGB.

Few would argue that the pontificate of John Paul II has been one of the most active of recent decades: it has seen the publication of numerous encyclicals on theological and social issues; there has been a punishing schedule of worldwide papal visits, including unprecedented recent trips to Cuba and Israel. Efforts have been made to reconcile the differences between the various Christian denominations as well as to forge closer ties with other monotheistic religions, notably Judaism and Islam. However, as a 21C Pope, John Paul II remains a controversial figure. His uncompromising stand on abortion, contraception, divorce, and the ordination of women priests is felt by many Catholics to be at odds with modern lifestyles. And dissenting movements within the Roman Catholic Church—such as liberation theology—have been silenced in a heavy-handed fashion.

Returning to ul. Grodzka, notice the corner house at **no. 26**, built in 1909 on the site of an older building from which only a figure of the *Virgin* (set below the first floor oriel) has survived. The attic was modelled on that of the Cloth Hall. Further down is the 14C **Lion House** (no. 32), so called on account of its Gothic emblem, a gilded bas-relief of a lion. Many buildings on the Royal Way possess such emblems, which were formerly used as a system of numbering. **No. 38**, for instance, has two from the 17C: an elephant and a rhinoceros. The first intersection is **ul. Poselska**, which in the Middle Ages delineated the limit of Kraków proper. Several restaurants are clustered around the stretch which goes off to the left: *Corleone*, *Orient Express*, *Taco Mexicano* and *Paese* (see *Restaurants*).

Heading right along ul. Poselska you reach a complex of buildings dominated by a former 19C prison. Today, the buildings house the **Geological Museum** (entrance from ul. Senacka, open Tues 10.00–17.30, Wed–Fri 10.00–15.00, Sat–Sun 10.00–14.00), and the more interesting **Archaeological Museum** (open Mon–Wed 09.00–14.00, Thur 14.00–17.00, Sun 11.00–14.00), entered from the attractive museum garden further west along ul. Poselska. The display is divided into four sections: Mediterranean culture in antiquity; the ancient and medieval history of Małopolska; Nowa Huta in prehistoric times; and the history of the former prison. The prize exhibit is a stone statue of the pagan Slav deity, Światowid, believed to date from the 10C. Classical concerts are occasionally held in the museum garden, which offers fine views of Wawel Castle.

Either return to ul. Grodzka and continue the Royal Way or head south along the parallel ul. Kanonicza (described in the next walk). Both streets bring you to pl. Św. Marii Magdaleny This delightful square, paved and renovated in the 1990s, is dominated by the grand façade of the SS Peter and Paul church and the more modest but no less interesting Romanesque church of St Andrew, which stands adjacent to it.

Church of SS Peter and Paul

The imposing **Church of SS Peter and Paul is the earliest and best example of Baroque architecture in the city.

The Jesuits arrived in Kraków in 1582 and set up their headquarters at ul. Grodzka 52 (now University departments). Work began on their church in 1596, and was completed by Giovanni Trevano in 1619. The overall design was modelled on the first Jesuit Baroque church in Rome—the Gesù: a Latin cross plan with two series of chapels in place of the aisles, but no galleries, and with a large dome above the crossing. Work on the interior continued until 1633, with Giovanni Battista Falconi executing the exquisite stuccoes in the apse, side chapels and dome.

Exterior Most interesting is the two-storey façade, consisting of three pedimented bays on top of five, and achieving a remarkable slenderness of proportion. Between the sculptures of saints are the coats of arms of Poland and of the Vasa line, as well as the Jesuit emblem. Due to the narrowness of ul. Grodzka in the 17C, the façade had to be set back from the street, thus forming a small court in front of the church. In 1715–22 Kacper Bażanka turned the space into a monumental enclosure preceded by rhomboidal stone plinths—a clever *trompe l'oeil* effect which disguises the fact that the church is not perpendicular to the street. The apostles on top of the plinths were originally designed by the Jesuit sculptor Daniel Heel in 1721–25, but owing to their poor condition, had to be replaced after the Second World War. Bażanka also designed the high altar (1726–35) and two of the funerary monuments inside the church.

Interior The interior is characterised by sharp architectural detail (not a single mural) and an austerity reminiscent of the Vasa style—a version of early Roman Baroque. Spartan chapels linked by a passageway run down the nave. In the chancel, before the high altar, is a **crypt** (open 10.00–17.00) containing the surprisingly modest tomb of the preacher Piotr Skarga (d. 1612), whose writings

Church of SS Peter and Paul

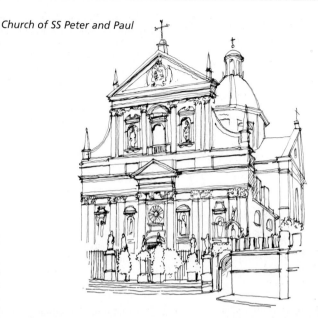

promulgated the idea of unity between the Eastern and Western churches. This theme is expressed in Bażanka's high altar, in the scenes in stucco relief on the apse ceiling, and indeed in the very dedication of the church: 'Peter, the first Pope, and Paul, the Apostle of the East'. On the left of the chancel is the funerary monument to Andrzej Trzebicki (d. 1679), with a bust of the bishop surrounded by cherubs and personifications of Faith and Valour.

Church of St Andrew

The stone towers to the south belong to the *Church of St Andrew, one of the few examples of completely preserved Romanesque architecture in Poland.

Built in 1079–98, St Andrew's was located at the centre of the medieval settlement of Okół. It was redesigned in the early 13C, receiving transepts, vaults and westwork. Initially, the church served a defensive as well as a religious purpose, as evidenced by the loopholes in the lower part of the façade. After transfer to the austere order of Poor Clares in c 1318, the church acquired a brick Gothic oratory (now the sacristy) and later, in the 17C, the towers were topped with copper lanterns. The convent was begun shortly after the arrival of the nuns, c 1325, though today the wing visible from ul. Grodzka bears the legacy of neo-Romanesque remodelling carried out in 1843.

The most interesting aspect of the exterior are the pairs of deep Romanesque windows in the towers and the arcaded frieze around the apse and chancel. The small interior, completely rebuilt in 1701, immediately surprises with its Baroque elegance and gilding. Especially good is the stucco decoration by Baldassare Fontana and the murals illustrating the *Life of the Blessed Salomea*.

St Andrew's church

Notice the Rococo pulpit in the shape of a gilded limewood boat with huge mast, meant to represent the boat of St Peter. The convent contains some unique 14C Nativity figures and a portable Byzantine mosaic of the **Virgin with Child** from the turn of the 12C.

There are two other buildings of interest on the square. **Collegium Iuridicum** (ul. Grodzka 53) was purchased by the University in 1403 and turned into a college of law; hence the name. It was remodelled in Baroque style in 1709, when arcades were added to the charming inner courtyard. Some Gothic elements have remained, though, notably the brick gable adjacent to ul. Kanonicza, as well as parts of the window frames, portals and vaulting. The house opposite Collegium Iuridicum at **no. 2** pl. Św. Marii Magdaleny originally dates from 1520. The portal supported by atlantes was added during remodelling in 1776. After recent renovation the ground floor was bought up by the Pizza Hut chain, which has thankfully managed to keep its neon signs discreet and disturb neither the aesthetic appearance of the building nor the square on which it stands.

4 • South of the Market Square ~ ul. Kanonicza

This walk leads south to Wawel along ul. Kanonicza, one of the most beautiful streets in Kraków, evoking the atmosphere of the medieval city. Mentioned in municipal documents as early as 1401, 'Canonicorum', today's ul. Kanonicza, is named after the Canons of the Cathedral, who from the 14C built their houses here. Most of the buildings date from the 14C–16C. The façades, attics and portals reveal a diversity of styles—Gothic, Renaissance, Baroque, Neo-classical—and conceal quiet courtyards reached by carriage gateways.

No. 3 has early Renaissance stone window frames, sgraffito decoration, and a fine Rococo portal. The Chapter House at no. 5 was founded in the 15C by Jan Długosz, who gave it over for use as a student hostel. Some fragments from this period have survived. The present building, formerly the headquarters of Tadeusz Kantor's Cricot 2 Theatre, is now the **Cricoteka Museum** (open Mon–Fri 10.00–14.00) documenting Kantor's life and work.

Tadeusz Kantor

Tadeusz Kantor (1915–90), painter, set designer, graphic artist, a leading light of the Polish avant-garde, was born in the village of Wielopole and educated at Kraków's Academy of Fine Arts (see p. 83). His first major undertaking was the experimental Independent Theatre he established during the Second World War, which operated underground at extreme risk to all involved (cultural activity was punishable by death in Nazi-occupied Poland). Following the 'thaw' of 1956, Kantor established what would come to be regarded as Poland's best avant-garde theatre—Cricot 2. Its precursor—the Cricot—began in the 1930s as an amateur theatre-cum-cabaret, whose surrealistic presentations became famous for their acid humour and merciless attacks on Cracovian philistinism. In 1960, along with the influential Kraków Group (see p. 103) with which it was closely tied, Cricot 2 moved to the cellars of the Krzysztofory Palace. These were the theatre's best years, when it staged a number of memorable productions including plays by the celebrated writer Stanisław Ignacy Witkiewicz (1885–1939).

Kantor's groundbreaking *Dead Class*, a play inspired by his own childhood and wartime experiences, appeared in 1976 (causing a sensation when it was staged at the Edinburgh Festival). It marked a new stage in his professional career, signalling a move into 'total art', in which theatre, painting and performance merged. As with subsequent plays—*Wielopole, Wielopole, Let the Artists Perish, Today is my Birthday, I Shall Never Return Here*—*Dead Class* was not only written, but also directed and choreographed by Kantor, who was always present on stage during performances. He meticulously designed the sets and costumes; even the props were works of art in their own right, as anyone visiting the Cricoteka museum will see. Kantor derived inspiration from what he referred to as his 'Poor Little Room of the Imagination'. As he wrote in *Credo*, 'The only truth in art to present one's own life, without fear or embarrassment, to discover one's own fate, one's own destiny'. Kantor realised this mission masterfully. His never-ending inward search acquired a universal meaning and he was able to captivate audiences regardless of the cultural context—from Paris and London to Kassel (the Documenta 8 festival) and New York (where in 1979 he won the New York critics' prize), Japan and Mexico. His plays touched on the most fundamental aspects of human existence: childhood, memory, love, the passing of time, nothingness, and death. Through his art, the 'Poor Little Room of the Imagination' became a vast monument of collective memory, a kind of labyrinth in which a lost soul could always find something familiar.

The **Three Crowns House** at no. 7, rebuilt in 1504 and in 1756–78, has a Renaissance façade and some fine late Gothic detailing in the vestibule. The ground floor accommodates the *U Literatów* café, with a pleasant summer garden-cum-courtyard at the back. **No. 9**, originally 14C, was once the home of Hugo Kołłątaj (1750–1812), a noted Enlightenment reformer. Preserved on the first floor are some fine 18C murals depicting seascapes. Following renovation in 1979–83, a branch of the National Museum was opened here, the **Wyspiański Museum** (open Mon–Fri 10.00–15.00), tracing the life and work of Stanisław Wyspiański one of the greatest figures in Polish literature and art.

Stanisław Wyspiański

At the turn of the 19C, Kraków was the cultural and spiritual capital of Poland and the main centre of the 'Young Poland' movement—the Polish version of 'Art Nouveau'—which encompassed all the arts and gave unequivocal support to the struggle for independence. Its leading representative was Stanisław Wyspiański (1869–1907), one of the 'greats' of Polish culture, who spent nearly all his life in Kraków and was deeply attached to the city. He studied at the School of Fine Arts (see p. 83) under, among others, Jan Matejko (see p. 92), and later at the Philosophy Faculty of the Jagiellonian University. This broad education, combined with an outstanding natural talent and versatility, allowed Wyspiański to express himself with equal ease through poetry, drama and painting. Despite his close association with Stanisław Przybyszewski (an advocate of 'art for art's sake') and fascination with West European Symbolism, Wyspiański lived and worked in his native land because he saw his art as a patriotic mission. He was the last Polish artist to create truly great works in response to the 19C notion of art in service of the nation. Like Matejko he took up historical themes, but used symbolic language rather than overt meaning to press the national cause.

Wyspiański considered monumental art—murals and stained-glass—to be his true vocation. His greatest achievement in this field was the decoration of the Franciscan Church (see p. 110), where he raised the art of stained-glass to heights not seen since the Middle Ages. Landscape painting occupied Wyspiański most intensively in 1904–1905, when he produced a series of pastels showing the changing view from his studio in different seasons and at different times of day. He also practised various types of applied art, designing furniture, posters, theatre sets and costumes, as well as books and magazines. Wyspiański exhibited frequently at home and abroad. He held several individual exhibitions during his lifetime and received many awards, but his works provoked controversy in traditionally-minded circles and, therefore, many of his monumental designs were never put into practice.

Wyspiański's contribution was equally important in the field of literature. As a poet and playwright, he carried on the Romantic tradition begun by the three great 'bards' of the mid-19C—Mickiewicz, Słowacki and Krasiński. In his literary works he combined history, symbolism, antiquity, Slavonic myths and folklore. His play, *The Wedding*, is the showpiece of neo-Romantic drama, often considered the most Polish of all Polish plays. It gives an iconoclastic account of the attitudes of the Cracovian intelligentsia at the turn of the century, revealed through a wedding feast in which reality and fantasy merge. In the course of the night the feast becomes a grand symbol of national tragedy and the impotence of Poland's would-be insurgents. The guests indulge in visions of rebellion, of the country's glorious past and radiant future, yet they flounder in a drunken and gibbering present. *The Wedding* is not only a drama of words, but also a powerful exercise in visual art, and to this day remains one of the most popular classics of Polish theatre.

In 1979, conservators discovered a treasure trove of iron hatchets (a pre-monetary form of payment), weighing a staggering four tonnes, buried underneath the house at **no. 13**. Next door, the portal of the **Szreniawa House** (no. 15) displays a variety of different styles. The original Gothic was supplanted in the 16C by a Renaissance frieze bearing plant motifs; in the 18C, above the frieze was placed a Rococo armorial cartouche, itself topped by a crown and then by a hat of the type formerly worn by higher members of the clergy. Go inside to visit the **Gallery of Ukrainian Art** (open Thur–Sun 12.00–16.00), with a collection of 17C–19C icons, and paintings by Jerzy Nowosielski. No. 16, a lavishly restored 14C house, is now the exclusive *Copernicus Hotel* (see *Where to stay*).

The **House of Bishop Erazm Ciołek** (no. 17) dates from the 16C when its eponymous founder integrated two Gothic buildings, one of which was a brick bastion, into his lavish town residence. The Renaissance portal has an armorial cartouche of the Jagiellon line consisting of a stone eagle and crown intertwined with the letter 'S', which refers to King Zygmunt (Sigismund) the Old. To the right of the portal is a Gothic window set askew to the façade in order to catch more daylight.

The 14C house at **no. 18** was remodelled in 1560–63 by Jan Michałowicz of Urzędów (the 'Polish Praxiteles'), who also designed the excellent Renaissance portal and the arcades around the inner courtyard supported on slender Tuscan columns.

The Neo-classical façade of the **Chapter House** at no. 19 disguises the 16C origins of the building. Suffragan Bishop Karol Wojtyła, later Pope John Paul II, lived here in 1951–63, and later in the Dean's House next door. Inside is a small **Archdiocesan Museum** (open Tues–Sat 10.00–15.00). The display, well-labelled in English, comprises altarpieces (15C–17C), liturgical vestments, paintings, including an excellent religious cycle by Hans Suess von Kulmbach (1514), and two items from St Mary's church: a Gothic sculpture of the *Adoration of the Magi*, and a predella illustrating the *Entombment of St John the Evangelist* (1516). Don't miss the room where John Paul II (see p. 111) once lived, complete with typewriter, skis and more of the Pontiff's personal belongings.

The 14C **Dean's House** at no. 21 is one of the best preserved buildings on the street. It was rebuilt in 1582–88 by the celebrated architect Santi Gucci (see p. 91). The façade has a sgraffito decoration and portal modelled on a Roman triumphal arch. Beyond it is a delightful arcaded courtyard containing a Baroque statue of *St Stanisław* (see p. 146). The ground floor arcades are supported on Ionic columns, the first floor ones on piers, above which are the armorial cartouches of various Cracovian Bishops.

No. 25, at the foot of Wawel, is the **House of Jan Długosz** (15C), where the historian lived from 1450 until his death in 1480 and where he wrote his seminal *Historica Polonica*, a 12-volume study of Polish history from ancient times to the late Middle Ages. On the façade facing the castle is a 17C painting on wood of the *Virgin and Child*. Further along the wall, notice the foundation plate marking the site of the Psalterists' House on Wawel hill (1480), which shows Długosz kneeling before the Virgin.

Here the Royal Way ends. Turning left into ul. Podzamcze, you reach the tiny 14C **Church of St Giles** at the intersection with ul. Grodzka. The church is usually only open during mass. There is a service in English on Sundays at 10.30.

5 • Wawel

Wawel hill lies to south of the Old Town. Spread across it is a complex of buildings dominated by the Royal Castle, the former seat of Poland's rulers, which overlooks the scenic 'Vistula bend', where the river turns at almost 90 degrees. When the Polish capital moved to Warsaw in 1595, Wawel remained the venue for royal coronations and funerals. Whole dynasties of rulers—the Piasts, Jagiellons, Vasas and Saxons—are buried in the Cathedral, their magnificent tombs made by the leading artists and architects of the day. During the so-called era of Partitions (1795–1918; see *History*), Wawel endured as a symbol of Polish statehood, a focal point of the struggle for national independence. Today, it is Kraków's most revered architectural monument, a reminder of the city's illustrious past, attracting thousands of tourists each day.

Panorama of Wawel Hill

• **Highlights** There is lots to see on Wawel and the tour can be exhausting. If you are pushed for time or patience, it is best to concentrate on the two most important buildings, the **Castle** and **Cathedral**. In the latter, you should not miss the Renaissance **Zygmunt Chapel** and the tombs of Polish monarchs. You can also climb the **Zygmunt Tower** for a fine view over the city. The highlights of the Castle are the **state apartments** on the second floor and a collection of magnificent 16C Brussels tapestries.

If you need a break at this point, stop in at the *Na Wawelu* (see *Restaurants*) situated inside a building of the former Austrian barracks (**20**), before moving on to the other exhibitions: the **Cathedral Museum**, which has a collection of items from the Cathedral Treasury, and '**Lost Wawel**', an archaeological display tracing the early history of Wawel.

• **Admission** Tickets for the Royal Crypts and the Zygmunt Tower, both entered from the Cathedral, can be bought at the Curates' House (**6**). Tickets to the Castle (including the Royal Chambers, Treasury, Armoury and Oriental

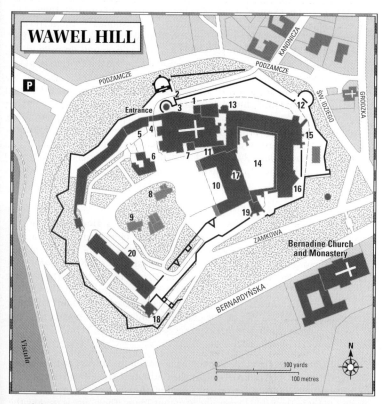

Exhibition) are sold at the office in the passageway of the Renaissance gate-house (**11**).

The **opening times** for the Cathedral (including the Royal Crypts and Zygmunt Tower) and Cathedral Museum are: Mon–Sat 09.00–17.30, Sun 12.15–17.30, summer; Mon–Sat 09.00–15.00, Sun 12.15–15.00, winter.

The **opening times** for the Castle are: Tues, Fri 09.30–16.30, Wed–Thur 09.30–15.30, Sat 09.30–15.00, Sun 10.00–15.00.

You can approach Wawel (pronounced *Vah-vel*) from several directions. From the Old Town, via ul. Kanonicza or the *Planty*, you will arrive at the foot of the hill (228m) along its north side, on the busy ul. Podzamcze. The brick fortifications, more massive further to the left, opposite ul. Grodzka, are reduced on this side to a round bastion and a wall running along the stone-lined path. These dark-red brick additions are the most recent in Wawel's history: in the mid-19C, after removing the last vestiges of medieval defences, the Austrians endeavoured to turn Wawel into a citadel.

Higher up, partly hidden by trees, looms the solid mass of buildings from other, more distant epochs. Most conspicuous are the two towers with copper crown-ings: the thicker and lower one, with spires, four corner turrets, a crown and a weather-cock in the form of a galloping horseman, is the **Zygmunt Tower** (1), named after its founder King Zygmunt Vasa. He commissioned Giovanni Trevano to reconstruct it after a fire in 1595, which destroyed its 14C predecessor. The tower houses the most famous **bell** in Poland—the 'Zygmunt', in memory of King Zygmunt the Old. Captured Italian cannons supplied the enormous quantity of bronze needed for the mammoth bell. It is 2.5m in diameter, weighs almost eleven tonnes and is covered with reliefs depicting SS Stanisław and Zygmunt, the Polish eagle, and the Lithuanian coat of arms ('*Pogoń*'). Pulling the bell up the tower was a considerable feat of engineering; an imaginary representation of the event can be seen in a painting by Jan Matejko. Unless some truly extraordinary occurrence takes place (say, the election of another Polish Pope), the bell's resounding D-sharp can only be heard a few times a year, on major church and state holidays. The **clock tower**, to the right of the Zygmunt, is a 15C structure resting on Romanesque foundations. Its graceful two-tiered Baroque crowning, designed by Kacper Bażanka in 1715, is moderately gilded and has four figures of saints in the corners.

Walk up along the stone-paved path towards the brick **Heraldic Gate** (2), erected in 1921 and decorated with the emblems of Poland, Lithuania and Ruthenia. At night it is barred with a wooden portcullis. Left of the gate, atop a polygonal bastion, stands a stately, equestrian **statue of Kościuszko** (3), designed by Leonard Marconi in 1921, and destroyed by the Nazis. The present one is a gift from the city of Dresden, and is modelled on the original. Turn to the arched **Vasa Gateway** (4). To the right of it is the gabled 14C Rorantist House, formerly used as a dwelling for the Cathedral cantors, which now houses the Cathedral Museum (entrance from the other side; see below).

Lower Castle

Passing through the Vasa Gateway you come out on the Lower Castle grounds. To your left is the Cathedral; to the right, the **Cathedral Museum** (5) clad in luscious vine, and, a little further on, the **Curates' House** (6), where you can purchase a ticket to the Royal Crypts and Zygmunt Tower. The house is used by the Cathedral clergy as living quarters.

Cathedral

The **Cathedral (open Mon–Sat 09.00–17.30, Sun 12.15–17.30, summer; Mon–Sat 09.00–15.00, Sun 12.15–15.00, winter) is a motley of styles, building materials and forms. The cream-coloured west façade is hemmed in between two towers, partly concealed in their lower sections by two Gothic sepulchral chapels. Three narrow windows in the gable, a 14C figure of St Stanisław (see p. 146), a Piast eagle and a huge 19C rosette window modelled on French cathedrals make for all the decoration.

Pass through the ornate Baroque entrance and walk up a flight of steps under a wooden coffered roof with rosettes (1643–44). A black marble portal frames a door of 1636 with characteristic inlaid iron decoration: a crowned capital 'K', the cipher of King Kazimierz the Great, repeated over and over again. By the door, bones of antediluvian animals are suspended on chains—a practice common in the Middle Ages—and below, in two small niches, are Gothic stone sculptures representing the dragon-slaying Archangel Michael and St Margaret.

Interior This is sparsely lit by the rosette and the dim clerestory windows, and seems short, as the chancel is concealed behind the large shrine of St Stanisław (see below) at the intersection of the nave and transept. Three bays of cross vaults rest on corbels supporting four sculptures of the Fathers of the Christian Church: SS Jerome, Ambrose, Gregory (all three late Gothic) and Augustine (1900). The walls are hung with somewhat faded Brussels tapestries (mid-17C), partly concealing the aisle arches.

The central place in the Cathedral is occupied by the **shrine of St Stanisław** (1), the most revered martyr of the Polish Catholic Church (see p. 146). His tomb has rested at this spot since the 11C, a fact which determined the unusual proportions of the church, with the chancel longer than the nave. The dome, supported on four pillars, was designed by Giovanni Trevano in 1626–29. Below it is a silver coffin (1669–71, Pieter van der Rennen), resting on the shoulders of angels, and bearing fine reliefs depicting scenes from the life of the saint.

On both sides of the nave, in the aisle arches, stand **royal tombs**: of Władysław of Varna (2) (a

Wawel cathedral

modern imitation of Gothic sarcophagi), and of Władysław Jagiełło (3). The latter, a marvellous work of the Florentine school (c 1420), is placed under a stone baldachin designed by Bartolomeo Berrecci, and supported on slender marble columns. The tomb, made of red Hungarian marble, is an excellent example of sepulchral art. It consists of a sarcophagus and a supine figure of the king, dressed in a belted coat, holding a sceptre and an orb, with a vanquished dragon at his feet. The reliefs at the sides of the sarcophagus depict members of the four estates bewailing the death of their monarch.

Pass around the shrine and enter the **chancel**, the site of many royal coronations. The prince would enter the church through the south entrance and first visit the Chapel of Bishop Zadzik in the south aisle (see below). There, he would be properly attired for the ceremony, and then led through the arched passage on the right of the chancel to assume his place in front of the **high altar** (4). The altar (c 1650), flanked by gilded columns, contains a large, mid-17C *Crucifixion*. In front of it stands the tomb of Cardinal Fryderyk Jagiełło (d. 1503), the brother of King Zygmunt the Old.

Return to the northwest corner of the church and begin the tour of the aisles and ambulatory. Of the 18 chapels in the Cathedral, almost all are usually closed and you can only peep through the grills; a pity, as the chapels contain some of the finest works of art to be found in Wawel, or indeed Poland. If you visit in May or June, beware—you may be swamped by hordes of noisy school children.

First is the 15C **Chapel of the Holy Trinity** (5) containing the tomb of Anna

Wąsowicz, who commissioned the renovation of the chapel in the mid-19C. The relief on the sarcophagus shows the benefactress reclining in a pose full of sensual charm, while on top kneels the figure of a naked child, lost in prayer. The Gothic vaults were reconstructed in the early 20C and covered with murals by Włodzimierz Tetmajer.

Crypt of St Leonard
Descend the stairs beyond the Czartoryski Chapel (6) to enter the *Crypt of St Leonard, which is covered with low vaults supported on eight pillars. It ends in a round apse with three narrow windows that used to supply light, as the crypt was originally above ground.

The Crypt of St Leonard is the most important remnant of the grand Romanesque Cathedral of St Wacław, begun at the end of the 11C and completed over fifty years later. The present, Gothic cathedral was begun by Bishop Nanker in 1320. While the west part of the old church was still being used, the Chapel of St Margaret (the present sacristy) and a new, square chancel surrounded by an ambulatory with radiating chapels appeared. In 1346–64, the new nave eventually swallowed up the rest of the Romanesque church, incorporating its towers and the Crypt of St Leonard. Chapels were added over the centuries, and the cathedral itself was repeatedly rebuilt and renovated; it has, however, been essentially preserved in the original Gothic form.

Today, the Crypt of St Leonard contains an altar by Eugène Viollet-le-Duc (1873) and several sarcophagi of Polish monarchs and national heroes. The oldest tomb is that of King Zygmunt the Old; the most ornate are the Vasa coffins, wrought by silversmiths from Gdańsk and Toruń; the most recent ones include the sarcophagi of Tadeusz Kościuszko (1832), Józef Piłsudski (1936), and Poland's wartime general Władysław Sikorski (1981), whose ashes were brought from England in 1994. Narrow passages take you to the other crypts which together hold the remains of most of Poland's royalty, with the Jagiellon, Vasa and Saxon dynasties all represented. You leave the church through the southwest gate; walk back through the main entrance and continue the tour from the entrance to the crypt.

From the short transept you can enter the vestibule of the **Chapter Library** (7) (here also is the exit from the Zygmunt Tower, see below). The library has one of the most valuable Polish collections of codices, incunabula and prints. Adjacent to it and entered through an identical portal with an ornate gate, is the domed **Chapel of Bishop Maciejowski** (8), with a columned tomb of the bishop high up in its west wall.

From the ambulatory you enter the underground **Crypt of the Bards** (9) containing the tombs of Adam Mickiewicz (1798–1855) and Juliusz Słowacki (1809–49), the greatest Polish poets of the Romantic period. The construction of the crypt was occasioned in 1890 by the return of Adam Mickiewicz's body to Poland from Paris, where he had lived in exile. Facing the entrance is the **Lipski Chapel** (10), with the tomb of Bishop Andrzej Lipski (d. 1631), by Sebastiano Sala, against the west wall. There are two more chapels before the sacristy: of the Skotnicki family (11), and of Bishop Zebrzydowski (d. 1620) (12). The latter is distinguished by the splendid tomb of the bishop, designed by Jan Michałowicz of Urzędów, who also considerably remodelled the chapel. The **sacristy** (13), a Gothic chapel from which the construction of the Gothic Cathedral began in 1320, was enlarged and acquired its present function in the 15C. The keystones of the vaults are decorated with Gothic reliefs, the oldest in Kraków.

Through the sacristy you can enter the 14C **Zygmunt Tower**, with one of the largest bells in Europe, the 'Zygmunt' (see above), and four smaller ones. From the top there is a good view over Kraków towards the Market Square: to the right you see the twin towers of St Andrew's (see p. 113) and the huge dome of the SS Peter and Paul's; slightly further away is St Mary's.

You leave the tower via the library vestibule. Opposite the entrance to the sacristy stands the **tomb of Władysław the Short** (14) (d. 1333), the first Polish monarch to be buried in the newly-built Gothic Cathedral. The supine effigy rests on a sandstone sarcophagus, at the sides of which figures are shown mourning the death of their king. Behind a Renaissance bronze grille at the northeast end of the ambulatory is the **Chapel of Bishop Gamrat** (15), which contains the bishop's tomb (1545–47), designed by Giovanni il Mosca. By the chapel, on the north wall of the ambulatory, notice the 15C **Crucifix of St Jadwiga** (16)—a sheet of beaten silver silhouetting the soft outlines of the International Gothic style.

The easternmost end of the Cathedral is occupied by the **Chapel of Our Lady** (17), which Santi Gucci converted into the sepulchral chapel of King Stefan Bathory in 1594–95; the same artist designed Bathory's tomb. The chapel is covered with tripartite 'Piast' vaults (c 1380) and late 16C painting. In the window jambs are the remnants of even older, Gothic murals. Opposite, on the west wall of the ambulatory, are Francesco Placidi's two 18C black marble memorials to Michał Korybut Wiśniowiecki (18) and Jan Sobieski (19). In the latter, two Turks with hands bound in chains are a reference to the battle that saved Vienna from the Ottoman siege in 1683. The **Chapel of Bishop Tomicki** (20), at the southeast end of the ambulatory, is a reduced version of the Zygmunt Chapel. It was designed in 1530 by Bartolomeo Berrecci, who also carved the bishop's tomb, which stands by the north wall.

The south aisle begins with the **Chapel of Bishop Załuski** (21), remodelled in Rococo style by Placidi in 1758–66. A black niche in its south wall holds a white marble figure of Bishop Grot (d. 1347), showing him as a rather corpulent man, poised flamboyantly on his right foot. Next is the **Chapel of Jan Olbracht** (22) (d. 1501), with the king's tomb standing against the west wall. The marble relief representing the monarch's figure, probably made by Veit Stoss's son, Stanisław, is still Gothic. The arcaded sandstone niche, however, with decoration meticulously carved by Francesco Fiorentino in 1505, is the earliest Renaissance monument in Poland.

Facing the Olbracht Chapel is the second oldest **royal tomb** in the Cathedral (23). It was commissioned in the 1370s by Louis of Hungary for his uncle, Kazimierz the Great. The supine king's figure, carved in Hungarian red marble, rests under a sandstone baldachin supported on eight columns. This motif, recalling the papal monuments in Avignon, symbolises the dome of heaven above the king. Next along is the 14C **Chapel of Bishop Zadzik** (24), converted into a sepulchral chapel in the 17C, probably by Sebastiano Sala, who also designed the bishop's tomb. The **Chapel of Bishop Jan Konarski** (25) contains

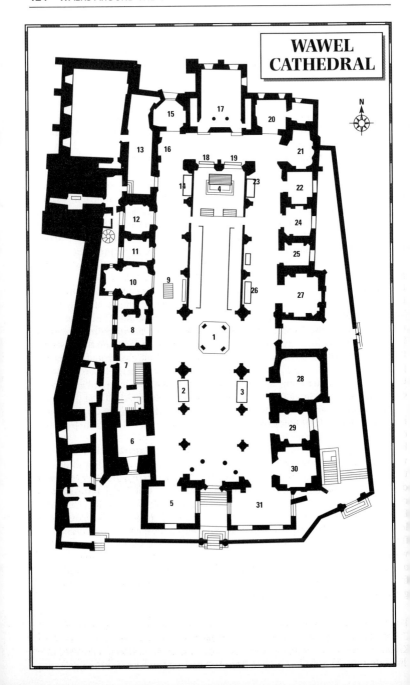

a marble tomb of the bishop (d. 1525), which probably originated in Berrecci's workshop. Note the glass case opposite the chapel containing Queen Jadwiga's wooden sceptre and orb—she donated the jewel-encrusted gold ones to the Jagiellonian University. Her sarcophagus (26), further west, with a white marble figure, was made in 1902.

The Zygmunt Chapel

Rightly known as the 'jewel of the Renaissance north of the Alps', the Cathedral's most famous chapel—the **Zygmunt Chapel (27)—has no equal outside Italy. Its pure Renaissance form, modelled on Tuscan architecture from the 15C and early 16C, is entirely the work of **Bartolomeo Berrecci**, whom Zygmunt the Old brought to Kraków in 1517 to work on the new royal castle (see p. 127). After the death of his first wife, Zygmunt decided to build a sepulchral chapel for himself and his former spouse. Little did he know that it would become the mausoleum of the last Jagiellons. Two years after Berrecci had shown the king a wooden model of the chapel, the foundations were already in place by the south aisle of the Cathedral. It took another fourteen years to complete the project.

Seen from the outside, the chapel immediately attracts attention with its **gilded dome**, cast in copper. The dome is surmounted with a tall lantern, topped by a spire and a gilded putto carrying a crown and cross. Equally striking is the **interior**, with its rich sculptural decoration and grotesque forms in bas-relief. The architectonic composition of each wall is based on the form of a Roman triumphal arch, popular during the Renaissance. Each of the deep, broad recesses is flanked by smaller niches containing sculptures of SS Peter, Paul, Wacław (Wenceslaus), Florian, John the Baptist and, the best of all, Zygmunt, the king's patron. The **marble effigy** of the king, Berrecci's true masterpiece, rests in the upper part of the west wall. The figure reclines in an uneasy pose, propped on its elbow, with a bent knee, as if about to wake up and rise.

The original sarcophagus was moved upwards in 1574–75 to make room for another monarch, Zygmunt August, whose similar figure rests in the lower part of the niche. It was sponsored by the king's sister, Anna the Jagiellon, and made by Santi Gucci, who simultaneously worked on his patron's tomb (c 1583), which was placed on the south side of the chapel a few years before her death. In the east niche is a silver altarpiece ordered by Zygmunt the Old in Nürnberg, and designed by Hans Dürer (Albrecht's brother). The six tondi in red marble with representations of the four evangelists, David and Solomon, are the work of Berrecci and his collaborators. Theirs, too, is the carved sandstone decoration, no less remarkable than the sculptures, with miniature scenes among a profusion of floral arabesques, evoking a mood of joy and earthly pleasures curiously at odds with their sombre ambience. Their subject-matter is derived largely from Greek and Roman mythology; the dolphin, a symbol of the immortality of the soul, is a frequently recurring motif. The chapel is closed off with an elaborate bronze grille (1530–32) from the renowned Vischer workshop in Nürnberg.

The sepulchral **Chapel of the Vasas** (28), the last royal mausoleum built in the Cathedral, was completed in 1676 after the death of the last Vasa king, Jan Kazimierz. The splendid bronze door is so thickly ornamented that you cannot see through to the chapel. The Baroque interior, decked out in black marble, exudes a severe Counter-Reformation spirit, characteristic of the Vasas, whose memorial slabs are contained within. Seen from the outside, the chapel is a mirror-image of the Zygmunt Chapel, save for the golden dome of the latter: the Vasa Chapel is more modestly clad in copper. Such imitation was not accidental: in their own century of wars, chaos and confusion, the Vasas wished to allude to the 'Golden Age of the Jagiellons'.

Behind a Baroque portal by Placidi is the cross-vaulted **Szafraniec Chapel** (29), forming the ground floor of the Silver Bell Tower (one of the few remnants of the former Romanesque cathedral). Rebuilt several times, it has nevertheless retained its Gothic style. The late 19C murals were painted by Józef Mehoffer, who also designed the stained-glass.

The domed **Potocki Chapel** (30) was refashioned by Jan Michałowicz of Urzędów as a sepulchral chapel for Bishop Padniewski. His alabaster tomb bears an inscription by the medieval poet Jan Kochanowski. The chapel became a mausoleum of the Potocki family in 1832–40, when it acquired its present Neoclassical form. Inside is a 19C statue of *Christ Giving a Blessing* by Berthel Thorvaldsen, and a 17C *Crucifixion* by the great Italian painter Giovanni Francesco Barbieri (Guercino).

Last is the **Chapel of the Holy Cross** (31), built in the 15C as a royal mausoleum. The tomb of its founder, Kazimierz the Jagiellon, stands in the southwest corner. Made by Veit Stoss in 1492, it is one of the most beautiful medieval sepulchral monuments in Poland. The tomb takes the form of a sarcophagus on which lies an reclining effigy of the king carved in spotted Salzburg marble. The natural veins in the marble add to the expressiveness of the piece: the king is shown close to death, his head tilted back in pain. Stoss and his assistant Jorg Huber of Passau made the rich baldachin resting on eight columns with religious scenes carved on the capitals. A larger tomb, standing by the west wall, was made in 1789. This Baroque classical composition is a reminder of the banishment of Bishop Kajetan Sołtyk for his defence of Poland against Russian interference: an eagle is struggling to get out of a coffin, which a malicious figure is trying to shut. The chapel also has stained glass by Józef Mehoffer and some rare late 15C Byzantine-style murals executed by artists from Pskov. The bosses of the vault are decorated with the crests of Lithuania, Poland and Austria.

Cathedral Museum

The Cathedral Treasury, whose beginnings reach back to the 11C, occupies a late Gothic building reached via the sacristy. The collection is not open to the public, although a few items are occasionally displayed in the Cathedral Museum (5; same opening times as the Cathedral). The highlight, rarely exhibited, is the spear of St Maurice, which Emperor Otto III presented to Bolesław the Brave in 1000 at the Congress of Gniezno.

Castle

Leaving the museum, proceed to the Renaissance **Castle (open Tues, Fri 09.30–16.30, Wed–Thur 09.30–15.30, Sat 09.30–15.00, Sun 10.00–15.00). You will pass the picturesque south side of the Cathedral, with the five chapels looking like fabulous boletuses huddled under the wall, and the golden dome of the Zygmunt Chapel (7 *Wawel Hill* plan) glowing brightly even on a cloudy day. To the right is the sloping expanse of the former Lower Castle, today a tidy, English-style lawn interspersed with flower beds and white stones marking the foundations of the medieval churches of St Michael (**8**) and St George (**9**). Walk between the former Royal Kitchen building (**10**) on the right (fronted by a display of cannons) and the Cathedral. Tickets to the Royal Chambers, Royal Treasury and Armoury, and oriental exhibition can be bought inside the long, vaulted passageway of the Renaissance gatehouse (**11**). You emerge onto the much-admired courtyard of the castle proper: an irregular pentagon, with three-tiered arcades all around, except for the west wing, most of which is taken up by the Royal Kitchen.

History of the castle

The Gothic castle on this part of Wawel hill was destroyed during a major fire in 1499. At the beginning of the 16C, King Zygmunt the Old commissioned a team of local stonemasons and Italian sculptors headed by **Francesco Fiorentino** to construct a new residence befitting the power and influence of the Jagiellon dynasty. After 1530, work was continued under the supervision of **Bartolomeo Berrecci**, another Florentine. In 1595, two towers were added—the Zygmunt Vasa (**12**) in the northeast corner, and the Sobieski (**13**), adjacent to the Cathedral Treasury. **Tomaso Dolabella** worked on the interiors, decorating them in Venetian Mannerist style.

Swedish troops ravaged the castle twice, most destructively in 1702, when they began a fire that raged for a whole week. The castle suffered during the Partitions, notably at the hands of the Austrian army, who used it as a barracks. It was only after 1905 that serious restoration work began, lasting until the 1960s.

The **courtyard** (**14**) is the best example of Italian Renaissance architecture in the castle. The arcades, directly borrowed from 15C Florentine design, are perfect semi-circles resting on slender columns, of equal length at the ground and first floor level, but twice as long at the upper level; they look so fragile, as if they were about to snap. The upper-storey columns are decorated with stone rings, which serve to visually shorten the shafts. Painted friezes depicting busts of Roman Emperors have been preserved just below the eaves in the south and east part of the arcades. The west wing has windows with intricate surrounds in pure Quattrocento style. Above the oriel are the crests of Poland, Lithuania and the Habsburg family.

Cross the courtyard diagonally to enter the Royal Chambers. The main part of the exhibition is on the second floor, the *piano nobile*.

The Royal Chambers could be a disappointment, were it not for the truly magnificent ****tapestries**, bequeathed to the Polish nation by the last of the Jagiellons, Zygmunt August, who commissioned them for the interiors of his Wawel residence. The tapestries were painstakingly woven in the mid-16C by several outstanding masters from Brussels to the drawings and designs of Michiel van Coxcie of Mechelen (1499–1592), nick-named the 'Flemish Raphael'. More than 350 pieces were made of which 136 have survived. It took a whole year for one craftsman to weave a single square metre of fabric. The largest tapestries are 5m x 9m in size.

The collection comprises three basic groups: figurative tapestries depicting Biblical scenes (***Adam and Eve***, ***Story of Noah***, ***Tower of Babel***); the so-called verdures—narrow and long, intended for the spaces between the windows, above the portals, and in the corners of the rooms, bearing images of plants, animals and usually hilly landscapes; and finally, the grotesque tapestries, smaller in size, with the cipher of Zygmunt August amid satyrs and other mythical creatures. The verdures abound in contrasts of light and shades of colour; a commonly used device is the representation of either bright or dark leaves against a contrasting background, creating a strangely scintillating effect. The huge Biblical scenes are rather tawny and subdued, almost faded, but stop for a minute or two in front of, say, *Noah's Offering*, and the fabric reveals its hidden riches. Bizarre creatures suddenly begin to assert their presence, assuming an astonishing depth of perspective. In some miraculous way, the texture of the fabric is for a brief moment transformed into that of smooth human skin, the fur of a dog, the lustre of water, the bark of a tree, or the thick, sticky warmth of fresh blood.

After the Third Partition of Poland in 1795 the tapestries were removed to Russia, where they remained until after the October Revolution. The Treaty of Riga (1921), ending Poland's victorious war against the Bolsheviks, ensured the tapestries' return a few years later. When Hans Frank arrived at Wawel to set up his residence as the head of the *General Gouvernement*, he discovered that the tapestries had vanished. In 1940 the collection surfaced intact, in Canada, and stayed there until 1962, when the Polish government managed to reclaim it (the Canadians only released the treasure after Khrushchev had given assurances that it would not be exported to the Soviet Union).

Royal Chambers

You begin the tour of the Royal Chambers with the Servants' Quarters on the ground floor. The main items of interest here are the original Gothic and Renaissance stone portals and wooden beam ceilings. From a room with a Renaissance fireplace you ascend a flight of stairs, first to the mid-floor landing and then, via the monumental Envoys' Staircase, to the **first floor**. Here you can see a 17C Brussels tapestry depicting a battle scene, after Rubens's painting, *The Death of Decius Mus*, in which vigorous movement, despair and suffering are portrayed with almost cruel realism. On the opposite wall hangs a large canvas showing a royal election. Several rooms on this floor, once used as private royal apartments of the Vasas, can only be visited by prior arrangement (☎ 422 1697, 422 5155 ext. 291, guided tours only, on the hour 10.00–14.00). They contain richly decorated portals ascribed to Master Benedykt, as well as some fine 17C–18C items: portraits by Italian masters, German, Flemish and Dutch canvases, furniture (mostly Italian), porcelain, and tapestries from Zygmunt August's collection.

Second floor The state apartments in the north and east wings consist of spacious, sparsely furnished rooms hung with Zygmunt August's splendid tapestries and decorated with richly gilded coffered or painted ceilings. Some of the rooms get their names from the subject matter of the broad friezes painted below the ceilings. Thus you have the Tournament Hall, the Military Review Room, the Zodiac Room, or the Planets Room. Some rooms are closed to the public; the best accessible ones are the **Audience Hall** and the Senators' Hall. The former, where the monarch would receive foreign envoys and preside over Coronation Parliaments, has a coffered ceiling remarkably decorated with carved wooden heads (1531–35). Of the original 194 heads only 30 have survived, but even that is enough to demonstrate the artist Sebastian Tauerbach's sweep of inventiveness and imagination. The purpose and intent of the work have so far eluded art historians. According to one theory, the heads were commissioned by Queen Bona Sforza, shown in several portraits on the second floor as a stern but kind-hearted elderly matron. She was brought up in Castel Nuovo in Naples and must have remembered the similar decoration of its entrance arch. However, unlike the stone reliefs in Naples, the wooden heads of Wawel are not merely a decorative ornament. Each is different; each testifies to the irreplaceable individuality of a human face, expressive of the character, inner life and story of its bearer. Some are solemn, lost in a quiet reverie, others seem bewildered, irritated, malicious or frightened. There is a philosopher, a warrior, a coquettish maid, a drunk, a lunatic. This panorama of human types is a fitting supplement to the frieze under the ceiling, painted in 1532 by Hans Dürer, showing the cycle of human life from the cradle to the grave.

The **Senators' Hall** originally hosted the Senate assemblies, lavish balls, theatrical performances, and other court festivities. It contains some of the largest tapestries from the royal collection.

Emerging on the second-floor landing of the Senators' Staircase, proceed to the **exhibition of oriental art** housed in the west wing, the oldest in the castle (1504–07). Most of the items on display were purchased, initially by Polish monarchs and eventually by museum curators, but some were taken as war booty, particularly by King Jan Sobieski (1674–96), the celebrated vanquisher of the Ottoman Turks at Vienna in 1683. The most captivating, and indeed most valuable, objects are the Turkish and Persian tents, which constitute one of the best collections of this kind in Europe. Of particular interest is a 16C Persian carpet depicting the Garden of Eden. It is known as the Paris-Kraków carpet, as only one half of it is displayed in Wawel (second floor), the other being found in the Musée des Arts Decoratifs.

Royal Treasury and Armoury

The Royal Treasury (mid-15C), originally housed on the ground floor of the Łokietek Tower, was where the crown jewels and most important state documents were once kept. In 1795, the Prussians plundered and melted down the most valuable items. Nowadays, the Gothic rooms on the ground floor of the Cockspur (15) and Danish (16) towers mainly contain items recovered from the Soviet Union after the Second World War. The highlights are the 13C coronation sword 'Szczerbiec', insignia bestowed on Sobieski by the Pope and Louis XIV, and an 11C golden chalice discovered in an abbot's tomb in Tyniec (see p. 163). The Armoury has unique 17C–18C Polish Hussar armour, 15C Nürnberg tournament armour, and Italian Renaissance parade shields.

'Lost Wawel'

Leave through the courtyard and return to the sloping grounds of the Lower Castle. The cellars of the former Royal Kitchen contain an archaeological exhibition called *Lost Wawel* (open Mon, Wed, Thur 09.30–15.30, Fri 09.30–16.30, Sat 09.30–15.00, Sun 10.00–15.00). There you can see the vestiges of one of Kraków's earliest stone churches, the pre-Romanesque **Rotunda of St Mary** (17), which predates even the establishment of the bishopric.

St Mary's was fairly typical of the many round stone temples built in Central Europe in the 10C. It had a sparsely-lit circular nave surrounded by four semi-circular apses, one of which housed the altar. Gutted by fire in 12C, the rotunda was merged with the castle later built by Kazimierz the Great. Further north there is an open grave with bones, and fragments of medieval fortifications. The second part of the exhibition (west) has glass cases containing various objects found in the former royal coach house and kitchen. The first exhibit on the left is a small stone sculpture of an animal that may be a 10C pagan relic. In the rooms on the ground floor you can see tiles from various stoves in the royal apartments and a lapidary with a fine selection of stonework by Bartolomeo Berrecci and other Italian masters.

Leave Wawel down the cobbled driveway which skirts the south side of the hill. You will pass, on your left, the former hospital building and the Sandomierz and Senators' Towers (**18** and **19**, respectively), relics of the medieval fortifications. The driveway brings you to the intersection of ul. Grodzka (leading back to the Market Square; walk 3), ul. Stradom (covered in 'Along the Vistula'; walk 4) and ul. Podzamcze, which skirts the hill and continues towards the river. There is a good view from this side onto the Austrian brick fortifications and the castle towers.

6 • The Old University Quarter

The historic university area is centred on three streets—**Św. Anny, Jagiellońska and Gołębia**—reached from the southwest corner of the Market Square. In the Middle Ages these streets formed the heart of the Jewish quarter, but after the establishment of the university (see below) the plots of land were gradually bought up to make way for colleges and faculties. Today, the university's main administrative offices and many of its arts and humanities departments are located here. The bars and cafés in the adjoining streets are a good place to meet Polish students. Cheap lunches are served at *Chimera* on ul. Św Anny (salads), *Piccolo* on ul. Jagiellońska (chicken and chips), and *Różowy Słoń* on ul. Straszewskiego (pancakes). For a more raucous student scene you could try the main campus area in the west of the city, where the *Świniarnia* and *Rotunda* clubs (see *Live Music*) and many halls of residence are located.

Collegium Maius
A short way up ul. Św. Anny (entrance facing ul. Jagiellońska) is one of Kraków's most renowned and architecturally complex buildings: **Collegium Maius, the earliest extant college of the Jagiellonian University.

History of Collegium Maius
As early as 1364, Kazimierz the Great founded the Kraków Academy, an educational institution pre-dated in Central Europe only by the Charles University in Prague, and initially comprising three faculties: law, medicine, and the liberal arts. Progress was temporarily halted by the death of Kazimierz in 1370, but a revival soon followed, thanks largely to Queen Jadwiga, who endowed the Academy with most of her considerable fortune. In 1400, Jadwiga's husband, Władysław Jagiełło, purchased a house at the corner of ul. Św. Anny and ul. Jagiellońska. A few months later the theological faculty set up its headquarters in the house, which took the name of Collegium Maius. During the 15C the Kraków Academy flourished, with enrolment rising to a peak of 500

students, of whom nearly half were foreigners. In time, teaching came to focus on the sciences, particularly astrology and astronomy. The Academy's most famous student, **Nicholas Copernicus** (see p. 132), studied and resided at Collegium Maius in 1491–95.

Though considerable damage was caused to the building through fires in 1462 and 1492, the latter in fact proved to be a blessing in disguise: during reconstruction carried out by the king's brother, Cardinal Fryderyk, the original corner house was integrated with buildings further down the street. This unified architectural whole was given a magnificent inner courtyard encircled by a late Gothic cloister, rather like the loggias of Italian universities. The 16C saw the construction of a new library wing (1518–40), as well as many other colleges around the University quarter.

Collegium Maius remained the University's chief building until the 19C. Under Austrian rule, it fell into decline. Much of the original late Gothic architecture and detailing was lost during restoration work carried out in 1840–60, after which the building housed the Jagiellonian library (until 1939). Fortunately, many of the neo-Gothic accretions were removed when the building once again underwent major restoration after the Second World War. Today's Collegium Maius is thus a mixture of authentic and 'new' Gothic elements.

Viewed from ul. Jagiellońska, the **façade** presents an unornamented mass of brick and stone, with three panelled gables topped by pinnacles and a delightful bay window at first floor level. The fragment of stone wall at the corner marks the extent of the original house from which Collegium Maius evolved.

The main entrance on ul. Św. Anny is used only for official ceremonies, so you should enter from ul. Jagiellońska. Beyond the vaulted vestibule you emerge onto the cool and peaceful courtyard. Around the rectangular space run pointed arcades, supported on round stone columns, with simple diamond vaults made up of faceted cells between the rib-lines. Above is a stone balustrade, which used to carry long wooden posts supporting the great projecting eaves of the roof. Walking

Courtyard, Collegium Maius

around the gallery, notice the impressive foundation tablet showing Cardinal Oleśnicki and his patron offering a model of the college building to St Mary.

The rooms off the courtyard accommodate the **Jagiellonian University Museum** (open Mon–Fri 11.00–14.30, Sat 11.00–13.30; guided tour in English), entered through the late Gothic *Porta Aurea*, or Golden Door. The largely ceremonial rooms on the first floor begin with the star-vaulted *Libraria*, the former library, currently used as an assembly hall by the University Senate. There are copies of astronomical instruments used by Copernicus here. Next is the Gothic *Stuba Communis*, or common room, which also served as a refectory. Standing by the bay window is a 14C statuette of Kazimierz the Great. An ornately carved wooden staircase leads up to the living quarters on the second floor.

The tiny **University Treasury** is housed in the two small rooms further on. Inside are various items of memorabilia, sceptres endowed by Queen Jadwiga (c 1400), Cardinal Oleśnicki (1454) and Cardinal Fryderyk (1495)—still wielded by the University Rector during official ceremonies—as well as the famous Jagiellonian Globe (1510), the first one to show America (though Australia is still missing), with a built-in calendar and clock. Next are the theology faculty's reading rooms, with Empire style and Biedermeier furnishings. The small **Copernicus Room** has a register of 1491 (copy) where the young Nicholas is entered as a student having paid his college fees. There is also a later edition of his greatest work *De revolutionibus* (the first edition is in the college library). The oddest exhibit, perhaps, is a photograph of the moon with the inscription 'To the Copernicus Museum in Kraków on the 500th birthday of a Giant', signed 'Neil Armstrong, Apollo 11'.

Nicholas Copernicus (Mikołaj Kopernik)

If one were to credit a single person with bringing the Middle Ages to a close, that person would be Nicholas Copernicus (1473–1543), whose theory of heliocentrism revolutionised the medieval understanding of the cosmos and—bolstered by the genius of Galileo, Kepler and Newton—begot modern science. Copernicus studied at the Kraków Academy and the universities of Bologna and Padua in Italy. In 1510 he became a canon and settled in Frombork, near Gdańsk, where he was able to pursue his astronomical investigations. At that time, astronomy, whose main practical function was the measurement of time and the preparation of calendars, was beset with difficulties that were growing in proportion to the precision demanded of it. Inspired by neo-Platonic cosmology, Copernicus assigned the central place of the universe to the Sun, and determined that all the planets, including the Earth, revolve around it on circular orbits—'and so the sun as if sitting on a throne, manages the family of planets busying around'. This bold move did away with all the complications of the Ptolemaic system, but, ironically, failed to produce better predictions of the movement of the planets. Copernicus set out the principles of heliocentrism in his famous treatise *De Revolutionibus Orbium Celestium*, a work so radical for its time that it had to be published posthumously (1543), and immediately earned its author an entry in the Papal Index for many centuries to come.

The last and largest room, facing ul. Św. Anny, is the 15C **Auditorium**, formerly the University's main assembly hall. Below the Renaissance coffered ceiling (16C) are professors' stalls, a rector's throne, and a richly carved wooden doorway of 1593 in a stone frame. In keeping with tradition, at the beginning of each academic year a procession of gowned professors begins at the auditorium and proceeds to Collegium Novum (see below). The ground floor *lektoria*, or lecture halls (usually closed to tourists), contain a unique display of scientific instruments, including an 11C Arabian astrolabe, donated to the Academy by the astronomer Marcin Bylica in 1492. Copernicus attended lectures in the *Galen Lektorium* and, according to legend, Faust and Twardowski (see p. 102) studied black magic in the Alchemist's Chamber, also on the ground floor. The museum also has a gallery of late 19C Polish painting (open Sat 11.00–13.30) and a collection of medieval sculpture.

Collegium Novum

Leave Collegium Maius and continue south to the first intersection—ul. Gołębia, where you should turn right towards the main University complex bordering the *Planty*. The group of buildings here is dominated by Collegium Novum, an imposing neo-Gothic structure designed in 1883–87. On the façade are the crests of the University and its greatest benefactors. The building houses the Rectorate and main administrative offices and lecture rooms. Feel free to wander in. Ascending the great staircase you reach the diamond vaulted auditorium (*Aula*), where there are portraits of Jadwiga and Jagiełło, famous University Rectors, and best of all, Matejko's **Copernicus**. An interesting detail among the many astronomical instruments depicted in this painting is the telescope, which Copernicus certainly never used, as it had not been invented at that time. A statue of the great astronomer (1900) stands to the left of Collegium Novum.

Church of St Anne

Return north along the *Planty* to see one of the city's finest buildings—the **Collegiate Church of St Anne—on ul. Św. Anny.

History of St Anne's

The history of St Anne's is closely connected to that of the University. Władysław Jagiełło funded the construction of a Gothic church here in 1407, which a decade later came under the patronage of the Kraków Academy. In 1689, the professors commissioned **Tylman van Gameren**, an architect widely admired for his work in Warsaw, to construct a new church modelled on San Andrea della Valle in Rome. Gameren finished the project in 1703, producing perhaps the greatest example of Polish classicised Baroque, an achievement all the more remarkable in the light of Poland's political and economic decline. As the façade had to be set perpendicular to the street, and could only be viewed from the side, Gameren profiled it in depth, with projecting columns, niches and recesses emphasised by an interplay of light and shade; his clever use of perspective and proportion, moreover, had the visual effect of shortening the nave and enlarging the dome. The building's appearance was further enhanced by **Baldassare Fontana**, who did the figural and ornamental sculpture, stuccoes, and main portal.

The **interior** of St Anne's (open 09.00–12.00 and 16.00–19.00) is laid out on the plan of a Latin cross, with three pairs of chapels along the broad nave and a dome above the transepts. The impression of space and light is accentuated by the pastel-coloured *trompe l'oeil* murals. Fontana's stuccowork immediately stands out for its intricacy and richness, particularly the medallion and fruit stuccoes on the nave piers, and his dynamic sculptures of saints and angels, recalling Bernini, around the altar. His best effort, however, is the **mausoleum** of the church's patron, St John of Kęty, a 15C theologian and cult figure, situated at the end of the south transept. The sarcophagus is supported by figures representing the four faculties of the University: Theology, Law, Medicine and the Liberal Arts. On top of the tall spiral columns surrounding the tomb are four of the Saint's namesakes: John the Baptist, John of Damascus, John the Apostle and John Chrysostom. In the north transept, opposite, there is another fine altar by Fontana with a *Pietà* in stucco relief. Next to it is a Neo-classical monument to Copernicus (1822).

Continue north along the *Planty*, turning left into ul. Karmelicka. In the late 19C, this was one of the city's showcase streets, lined with tall, at times even palatial, tenement houses. The cobbled pavements were restored in the 1990s, when the street was given a major facelift. A short way down on the right is the **Carmelite Church of the Visitation of Mary**, a Baroque church built in 1657–79 on the ruins of a Gothic aisled hall. The darkness of the interior is broken by the richly gilded high altar (1698–99), around which are wooden saints and prophets belonging to the best Polish figural sculpture of the 17C. Abutting from the south is the domed Chapel of the Virgin Mary (16C), probably rebuilt by Giovanni Trevano in 1634–37. Notice also the Rococo painted decoration (1756) and fine chancel stalls. On the wall outside, a fading plaque behind bars contains a footprint preserved in stone. According to legend it belongs to Queen Jadwiga, who frequently visited the church while it was under construction.

Backtracking to the *Bagatela* Theatre, you could take a short detour along ul. Krupnicza to the **House of Józef Mehoffer** (no. 26), opened in 1996 as a branch of the National Museum (open Tues, Thur–Sun 10.00–15.30, Wed 10.00–18.00). Mehoffer was an exponent of the 'Young Poland' movement (see p. 83), and is considered to be one of the major Polish painters. The house has been thoroughly restored and is furnished with memorabilia and numerous paintings from the artist's private collection. Chamber concerts are occasionally held inside the reconstructed turn-of-the-century parlour.

7 • Around the Planty Park

This walk begins on pl. Szczepański, west of the Market Square, and roughly follows the medieval city walls around the northern part of the Old Town. The highlight is the Czartoryski Museum, contained inside the former city arsenal.

There are a number of fine Art Nouveau buildings on pl. Szczepański, though the square itself dates from 1801. The south side is dominated by the **Old Theatre** (*Teatr Stary*; no. 1), the oldest in Kraków and still one of the best. Some of the most acclaimed productions of the 1990s were put on here, including *The Wedding* (see p. 116), directed by Andrzej Wajda (see p. 150), *Lunatics*, directed by Krystian Lupa, and an especially memorable adaptation of Sławomir Mrożek's *Love in the Crimea* (see below). The building's fine Art Nouveau façade, with a broad stuccoed frieze under the eaves, is the late 19C work of the architects Tadeusz Stryjeński and Franciszek Mączyński. In the basement (entrance from ul. Jagiellońska 1) is the up-market *Maska* bar (see *Late-night bars*

The Old Theatre

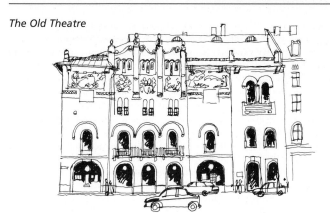

Sławomir Mrożek

Sławomir Mrożek, one of the most original Polish writers of post-war period, was born in a village near Kraków in 1930. He began his literary career as a journalist and satirist, collaborating with, among others, the Piwnica Pod Baranami Cabaret (see p. 99). His first play, *Police*, published in 1958, received mixed reviews, but he shot to fame in the 1960s with *Tango*, becoming the most widely-performed Polish playwright outside Poland. *Tango* was shortly followed by *The Emigrants*, in which Mrożek chronicled his own experiences of exile—he left his native land in 1963, moving first to Italy, then France, before finally settling in Mexico.

Mrożek is often—and perhaps wrongly—associated with the Theatre of the Absurd, his work compared to that of Beckett and Ionesco. He is at his best when portraying the grotesque, almost surreal world of the People's Republic (1948–89), a world distorted and undermined by a stupidity that bears many names. Mrożek satirises communist Poland to great comic effect, but often the humour has a terrifying metaphysical and existential depth. This, combined with his irony and scepticism of tradition, won Mrożek the reputation of an iconoclast, a destroyer of national myths. Others see him as a moralist, an acute observer of social and cultural change in the modern world.

Mrożek's works were banned for several years during the communist period. After the imposition of Martial Law in 1981, he himself refused to publish in Poland through official channels. Instead, his works appeared in various émigré journals (such as the Paris-based *Kultura*) and in uncensored, 'underground' publications. At the end of the 1990s, Mrożek returned to Poland and settled in Kraków, resuming his place as one of the most prominent figures in the literary life of the city. He has also written novels, short stories (the best-known are *Wedding in Atomice* and *The Elephant*) and a series of philosophical fables in which the protagonists are animals. His latest play, *Love in the Crimea*, was premiered at the Old Theatre in Kraków, to wide critical acclaim.

and clubs), a good place for refreshments and snacks, and upstairs, a small **Theatre Museum** (open Tues–Sat 11.00–13.00, and an hour before performances).

An equally impressive example of Cracovian Art Nouveau is the **Palace of Art** (*Pałac Sztuki*), which borders the *Planty* on the west side of the square. On the façade are niches containing busts of famous artists, notably Jan Matejko (pl. Szczepański side) and Stanisław Wyspiański (*Planty* side). Running round the building, below the mansard roof, is a decorative frieze by another turn-of-the-century artist, Jacek Malczewski. Exhibitions of graphic art, sculpture and painting—often the best in Kraków—are held inside (open daily 08.15–20.00).

The neighbouring **Arts Pavilion** (*Bunkier Sztuki*) at pl. Szczepański 3, facing the *Planty*, is where the International Graphic Art Triennale is held in September. The pavilion also hosts exhibitions of modern art (open Tues–Sun 11.00–18.00).

The house at no. 9, on the east side of the square, was donated to the city by the Szołayski family at the end of the 19C. It is now a branch of the *National Museum (open Tues 10.00–18.00, Wed–Sun 10.00–16.00, but closed for renovation at the time of writing, and the layout may change when it re-opens). The display consists of a broad and impressive selection of Polish sculpture and painting, with particular emphasis on medieval art from the Małopolska region. The prize exhibit on the first floor is an exquisite wooden sculpture of the Virgin, known as *The Madonna of Krużlowa* (c 1410) after the village where it was found. It is a masterpiece of the International Gothic style and, like other 'Beautiful Madonnas' of the early 15C, embodies the courtly ideal of female beauty, both physical and spiritual. Other sculptures on the first floor include an almost life-size *Jesus Riding a Donkey* (c 1470), and two reclining figures of knights (c 1480), attributed to Veit Stoss. There are also some fine epitaphs, notably *Wierzbięta of Branice* (c 1425), in which Grzegorz Wierzbięta, the steward to the royal household, is shown as a knight kneeling before the Virgin and Child.

Upstairs, the story is taken up to the 18C, with Hans Dürer's miniature *St Hieronymus* (c 1526), Sarmatian portraits (see below) and votive paintings. The highlight is a huge, anonymous polyptych of *St John the Almoner* (c 1504), brought here from St Catherine's church. The centrepiece shows St John, a 7C Egyptian patriarch, distributing alms to the poor, with scenes from the life of the saint in the inner wings, and scenes from the lives of the hermits of the Eastern church in the outer ones.

The street leading northwest off pl. Szczepański is ul. Reformacka, which brings you to the 17C **Reformed Franciscans' Church and Monastery**. The buildings themselves are of little interest, but in the crypts below the monastery there are over 1000 tombs dating from 1667 onwards. Due to the special atmospheric conditions, the mummified corpses, including one of a Napoleonic soldier, are almost perfectly preserved. The tombs were recently closed to the public when it was discovered that various skulls and bones had gone missing, but the monks may still show you round. Ask at the vestibule for a private tour. Visits must be short, though, to protect the relics from further decomposition.

Turning right along ul. Św. Marka you reach a 13C **church** of the same name, at the junction with ul. Sławkowska. Originally a Gothic aisled hall, the interior of St Mark's was completely rebuilt in 1624–47 with the addition of the nave arcades and early Baroque decoration. The Mannerist **high altar** (c 1618) was built at roughly the same time as the monastery. Adjoining the chancel is

Sarmatian Art

During the 16C–18C in Poland there evolved a local cultural style known as **Sarmatism**, pervading not only art, but also literature, rhetoric, music, fashion, military and civil customs. It was based on the erroneous belief that Poles were descendants of the ancient Sarmatians, a nomadic people living in the Black Sea Steppe, who supposedly settled along the Vistula having conquered the indigenous tribes, and were the forebears of the Polish and Ruthenian peasantry. As the successors to the bold and warlike Sarmatians, the nobility felt they were entitled to a privileged position and exclusive power in the state. They displayed an inflated belief in their historic mission, xenophobia and megalomania, and cultivated the orientalisation of their aesthetic tastes.

The Sarmatian myth went hand-in-hand with a cult of ancient Rome, in which the nobles detected the origins of their ideals and beliefs. The Sarmatian nobles easily assimilated Mannerist, Baroque and Neo-classical forms, adapting them to suit their own needs in the chapels, triumphal arches and monumental sarcophagi—the *castra doloris*—which they commissioned.

The Sarmatian style—a fusion of Mannerism and Baroque with Oriental culture—was most prominent in objects of everyday life such as dress, military equipment, riding gear, crockery and cutlery. It also influenced the interior design of innumerable manor houses and estates. The main elements of Sarmatian interior decoration were tapestries, drapes, rugs, carpets, often decorated with weapons, hunting trophies, gorgets, ancestral portraits, candleholders and mirrors, pewter, silverware and faience. Polish art was at its most original in these areas. To this day its achievements are inseparable from the notion of national culture and clearly originate in the heritage of the nobility.

a square bell tower set askew to the street, and between the external chancel buttresses—a copy of a Gothic sculpture of *Jesus flanked by the Virgin and St John the Evangelist* (c 1500) (the original is inside the church).

The bustling ul. Sławkowska has many *kantors* and is a good place to change money. The building at no. 17, opposite St Mark's, is the neo-Renaissance **Academy of Sciences** (1857–64), accommodating an extensive library and the *Ossolineum* bookshop selling academic texts.

Continue east along ul. Św. Marka to the next junction. The **Palace of the Cistercian Abbots of Jędrzejów** at ul. Św. Jana 20 is an amalgamation (1735–44) of three Gothic burghers' houses, which accounts for its sizeable proportions. Francesco Placidi added the Rococo façade. The impressive stone portal, with caryatids supporting the moulding, is also Rococo (c 1744). In the basement is a **gallery** (open Mon–Fri 11.00–18.00 Sat 11.00–14.00) run by the well-known Cracovian sculptor, Dominik Rostworowski (see *Contemporary Polish Art*). The small shop at no. 14 (open Mon–Fri 11.00–17.00, Sat 10.00–14.00) further down the street sells posters and postcards by satirical cartoonist Andrzej Mleczko (see *Contemporary Polish Art*).

Looking left, you will see the picturesque outline of the Piarist church, which closes the north end of ul. Św. Jana. Walk towards it passing, at no. 15 (right), the 17C **Lubomirski Palace**, named after its 19C owner, who remodelled the façade in an eclectic spirit. Preserved are an 18C portal and 17C stuccoes inside the vaulted vestibule. The elegant, turn-of-the-century house at the junction with ul. Pijarska (left) is the *Orbis-Francuski Hotel*, with a French restaurant inside.

The Piarists settled in Kraków in 1654, organising theological schools and teaching. Their Baroque **Church of the Transfiguration** (ul. Pijarska 2–4), with adjoining monastery, was designed by Kacper Bażanka in 1714–27. **Francesco Placidi**, the last and best Baroque architect in Kraków (active 1742–82), completed the project, adding the tall white façade (1761). Below the front stairs an entrance leads down to the church crypts, where exhibitions of religious sculpture are occasionally held. Above, on the stone balustrade, stands a marble bust of the Piarist monk, Stanisław Konarski, school reformer and co-author of the 3 May Constitution (1791); his heart is embedded in the south aisle wall (1882). Inside the church, notice the *trompe l'oeil* murals executed by the Moravian, Franciszek Eckstein, in 1727–33, which recall the decoration of the church of St Ignatius in Rome.

The Czartoryski Museum

The former monastery, to the east of the church, is linked to the Czartoryski Palace via a delightful covered passageway across ul. Pijarska. Together, these buildings constitute the *Czartoryski Museum (ul. Św. Jana 19), the highlight of the walk.

The history of the collection

The Czartoryski Museum, the oldest in Poland, began as the private initiative of Princess Izabela Czartoryska (1746–1835), who amassed at her home in Puławy (eastern Poland) a large collection of Polish art and memorabilia. Spurred by a Romantic interest in the past, Czartoryska sought to protect her nation's cultural heritage from plunder by the Partitioning powers, particularly Russia. Two museum pavilions were erected in the park in Puławy: the Temple of the Sybil, where items connected with Polish royalty and the struggle for independence were displayed, and the Gothic House, accommodating European art and relics. Fearing reprisals after the failed November Uprising in 1831, Czartoryska managed to secretly transport the collection to Paris, where it remained at the family's residence—the Hôtel Lambert on the Ile-Saint-Louis—for the next half century. Thanks to the efforts of her grandson, Władysław Czartoryski, the collection was enriched with the addition of ancient, medieval and early Renaissance art, Italian majolica, Meissen porcelain, and other works. In 1876 Władysław moved the collection to Kraków. He purchased the Piarists' monastery, the City Arsenal, and three other buildings on ul. Pijarska, which the French architect, Maurice Ouradou, converted into a unified museum complex (1879–84). During the Second World War, the Nazis looted the most valuable items. The greatest loss was Raphael's *Portrait of a Young Man*, possibly a self-portrait, which was never recovered.

Today, the Czartoryski Collection is a branch of the National Museum (open Tues–Fri 09.00–17.00, Sat–Sun 10.00–15.30). It occupies three buildings—the Palace, Arsenal, and 'Small Monastery' (*Klasztorek*)—and exudes the atmosphere of a 19C museum, preserving even the original French-Polish labels and oak showcases. The permanent display is accommodated on the upper floors of the palace.

First floor This floor is devoted to the history of Poland from the 14C–18C: memorabilia of the Polish Jagiellons and Vasas, portraits, including a group of ten miniatures of Zygmunt the Old's family from the workshop of Lucas Cranach the Younger, Persian and Turkish art, such as an Ottoman tent captured at Vienna in 1683, Polish scale armour, or *Karacena*, sabres belonging to Kościuszko, ceremonial shields, horse trappings and coffin portraits (c 1700). In addition there is a display of European decorative art—medieval French enamels, ivory, silverware, pottery, porcelain, a 16C Persian carpet, and an early 16C Brussels tapestry, *The Shower of Gold*.

Second floor This section accommodates a gallery of European sculpture and painting (13C–19C). Pride of place goes to **Leonardo da Vinci**'s *Lady with an Ermine* (c 1485), painted shortly after he had arrived at the court of Lodovico Moro. Other highlights include Rembrandt's *Landscape with the Good Samaritan* (1638), Alessandro Magnasco's *Temptation of Monks* and *Washerwomen*, and Vincenzo Catena's sculpture, *Madonna and Child with Saints* (1508).

Continue east along ul. Pijarska, skirting the medieval town walls and St Florian Gate (see p. 105). You will emerge onto a broad square—pl. Św. Ducha—dominated by the eclectic **Słowacki Theatre**. Named in honour of the great Romantic poet, Juliusz Słowacki, the theatre was built in 1891–93. The architect in charge, Jan Zawieyski, modelled it on the Paris Opéra, introducing a few local motifs like the parapet around the dome, whose grotesque masks echo the Cloth Hall. Impressive, if overdone, is the rich west façade decorated with groups of allegorical figures: on the right, Music, Opera and Operetta; on the left, Poetry, Drama and Comedy. At the very top stand the figures of Tadeusz and Zosia, the main protagonists of Adam Mickiewicz's (1798–1855) epic poem, *Pan Tadeusz*, about the twilight years of the Polish nobility. The highlight of the interior is the exquisite **stage curtain** painted by Henryk Siemiradzki and adorned with allegorical figures representing the arts. Before the First World War, the Słowacki rose to prominence as the leading Polish theatre, staging uncensored plays and developing a national repertoire. All the Romantic classics were premiered here, as well as contemporary plays, such as Wyspiański's *The Wedding* (1901), and even the first film show in Kraków (1896). Before the building stands a monument to the grandfather of Polish comedy, Aleksander Fredro (1793–1876).

The east side of pl. Św. Ducha encloses the irregular brick shape of the Gothic **Holy Cross Church**, its west tower and steep pointed roof forming a charming silhouette. Most impressive is the late Gothic palm vault, whose sixteen ribs spread out from a single central pillar. Notice, also, the 15C–16C murals and paintings, restored and complemented by Stanisław Wyspiański in the early 20C. The furniture is Mannerist and Baroque except for a Gothic bronze font of 1420.

You can return to Market Square along ul. Szpitalna (Hospital Street), which runs south off pl. Św. Ducha. The building at no. 21 with a Mansard roof is the 15C **House under the Cross**, the only surviving building of a former medieval hospital. Inside is a small **museum** (open Wed 11.00–18.00, Thur–Sun 09.00–15.30) devoted to the history of theatre in Kraków.

Walks beyond the Old Town

1 • Jewish Kazimierz

This walk begins south of the Market Square and explores the former Jewish town (now district) of Kazimierz, roughly delineated by the ul. Dietla to the north, ul. Starowiślna to the east, ul. Krakowska to the west, and the river to the south.

Even after its formal incorporation into the city in 1791, Kazimierz retained its distinctive character, its culture providing a sharp contrast to the splendour and pageantry of its royal neighbour—Kraków. As late as the 1930s, it was still an exotic and bustling mix of synagogues and workshops, dog markets and beggars, narrow winding lanes and alleyways; an impoverished and overpopulated world with something of the flavour of a Middle-Eastern bazaar. The war years, however, changed Kazimierz beyond recognition. Its Jewish population was entirely wiped out, and today the district is a shadow of its former self. The film show at the Ajzyk (Isaac) Synagogue (see p. 144) will give you some insight into this lost world and the tragic fate of its inhabitants.

When the ambitious renovation programme properly gets under way, Kazimierz may yet rival the Market Square as the city's main tourist attraction, but a major problem is the unknown ownership status of many of the dilapidated and disused buildings. The local authorities cannot sell off these buildings for fear that the former (pre-war) owners may suddenly appear to reclaim their property. Efforts are being made to trace former owners or their relatives in various countries around the world, but as so many disappeared or were killed during the Second World War, the authorities face an almost impossible task. The situation is set to improve after 2004, the last year for submitting legal claims to property in the district.

History of Kazimierz

Established in 1335, the town of Kazimierz was named after its founder, King Kazimierz the Great (1310–70). A spacious market square (now pl. Wolnica), almost as large as Kraków's, was laid out at the centre. The square was bisected by the main thoroughfare—ul. Krakowska—and in its northeast corner the parish church of Corpus Christi (see p. 144) was built, followed in the 15C by a town hall. Encircling the town were huge stone walls—2850m long, 1.8m thick and 4m–5m tall—interspersed with four gates and two defensive towers. A separate wall later divided Kazimierz into its Christian and Jewish parts. The town remained an island until 1878–80, when the arm of the Vistula separating it from Kraków was drained to form today's ul. Dietla. An old viaduct can still be seen at the east end of the street.

The history of Jewish Kazimierz begins in the late 15C. Following a ruling by the royal court, Kraków's Jewish population was resettled in the east part of the new town, around ul. Szeroka and pl. Nowy. Synagogues, publishing houses and a cemetery appeared. The Jewish community, headed by the Kahal, or council of elders, rapidly came to be associated with scholarship and academic excellence. It established first-rate centres of learning, notably a Talmudic school of European repute. For centuries Kazimierz retained its position as the most important cultural centre of the largest Jewish community in Poland. In 1939 there were over 45,000 people in the district who spoke Yiddish as their native language.

Begin on **ul. Szeroka**, the most famous street of Jewish Kazimierz and today the hub of social life in the district. Almost the entire east side is occupied by cafés and restaurants. Two of these (nos 17 and 18) offer Jewish cuisine in pleasant surroundings and put on evenings of Klezmer music. *Alef* (no. 17), the smaller and better establishment, also has a few guest rooms (see *Hotels*). Another option for accommodation is the newly-opened *Ester Hotel* at no. 20 (see *Hotels*), which has rooms facing the Old Synagogue (see below). Ul. Szeroka really comes alive in June, when it hosts the final concert of the Festival of Jewish Culture (see *Festivals*), attended by vast crowds.

The Old Synagogue and High Synagogue

The most important building on the street is the ***Old Synagogue** at the south end (no. 24), which houses a **museum** (open Wed–Thur, Sat–Sun 09.00–15.00, Fri 11.00–18.00) devoted to the history and culture of Kraków's Jews. It was built in Renaissance style in c 1557–70 by Matteo Gucci. The almost empty Hall of Prayer has rib vaults arising from two pillars, in clear imitation of the Staronová Synagogue in Prague. In the middle stands a small podium encircled by an exquisite *bema*, or wrought-iron grating in the shape of a cage. On the east wall, facing Jerusalem, is a 17C Ark of the Covenant bearing the scrolls of the Torah. The two remaining rooms on the ground floor are devoted to an exhibition of Jewish decorative arts. On the upper floor numerous photographs, posters and documents offer a grim reminder of the extermination of Polish Jews during the Nazi occupation, when the building was desecrated and many of its works of art looted. The original chandeliers, for example, were used to decorate the wartime residence of Hans Frank.

Old Synagogue

The alleyway by the Museum, actually an extension of ul. Józefa, leads to the dilapidated 16C **High Synagogue** (ul. Józefa 38), disused since 1939. It faces a large yellow building on ul. Wąska (nos 5–7), formerly the headquarters of the Gestapo in Kraków, which bears a plaque to the scores of victims who were tortured here.

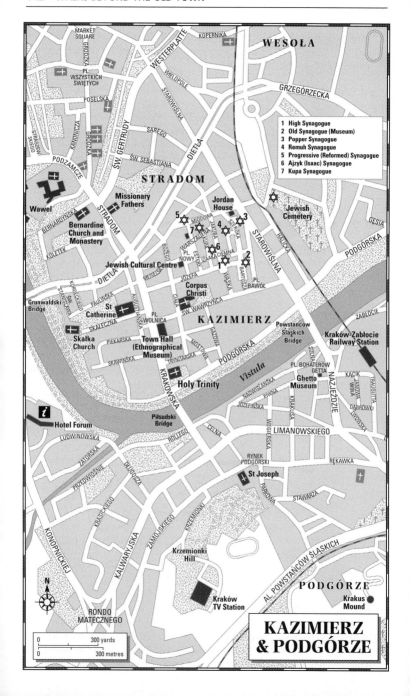

1 High Synagogue
2 Old Synagogue (Museum)
3 Popper Synagogue
4 Remuh Synagogue
5 Progressive (Reformed) Synagogue
6 Ajzyk (Isaac) Synagogue
7 Kupa Synagogue

KAZIMIERZ & PODGÓRZE

The Remuh Synagogue

Returning to the west side of ul. Szeroka, do not miss the small *Remuh Synagogue at no. 40, which continues to perform a religious function (services on Friday afternoon and Saturday morning). The curator is usually willing to show visitors around and will provide skullcaps for men wishing to enter the synagogue or adjoining cemetery. Constructed in 1553 when Israel Isserles, a trusted banker to King Zygmunt August, converted one of his properties into a house of prayer, the Remuh nevertheless came to be associated with his son, the famous scholar and philosopher Rabbi Moses Isserles (1525–72), who is buried here.

> The origins of the cemetery, which served the Jewish community until 1799, are the subject of local legend: one Friday a wedding was organised on ul. Szeroka. When dusk fell and the Sabbath was not far ahead, Rabbi Remuh called for the celebrations to be stopped. After the rabbi's third warning to the bridal couple went unheeded he cast a curse on the revellers, who immediately sank with their house into the ground. To this day, so the legend goes, the place is ringed with a wall, behind which there are a dozen or so graves.

The inscription on the rabbi's tomb reads 'From Moses [the prophet] to Moses [Isserles], there was no greater Moses'. In 1939, with war imminent, local Jews covered the rabbi's and other important tombs in the cemetery with earth. Thus concealed, the tombs managed to survive the Holocaust, and were unearthed by conservationists in the 1950s; the remainder were all destroyed by the Nazis. After the war the shattered gravestones were cobbled together to form a Wailing Wall.

The modern building next door to the Remuh synagogue (no. 39) was renovated in the early 1990s by US-based Nissenbaum Foundation and on the first floor houses the only kosher restaurant in Kraków—*Na Kazimierzu* (see *Restaurants*), set in a rather characterless interior.

Across the street at no. 16, concealed behind trees and an iron gate, stands the early 17C **Popper Synagogue**, today housing an art studio. Of more interest is the **Jordan House** (no. 2), which closes the north end of ul. Szeroka. The building dates from the 16C and according to legend is a remnant of Kazimierz the Great's efforts to set up a university in the district. Inside is the small *Jarden* bookshop (Jewish culture and history) and adjoining *Arka Noego* café with elegant, pre-war furniture.

From the north end of ul. Szeroka you could make a short detour to a more recent but no less fascinating **Jewish Cemetery**, actually outside Kazimierz proper. Go right along ul. Miodowa, across ul. Starowiślna and walk under the rail bridge. This peaceful and secluded spot with its beautiful gravestones and tree-lined alleys makes for a delightful afternoon walk. If the gates are locked, enter the building at no. 55: the back entrance leads conveniently onto the cemetery.

The Progressive, Kupa and Ajzyk Synagogues

Returning along ul. Miodowa you will come to the **Progressive (Reformed) Synagogue** (no. 24), so-called because services were given here in Polish and German as well as Hebrew. Built in 1862, it is a venue for organ concerts and religious ceremonies attended by Jews from all over the world.

Two more synagogues are hidden in the maze of streets directly south. Turn left into ul. Estery and left again at the first junction (ul. Warszauera) to get to the derelict **Kupa Synagogue** (no. 8), so named because it was financed with Kahal funds (*kupa*—purse). Here too is a stretch of medieval town wall (another fragment runs along ul. Paulińska). Straight down ul. Kupa, at the intersection with ul. Izaaka, is the more interesting **Ajzyk (Isaac) Synagogue** (no. 16), an early Baroque building of 1640. Thanks largely to the efforts of its curator, Dominik Dybek, the synagogue has been thoroughly renovated to reveal Giovanni Battista Falconi's original stucco decoration. The former gallery for women, located on the first floor, is separated from the main room by an ornamental wooden wall with five arcades. Most interesting is the continuous film show, based on German archive footage, which traces the life of Kraków's Jews before the Second World War.

Ul. Izaaka opens out onto pl. Nowy, a square devoid of historic buildings but at weekends occupied by a fruit and vegetable market around the circular abattoir in the middle. Stop in for refreshments at the *Singer* (see *Late-night bars and clubs*), which faces the square at ul. Estery 20, or walk up ul. Meiselsa to the **Jewish Cultural Centre** (no. 17), which has a café in more sterile surroundings, as well as gallery and cinema. The next junction is ul. Bożego Ciała. Turning left you reach pl. Wolnica, where the next walk begins.

2 • Christian Kazimierz

The Christian half of Kazimierz occupies the area roughly to the west of ul. Bożego Ciała. It perhaps lacks the distinctive ambience of the neighbouring Jewish quarter, but is well worth visiting on account of its two medieval **churches of St Catherine** and **Corpus Christi**. These magnificent buildings, their lofty spires visible from afar, were raised in the 14C–15C, in part as an attempt to convert the city's Jews. Equally interesting is the **Skałka church** by the riverside, associated with the cult of St Stanisław, where many famous Poles are buried. A tour of all the sites will probably take no longer than a couple of hours. If you want to finish off with a meal, the *Thien Long* (Chinese) and *Ganges* (Indian) are conveniently located, but in truth the area is rather short on good places to eat: either return to ul. Szeroka in Jewish Kazimierz, or head north to ul. Stradom, in the vicinity of which is the excellent *Chłopskie Jadło* (see *Restaurants*).

Corpus Christi Church

You will probably approach pl. Wolnica along ul. Bożego Ciała or ul. Św. Wawrzyńca. At the junction of these two streets rises the imposing *Corpus Christi Church, set amongst greenery behind a high stone wall. It was one of the first churches in Kraków to achieve truly late Gothic proportions, with the nave more than twice as high as it is broad, and the external buttresses of the long aisleless chancel and apse further emphasising the height. The oldest parts visible today are the late Gothic nave vault and pretty pinnacled west gable (c 1500). The northeast tower, dating from 1566–82, is topped with a Baroque crowning. Skirting the wall anti-clockwise you will pass under a huge arcade on which rests a covered passageway linking the church with the adjoining monastery. Further on, near the main entrance, is the only remnant of the former graveyard—the Chapel of Gethsemane, enclosed by an iron grating, containing a number of late Gothic and Baroque wooden sculptures.

The magnificently gilded **interior** of the church juxtaposes severe Gothic architecture with exceptionally rich wood carving. Of particular interest are the lavishly decorated stalls of 1624–32 and the **pulpit** shaped in the form of a boat with a mast and oars, supported by two mermaids. The huge high altar, completed in 1634, contains two paintings—*Nativity* and *Descent from the Cross*—attributed to Tomaso Dolabella. The other, predominantly Rococo, altars bear fine sculpted figures, probably designed by Anton Gegenpauer. Of the many 17C paintings in the chancel and aisles, those near the Renaissance memorial slab of Bartolomeo Berrecci (c 1480–1537) in the Chapel of St Anne, merit special attention.

Pl. Wolnica is dominated by the 14C–16C Renaissance **Town Hall**, with an octagonal tower and crenellated attic. The building was extensively altered in the 19C and turned into a Jewish school. Since 1947 it has housed the **Ethnographical Museum** (open Mon 10.00–18.00, Wed–Fri 10.00–15.00, Sat–Sun 10.00–14.00) containing a rich collection of folk art, particularly from the south of Poland.

Walking down ul. Krakowska towards the Piłsudski bridge you will notice the distant outline of the Kraków TV tower. The Ethnographical Museum has a tiny **exhibition centre** at no. 46 (open Mon–Fri 09.00–15.00), but of greater interest is the **Church of the Holy Trinity**, further down on the left. Constructed in 1752–58 for the Trinitarians, this is Francesco Placidi's Cracovian showpiece, surpassing even his Piarist church on ul. Św. Jana (see p. 138). Most impressive is the façade, replete with recesses and projections, echoing Chiaveri's Hofkirche in Dresden. The pediment over the west entrance is turned outwards with the broken ends projecting forward on pilasters. Above it, the top tier of the 'tower' has two long concave sides framed by columns and two short convex ones. The modest interior has a fine vault mural (c 1750) depicting the ransoming of prisoners captured by the Turks.

Returning north along ul. Krakowska, you should not miss the area enclosed by ul. Paulińska, ul. Augustiańska and ul. Skałeczna, home to the lush, but inaccessible gardens of the Augustinian monastery (ul. Augustiańska 9), bordered by a high limestone wall. Overlooking the gardens is the Church of St Catherine, the purest example of Cracovian Gothic.

Church of St Catherine

The *Church of St Catherine was a gift from Kazimierz the Great to the Augustinian Order, brought from Prague in 1343. First to go up was the chancel, completed in 1378, followed by the main body (1426). The oldest extant vaults, designed by Master Hanusz (1503–05), are in the chancel, whose external buttresses are topped with intricate stone pinnacles. The towerless west façade faces the monastery gardens, so you enter the church from the north aisle or through the cross-vaulted cloisters.

Tall and empty, the plan of the **interior** is very similar to that of the Corpus Christi church (see p. 144). The rectangular chapel in the southwest corner, its magnificent vault resting on a single pillar, is known as the Hungarian Chapel after its founder, the Palatine Ścibor, a condottiere in the Hungarian army. Built in 1402–14, it is still used by the Augustinian nuns and is connected to their convent by an arch which crosses ul. Skałeczna. Especially fine is the church's south porch, with its rich portal, pinnacles, and sumptuous stone detailing (1430). Notice, also, the large Mannerist high altar of 1636 with a painting of the mystical wedding of St Catherine (1674). In the south aisle stands the fine tomb of the magnate Spytek Jordan (1600), a vigorous patron of the arts whom Vasari referred to as '*il grandissimo signore in Polonia*'. A rustic belfry with a wooden roof (15C) stands in the church grounds.

The adjoining monastery (south) has beautiful **cloisters** (1378) with elaborate piers and recently discovered medieval murals. At their east end is the Gothic Chapel of St Thomas, currently the sacristy. The vault, again resting on a single pillar, has the name of Kazymirus (Kazimierz the Great) emblazoned on the bosses. Here, too, you will find the impressive Chapel of St Dorothy (the former chapter house), its vault carried on two slender pillars.

Ul. Skałeczna, one of the city's most picturesque streets, terminates at an elaborate wrought-iron gate. Walking down, parallel to the monastery's garden wall, you will notice in the distance the silhouette of the Church of St Michael the Archangel and St Stanisław, commonly known as the 'Skałka' church after the hillock of Jurassic limestone (skałka) on which it stands.

Skałka Church

The original Romanesque rotunda was replaced with a twin-towered Gothic church in the 13C. Some 500 years later, the Pauline monks, influenced by the cult of St Stanisław (see below), built an adjoining monastery and in 1733 commissioned Georg Müntzer to redesign the *church in Baroque style. The final version was completed by Antoni Solari in 1740–42.

The **interior** has some fine 18C stucco decoration and sculpture, but the main attraction, situated below the entrance stairs, is the **Crypt of Honour**. This national pantheon was built in 1880 to commemorate the 400th anniversary of the death of Jan Długosz (1415–80), whose ashes were the first to be moved to the crypt. Other famous names at rest here include the painter and playwright Stanisław Wyspiański (see p. 116), the novelist Józef Ignacy Kraszewski, the composer Karol Szymanowski, and the painters Henryk Siemiradzki (see p. 139) and Jacek Malczewski (see p. 91).

History of the Skałka Church

The history of the church is interwoven with the legendary struggle between secular and ecclesiastical power, represented respectively by King Bolesław the Bold (c 1040–81) and Stanisław Szczepanowski, Bishop of Kraków (c 1030–79). In 1079 the bishop was accused of treason and executed—according to legend, in the 'Skałka' church, later to become the centre of his cult. He was recognised as a saint and canonised by Pope Innocent IV at Assisi in 1253 and his remains are now kept in Wawel Cathedral. Significantly, the crowning of Polish kings took place in front of the bishop's tomb in the cathedral (see p. 121). The ceremony included a penitent pilgrimage to the 'Skałka' church, which each king would perform on the day before his coronation. Nowadays the tradition is observed each year on 8 May, when a reliquary containing the bishop's remains is ceremoniously brought from the cathedral to the 'Skałka' church where he was killed (see *Festivals*). The bishop's decapitated corpse is said to have been cast into the pool outside, since known as the Stoup of Poland. A statue of St Stanisław stands on a plinth in the middle, surrounded by water. Silver eagles on obelisks—guardians of the bishop's remains—adorn the four corners.

You can leave the site through the gate by the north side of the monastery, which brings you onto the banks of the Vistula. Crossing over the Grunwaldzki bridge, you may want to get a bird's eye view of the area. For this purpose *Hotel Forum*, a monstrous vestige of 1970s planning, is excellently suited; the appropriately named *Panorama* café at the top offers a splendid view over Wawel Castle, Kazimierz and its environs.

3 • Podgórze

Facing Kazimierz on the south bank of the Vistula is the district of Podgórze, which lies at the foot of a wooded hill known as Krzemionki. The hill is occupied in its northern part by the Kraków TV station and surrounding park, and in its southern part, beyond al. Powstańców Śląskich, by a large cemetery, allotments, and the mysterious **Krakus Mound** (16m). The origins of the mound have been traced to the 8C and it is said to contain the grave of Krak, the legendary founder of the city that bears his name. A popular church fair known as 'Rękawka' (sleeve)—so-called because the locals who raised the mound carried earth up the hill in their sleeves—is held here on the first Tuesday after Easter.

During the 19C Podgórze developed as an Austrian town (Josephstadt), primarily noted for its industry, but always eclipsed by its richer neighbour, Kraków, to which it was joined in 1915. This partly explains the absence of historic buildings, though the Austrians did leave a number of 19C houses on ul. Limanowskiego and ul. Józefińska, and the large neo-Gothic **Church of St Joseph** (1909) on the main square—Rynek Podgórski. By far the most interesting aspect of Podgórze, however, is its association with the fate of Kraków's Jews during the Second World War. Their story is told in Thomas Keneally's novel *Schindler's Ark*, filmed by Steven Spielberg in the original Kraków setting. Some of the city tourist agencies still run a 'Schindler's List' tour, which takes you round the original sites, as well as those recreated for the purposes of the film. Schindler's factory was located on ul. Lipowa near Kraków Zabłocie station.

Jewish Podgórze

The war years were a catastrophic turning point in the history of Kraków's Jews. In 1941, the Nazis set up a new 'Jewish District' in Podgórze, into which Jews from Kazimierz and other areas of Kraków were moved. The ghetto was delineated by today's Rynek Podgórski, pl. Bohaterów Getta, and the intersection of ul. Limanowskiego and ul. Wielicka. Enclosed by a ring of walls and barbed wire, nearly 17,000 people were crammed into the ramshackle buildings. In 1942, the inmates were systematically moved out to a new concentration camp erected in nearby Płaszów, after which the ghetto was liquidated (13 March 1943). Escape from the Płaszów camp was virtually impossible. The fifty wooden barracks, symbolically erected on the site of two Jewish cemeteries, were guarded by electric fences, ditches, dogs and watchtowers. Between 1942 and liberation in 1945, Płaszów housed approximately 150,000 inmates; most perished. The Camp Kommandant, Amon Leopold Göth, was found guilty of crimes against humanity and executed in Kraków in 1946.

Today, there are few visible remnants of Jewish Podgórze. During the war, pl. Zgody (pl. Bohaterów Getta) was the most gruesome and feared area of the ghetto. It was here that Jews were selected for execution or transportation to the concentration camps. Today, the square is dominated by the ugly mass of tinted glass that is the BPH Bank building. The house at **no. 6**, now a mini-market, bears a plaque commemorating the Jewish Resistance Organisation, which had its headquarters here in 1942–43. **No. 18** was formerly a pharmacy, whose Polish owner, Tadeusz Pankiewicz, received permission from the Nazi authorities to do business here. It was chiefly through Pankiewicz and his staff that food, medicine, false documents, and other kinds of aid were brought in from outside. In 1983 the house was converted into a **museum** (open Mon–Fri 10.00–16.00, Sat 10.00–14.00) documenting life in the ghetto.

4 • Along the Vistula

This walk begins by Wawel at the intersection of ul. Bernardyńska and ul. Stradom. You first visit a couple of churches (the Bernardines' and Missionary Fathers'), before crossing the river to see the Manggha Centre of Japanese Art and Technology. It is best to do this walk on a sunny day, when you can stroll along the riverside, getting a good view of Wawel Castle and the Kraków skyline.

Nestling at the junction is the **Bernardine Church**. Its ivy-clad façade, with two modest octagonal towers and niches filled with saints, bears some resemblance to SS Peter and Paul's on ul. Grodzka (see p. 112). The church dome was set below the roof, apparently to widen the firing range from the battlements of Wawel.

The once-wooden church was rebuilt in stone in 1455. Five years earlier, royal emissaries had brought from the Silesian town of Wrocław the renowned Italian preacher, Giovanni Capistrano. A hundred or so of Capistrano's devotees established the Order of the Observers of the Rule of St Francis in 1453, popularly known as the Bernardines. Their church was destroyed during the Swedish siege of Wawel in 1655 and later rebuilt in Baroque style (1670–80).

Furnished in stages during the 17C–18C, the **interior** includes a sculpture of the *Virgin and Child with St Anne*, ascribed to one of Veit Stoss's pupils, found in the Chapel of St Anne at the east end of the north aisle. The highlight, however, also in the chapel, is a 17C oil painting of the *Dance of Death*, in which skeletons are shown dancing with elegant courtiers, while Death looks on and invites members of the four estates (clergy, nobility, bourgeoisie, peasantry) to take part. Around the scene are rhymes—full of black humour—reminding us that, in the end, no one can escape the terrible dance. The sacristy contains the reliquary of the Blessed Szymon of Lipnica, whose marble tomb, sporting a reclining figure, stands in a south aisle chapel parallel to the chancel. Huge *Passion* paintings by the Bernardine monk Franciszek Lekszycki (d. 1668), based on etchings by Rubens and Van Dyck, fill the aisles.

Originally a paved road leading across marshland to the Old Vistula bridge, **ul.**

Stradom benefited from its location on the main trade route to the south of Poland, gradually acquiring inns, bath-houses and a customs house. The newly-weds Honoré de Balzac and Ewelina Hańska stopped at the *White Rose Hotel* (no. 13; no longer extant) in 1850. The street is now the main thoroughfare linking the city centre with the Kazimierz district (walks 1 and 2, *Beyond the Old Town*).

A short way down on the left is the ***Church of the Missionary Fathers** (no. 4), considered to be one of the finest examples of late Baroque architecture in the city. Brought to Poland in 1651, the Missionary Fathers found their way to Kraków a year later. A small monastery soon appeared, bordered by a beautiful formal garden, which has survived to the present day (often inaccessible). The church, completed in 1719–32, was designed by **Kacper Bażanka**, whose Roman education no doubt inspired him to base the façade (unfinished) on Bernini's Sant' Andrea al Quirinale. Above the entrance is a protruding semi-circular portico resting on columns, itself encased in a monumental aedicule composed of colossal order pilasters and crowned by a triangular pediment. The **interior** is modelled on the Chapel of the Magi in Borromini's Collegio di Propaganda Fide in Rome. Tadeusz Konicz, who, like Bażanka, drew his inspiration from Roman art, executed the painting at the high altar, as well as others around the church.

Backtrack to the junction and proceed down ul. Bernardyńska, which brings you to the riverside. A short distance to the right, by the castle walls, is the entrance to the *Smocza Jama*, or **Dragon's Cave**, a children's attraction of the pre-virtual reality age. According to legend, the grotto was once inhabited by a ferocious maiden-eating dragon, who died of poisoning after a cobbler's apprentice had treacherously fed him a sulphur-stuffed sheep. Another version attributes the death to excessive drinking, with the dragon attempting to quell the fire in his belly by consuming vast amounts of water from the Vistula (these days a few pints would be lethal!). The copper effigy of the dragon, which occasionally breathes fire (gas flame), was designed by Bronisław Chromy. Feel free to enter the cave (open 10.00–17.00, summer only), but there is nothing to see inside.

For a more rewarding experience you could visit the **Manggha Centre of Japanese Art and Technology** (open Tues–Sun 10.00–18.00) visible across the river at ul. Konopnickiej 26. To get there, backtrack along the riverside and cross the Grunwaldzki bridge. The impressive modern building was designed by the outstanding Japanese architect Arata Isozaki, and funded by Polish film director Andrzej Wajda (see below), whose work is particularly admired in Japan. The Centre puts on frequent concerts and cultural events, but at other times you should not miss the unique collection of Japanese art, comprising some excellent 18C woodcuts, Samurai weaponry, porcelain and jewellery. The collection was assembled by Feliks Jasieński (1861–1929), a writer and intrepid explorer, nick-named 'Manggha' after his passion for the culture of the Orient. Jasieński described his travels in the Far East in his magnum opus—*Manggha. Promenades à travers le monde, l'art et les idées*—and he is credited as the first person to bring Japanese, Hindu and Persian culture to Poland. Familiarising the hostile, turn-of-the-century Polish public with Oriental culture became something of a lifetime mission for Jasieński. 'I have shown you Japan,' he wrote in a letter to a friend, 'so that you can learn to think about Poland in the same way as those artists who thought for two millennia about Japan in Japanese terms'.

Andrzej Wajda

Andrzej Wajda, regarded by many as the greatest Polish film director, was born in 1926 in Suwałki, northeast Poland. After the Second World War, he studied painting at the Academy of Fine Arts (see p. 83) in Kraków, a city with which he has maintained strong connections throughout his life. Like his friend and fellow film-director Roman Polański, Wajda graduated from the famous Łódź Film Academy in the 1950s, becoming one of the leading figures of the 'Polish School', which produced some of the best films ever made in the country. In *Pokolenie* (*A Generation*, 1954), *Kanał* (*Canal*, 1957), *Popiół i diament* (*Ashes and Diamonds*, 1958) and *Lotna* (1959) Wajda explored the devastating effect of the Second World War on the minds of young Poles and laid bare the Polish myth of heroism inherited from the Romantic tradition. The recurring motif of the white horse in Wajda's films evokes a world of traditional values destroyed by war.

Wajda achieved great success with his film adaptations of Polish literary classics: Stefan Żeromski's *Popioły* (*Ashes*, 1965), Jarosław Iwaszkiewicz's *Brzezina* (*The Birch-wood*, 1970), Stanisław Wyspiański's *Wesele* (*The Wedding*, 1972) and Władysław Reymont's *Ziemia Obiecana* (*Promised Land*, 1974), all artistically sophisticated and superbly performed. *Promised Land* and *Panny z Wilka* (*The Girls From Wilko*, 1979) were nominated for Oscars in the 'best foreign film' category.

In the 1970s and 1980s, Wajda's films became increasingly concerned with contemporary social and political issues. The groundbreaking *Człowiek z Marmuru* (*Man of Marble*, 1976) and the French-made *Danton* (1982) condemned the excesses of totalitarianism and examined the loneliness of the individual in the face of historical change. *Man of Marble* was an overt record of the social ferment that culminated in the emergence of the Solidarity movement, but even *Danton*, ostensibly about the French revolution, was full of penetrating references to Poland's past and present. *Człowiek z Żelaza* (*Man of Iron*), made in 1981, was nominated for an Oscar and won the *Palme d'Or* at the Cannes film festival, establishing Wajda as a director of international repute. The film specifically addressed the political changes occurring in Poland and the great hopes vested in the birth of Solidarity. Subsequently persecuted by the communist authorities, Wajda moved abroad, but in Western Europe he rarely managed to repeat the spectacular success of his earlier work.

For over 30 years Wajda's films had a huge impact on the Polish national consciousness, yet his near-prophetic role during the communist period inevitably changed with the commercialisation of the Polish film industry in the 1990s. Politics now ceased to be a burning issue, and in the absence of state censorship metaphorical language was no longer so poignant. As a result, Wajda's output became increasingly out of touch with the cinema-going public. Bizarre experiments such as *Nastazja Filipowna*, an avant-garde version of Dostoyevski's *The Idiot* performed in Japanese, or his adaptation of the teenage bestseller *Panna Nikt* (*Miss Nobody*), were not well received. However, in 1999, Wajda confounded his critics with an excellent film adaptation of Adam Mickiewicz's epic poem *Pan Tadeusz*, one of the great classics of Romantic literature.

5 • East of the Market Square ~ ul. Kopernika

This short walk takes you east of the Market Square to the former suburb of Wesoła, which begins just the other side of the *Planty*. Founded in 1639 by Katarzyna Zamoyska, Wesoła was originally composed of palaces, mansions and gardens, the best ones lining its main axis—ul. Kopernika. In 1780–88, the Discalced Carmelites' Monastery at no. 19 was converted into the St Lazarus General Hospital, the first of its kind in Poland. This marked the beginning of a trend which saw Wesoła evolve into the main hospital district of Kraków, and today ul. Kopernika is where the clinics and administrative buildings of the city's Medical Academy are based. Walking up the pleasant, tree-lined street, you will also pass four churches of note: **St Nicholas's** (no. 9, right), Baroque, 1656–84 (originally Romanesque, 12C), with a solitary Gothic column in the churchyard, brought here from a hospital set up for the victims of leprosy, and inside—a beautiful 15C polyptych; the **Jesuit Church**, 1909–21 (left past the railway bridge), with impressive modern sculptures by Xawery Dunikowski (1875–1964) and a huge slender brick tower; the **Church of the Immaculate Conception** (no. 19), early Baroque, 1634–80 (next to the former hospital of St. Lazarus); and **St Theresa's**, 1720–32, designed on a cruciform plan, which stands behind a wall on the left, next to the **Discalced Carmelites' Convent** (no. 44). The street's highlight is the small but well-managed **Botanical Garden** at no. 27 (open Sat–Thur 09.00–19.00; greenhouses 10.00–13.00), with a wide variety of Central European and tropical plants and a 500-year old oak. Just before it is a former astronomical observatory (1784–88), one of the few examples of Neo-classical architecture in the city, today housing a small **Botanical Museum** (open 09.00–16.00 Sun only).

6 • Nowa Huta

Ten kilometres east of the city centre lies **Nowa Huta** (New Steelworks), the largest district in Kraków, with a population of 220,000. Its main 'attraction' is the massive Sendzimir (formerly Lenin) Steelworks, a fully-preserved Stalinist monolith of the type that is thankfully fast disappearing in Eastern Europe. Of interest, too, is the urban layout of the district, formerly a town in its own right (until 1951) and the first to be built in post-war Poland.

• **Transport** Unless you only want to visit some of the sites, Nowa Huta is best visited by car. The main square—pl. Centralny—can be reached by tram nos 4, 15 and 22, or by bus nos 502 and 511 from the main railway station.

History of Nowa Huta

The origins of Nowa Huta should be sought in the uneasy relationship between Kraków and the post-war communist state. Unlike so many other Polish cities, Kraków survived the war years physically intact and its population suffered little displacement. Moreover, it entered the new era as Poland's leading cultural centre, a status it had retained for centuries. These two facts spelt danger to the communist authorities, who saw Kraków as a hotbed of bourgeois values and reaction. Consequently, it was felt that the ancient royal capital had to be symbolically punished, its conservative, largely Catholic intelligentsia 'proletarianised' and thus rendered harmless, or so it was hoped. To this end, in 1949, the decision was taken to build a huge iron and steel works, serviced by a model 'workers' town', on the periphery of the city. A site was chosen on open fields between the villages of Mogiła, Krzesławice, Bieńczyce and Łęg. The fact that this spot was far away from natural resources and adequate supplies of water, and that Kraków lies in a valley, had no impact at all on the choice of location. Ideological concerns were paramount, and the consequences were predictably disastrous, not least for the proletariat, who had to suffer decades of illness and disease caused by the noxious fumes. The construction of the Lenin Steelworks began in 1951. At its completion four years later it was the largest steelworks in Poland. By 1976, its 37,000 staff were producing on average 6.5 million tons of iron and steel per year. Yet the communists' plans for bourgeois Kraków backfired somewhat when, in the 1980s, Nowa Huta became a stronghold of the Solidarity movement.

'Colourful housing estates set amongst greenery and flowers, modern blocks of flats, market pavilions, an abundance of happy young people on the streets' is how a 1978 Polish guide book to Kraków describes the district of Nowa Huta. Today, the impression one gets of this showpiece of Stalinist planning is rather different. The 'model' housing estates—grey, uniform, run down—still carry names redolent of the past, in some cases sounding almost as if they were borrowed from Orwell's novel, *1984*: the Estate of Youth, the Estate of Peace, the Estate of Enlightenment. For decades, the black smoke billowing from the chimneys of the steelworks did untold damage to Kraków's architectural heritage; more importantly, pollution was a major cause of death and disease among the city's inhabitants. There exists no more poignant reminder of the scale of the problem than the steelworkers' cemetery in the shadow of the rolling mill: looking at the dates on the graves one sees that very few of the workers buried there made it to old age. The environmental situation has greatly improved in recent years with the most polluting sections of Nowa Huta being closed down, but this, in turn, has caused new social problems in the form of poverty and unemployment. Frustrated also by the lack of civic amenities, many young people have turned to violence and petty crime. Unless you know your way around, Nowa Huta is not the place to be after dark.

Your walk begins at pl. Centralny, from which the main thoroughfares of the district fan out in all directions.

Going north along al. Róż you pass the spot where there once stood (until 1990) a giant statue of Lenin. Many demonstrations against the communist regime took place here. In the late 1970s, a small explosive charge ripped off Lenin's heel. The statue was speedily repaired, which gave rise to the joke: 'Lenin tried to take a Great Leap Forward, but they welded him back into place'.

Turning left off al. Róż into ul. Żeromskiego you reach the **People's Theatre** (*Teatr Ludowy*, Os. Teatralne 34), a grim example of 1950s architecture. The first performance staged here (1955) was Wojciech Bogusławski's (1757–1829) *Cracovians and Highlanders*, a comic opera set in the nearby village (now suburb) of Mogiła. In the 1990s, the theatre put on a series of highly acclaimed performances involving a local neighbourhood cast.

The construction of new churches in Nowa Huta was forbidden for many years as

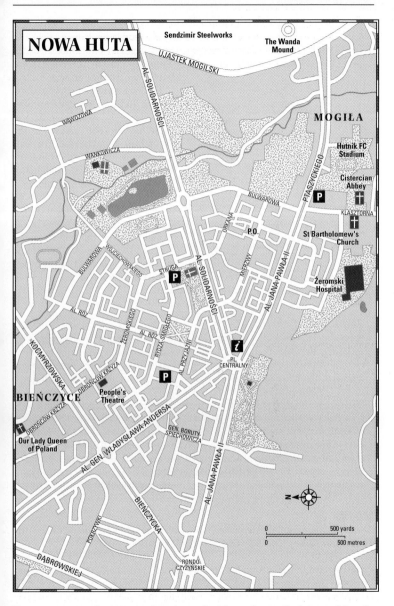

NOWA HUTA

Sendzimir Steelworks

The Wanda Mound

UJASTEK MOGILSKI

AL. SOLIDARNOŚCI

WAWOZOWA

WANKOWICZA

MOGIŁA

Hutnik FC Stadium

PTASZYCKIEGO

Cistercian Abbey

KLASZTORNA

BULWAROWA

ORKANA

P.O.

St Bartholomew's Church

BULWAROWA

WOJCIECHOWSKIEGO

STRUGA

AL. SOLIDARNOŚCI

MIERZWY

AL. JANA PAWŁA II

Żeromski Hospital

AL. RÓŻ

ŻEROMSKIEGO

AL. RÓŻ

RYDZA-ŚMIGŁEGO

AL. PRZYJAZNI

PL CENTRALNY

KOCMYRZOWSKA

OBROŃCÓW KRZYŻA

People's Theatre

BIEŃCZYCE

OBROŃCÓW KRZYŻA

Our Lady Queen of Poland

AL. GEN. WŁADYSŁAWA ANDERSA

GEN. BORUTY SPIECHOWICZA

AL. JANA PAWŁA II

N

BIEŃCZYCKA

500 yards

0

0

500 metres

POKRZYWKI

DĄBROWSKIEJ

RONDO CZYŻYŃSKIE

the communist authorities sought to prove that the proletariat had no need for religion. Needless to say, the ban led to numerous riots and demonstrations, with especially fierce street battles taking place in November 1982. In the spate of building that followed the lifting of the ban, the **Our Lady Queen of Poland Church**, further north along ul. Obrońców Krzyża in the district of Bieńczyce, stands out for its

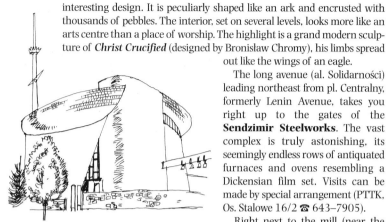

interesting design. It is peculiarly shaped like an ark and encrusted with thousands of pebbles. The interior, set on several levels, looks more like an arts centre than a place of worship. The highlight is a grand modern sculpture of *Christ Crucified* (designed by Bronisław Chromy), his limbs spread out like the wings of an eagle.

The long avenue (al. Solidarności) leading northeast from pl. Centralny, formerly Lenin Avenue, takes you right up to the gates of the **Sendzimir Steelworks**. The vast complex is truly astonishing, its seemingly endless rows of antiquated furnaces and ovens resembling a Dickensian film set. Visits can be made by special arrangement (PTTK, Os. Stalowe 16/2 ☎ 643–7905).

Our Lady Queen of Poland, Nowa Huta

Right next to the mill (near the junction of ul. Ujastek Mogilski and ul. Ptaszyckiego), amid tramlines and shrubbery, is a more ancient site—the prehistoric **Wanda Mound**, one of four in the city, whose origins are enshrined in popular myth.

The Myth of Wanda

Following the death of her father, Krakus (the legendary founder of Kraków), Princess Wanda was subjected to incessant courtship by the German Prince Rytygier (Rytogar). Repelled by this Teutonic upstart but fearful of forfeiting her lands (Rytygier threatened to invade if she did not marry), Wanda threw herself into the Vistula to avoid an even more terrible fate. She was buried close to the spot where she drowned. Local people covered her tomb with a mound of earth, known till this day as the Wanda Mound. In deference to tradition, each year on the Feast of Wanda young men are entitled to hurl into the Vistula all unsuspecting women so-named.

On top of the mound (14 m), until 1970 enclosed by Austrian fortifications, is a small marble monument, designed by Jan Matejko (see p. 92). The emblem of Princess Wanda is inscribed on the marble block in bas-relief.

Mogiła

Returning along ul. Ptaszyckiego, turn left into ul. Klasztorna to see the **Cistercian Abbey** (Opactwo Cystersów) in Mogiła.

Bishop Iwo Odrowąż founded the abbey in 1225 for the Cistercians, who settled in the village of Mogiła. Their church of St Wenceslaus, an early Gothic basilica on a Latin cross plan, went up in c 1266, remaining largely unchanged until the late 18C, when it was rebuilt in Baroque style and received a new façade. A 13C miniature arcaded frieze and three pointed arch windows have been preserved at the east end (visible from the garden).

The Baroque west front of the church masks some fine 13C stone detailing within, notably sculpted early Gothic bosses in the aisle vaults. The chancel, unusually flanked on one side by a pair of chapels, features a late Gothic polyptych of 1514 which serves as the high altar. Highlights include the Renaissance **murals** in the transept and chancel, executed in the early 16C by Stanisław Samostrzelnik, a monk at the abbey and also a talented artist, who did a number of royal prayer books and miniatures. A 13C portal (often closed) in the south aisle leads through to the cross-vaulted 14C cloisters, where Gothic and Renaissance tombstones are embedded in the walls. Here, and in the library (c 1533), are more murals by Samostrzelnik, notably his monumental *Crucifixion* of 1538, now looking very time-worn. The library itself (ask the porter for permission to enter) contains over 15,000 documents amassed by the Cistercians over the centuries. In the oldest, east wing there is an early Gothic chapter house (late 13C). From the cloisters you may enter the pleasant monastery garden.

Opposite the abbey, hidden among trees, is the small **parish church of St Bartholomew** (Kościół Św. Bartłomieja), an early and very well-preserved example of Polish wooden architecture. It was built in 1466 by the royal carpenter Maciej Mączka. Of note inside is a Gothic portal, carved in wood and bearing Mączka's signature, as well as Rococo murals. Above the entrance gate rises a domed belfry.

St Bartholomew's church, Mogiła

7 • The Rakowicki Cemetery

A pleasant afternoon may be spent at the extensive Rakowicki Cemetery, situated to the north of the Old Town. The first plots appeared in 1802. Over the next two centuries the Rakowicki became the city's most elite cemetery, where today many famous Cracovians are buried (al. 29 Listopada; bus nos 105 or 129 from the main railway station).

The broad central alleyway, which begins near the chapel, is lined with many 19C–20C graves, some plain and unpretentious, others very grand and ornate, such as the Neo-classical sepulchral monument to Jan Matejko (see p. 92).

To the right of the main entrance you reach the Lane of Honour, containing the graves of people honoured by the communist state: workers, party officials, militiamen etc. To the northeast is the adjoining Military Cemetery, with the graves of soldiers who died during the First and Second World Wars, and a separate section for British RAF pilots.

Visiting the Rakowicki Cemetery on All Saints' Day and All Souls' Day (1–2 November) is an unforgettable experience. On these public holidays Poles traditionally turn out *en masse* to pay their respects to the dead. Relatives meticulously tidy the graves of their loved ones, forgotten tombs are suddenly lavished with an abundance of flowers, and crowds wander the alleyways bathed in the light of a million candles.

8 • The New University Quarter

During the 20C the University expanded beyond the perimeter of the *Planty* and the Old Town. New buildings, departments and halls of residence sprang up in the 1960s in the west and northwest areas of the city. While these are of little interest, the slightly older university complex (1930s) along al. Mickiewicza is well worth a visit.

Begin at Collegium Novum (see p. 133) and head down ul. Piłsudskiego in the direction of the Kościuszko Mound (see p. 158), visible in the far distance. By the junction with ul. Retoryka, you pass a group of impressive Historicist buildings designed by Teodor Talowski (1857–1910), the most prominent architect of late 19C Kraków. The large red brick building on the corner (no. 1) is adorned with wavy masonry ornamentation and is called the '**Singing Frog House**' after the figure of a mandolin-playing frog placed on one of the window sills.

Cross the busy thoroughfare—al. Krasińskiego—to the *Cracovia Hotel*. Stretching out before you is a huge expanse of greenery known as the **Błonia** (48ha). From the 15C it served as the city common, and even today, farmers from the outlying villages retain the ancient right to graze their cattle here (and sometimes do). Due to its sheer size, the Błonia is often a venue for large-scale ceremonies: in 1979 a staggering two million turned out to see John Paul II on his first visit to Poland. The first football matches in Kraków were played on the Błonia—the local clubs, Cracovia and Wisła, have their stadiums close by.

At the edge of the common, across from the hotel, stands a branch of the **National Museum** known as the 'New Building' (open Tues, Thur–Sun 10.00–15.30, Wed 10.00–18.00), with a display of painting and sculpture from the 'Young Poland' period. There is a particularly rich collection of works by Wyspiański (see p. 116), including his stained-glass designs for Wawel Cathedral (never executed) and numerous portraits. This is followed by 20C art and sculpture, including some fine abstract pieces, and finally post-war Polish art.

The building dates from the 1930s, when classicism was still the prevailing architectural style. There are other fine examples from the period further to the north: the **Jagiellonian Library** and the **Academy of Mining and Metallurgy**, the latter with two statues of brawny workers flanking the entrance. These magnificent buildings, both designed by Wacław Krzyżanowski, form part of the new university quarter, which emerged in the 1930s along al. Mickiewicza. In terms of standards of workmanship and the quality of building materials used, they stand out from the many post-war University buildings nearby.

9 • Salwator, the Kościuszko Mound and Przegorzały

Salwator, in the west part of Kraków, rivals Wola Justowska as the city's richest and most exclusive suburb. It borders an area of fields and woodland, ideal for walks, yet is only ten minutes' ride from the city centre.

- **Transport** For Salwator, take tram no. 1, 2 or 6 from pl. Wszystkich Świętych and get off at the terminus.

If you want to go straight to the Kościuszko Mound, take bus 100 which leaves every hour from Plac Matejki (opposite the Barbican).

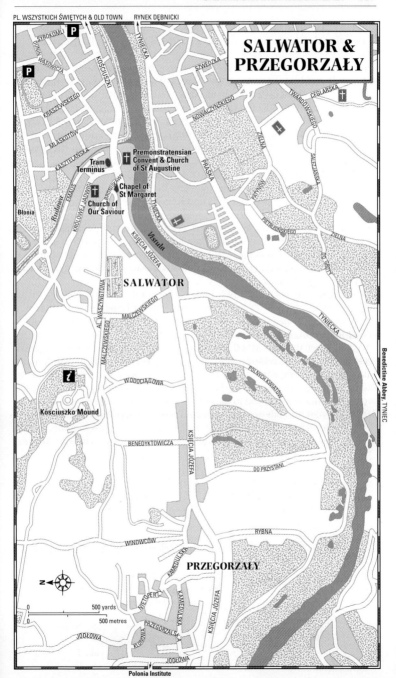

SALWATOR & PRZEGORZAŁY

Premonstratensian Convent & Church of St Augustine

Tram Terminus

Chapel of St Margaret

Church of Our Saviour

Błonia

Vistula

SALWATOR

Kosciuszko Mound

PRZEGORZAŁY

0   500 yards

0   500 metres

Polonia Institute

Benedictine Abbey, TYNIEC

For Przegorzały, take bus nos 109, 209, 229, 239, 249 or 259 from Salwator. Get off at the stop near the junction with ul. Jodłowa and walk up the hill.

To the left of the tram terminus in Salwator, in a picturesque setting at the fork of the Vistula and Rudawa rivers, is the Premonstratensian Convent (ul. Kościuszki 88), one of the oldest in Kraków, founded in 1162. From here, the ancient district of Zwierzyniec, owned by the convent as early as the 12C, stretches northwest along ul. Królowej Jadwigi and west up to the Kościuszko Mound, a walk of about 25 minutes. Salwator's understated charm is revealed in the fine Secessionist villas stretching up the hill and along the river. On Easter Monday the popular Emaus fair takes place near the convent, and in June the Lajkonik parade (see p. 90) assembles here before moving on to the Market Square.

The **Church of St Augustine**, adjoining the convent, dates from the early 13C. Initially it served both the male and female rule of the Premonstratensian order, as evidenced by the oratories situated on either side of the chancel, to which they are connected by open-work arcades. Thorough rebuilding carried out in 1596–1626 preserved only a late Romanesque portal (north entrance) from the former church and gave the convent its present fortress-like character. The spacious grounds are enclosed by a late Renaissance decorative parapet wall with towers and loopholes.

Walk up the hill along ul. Bł. Bronisławy, a beautiful cobbled avenue lined with trees and villas. On the left you will pass the deserted **Chapel of St Margaret**, a small, wooden, domed octagon of 1690 associated with pagan worship, which stands in an overgrown garden.

Further up on the right is the 12C **Church of Our Saviour** (only open for mass), set in its own grounds behind a wall. Inside are a *Crucifixion* (1605), which shows Christ giving his golden shoe to a minstrel, and two Renaissance pulpits, the one by the entrance in the shape of a chalice. Of greater interest is the underground archaeological site, now open to the public, where excavations were carried out in 1962. Amongst the finds were a stone mensa and fragments of early Gothic murals.

Ul. Bł. Bronisławy soon merges with the car-free al. Waszyngtona, a long avenue leading up Bł. Bronisławła Hill (333m) to the **Kościuszko Mound**

Kościuszko Mound

(34m). Raised in 1820–23, the mound contains earth from many of the battle sites where Tadeusz Kościuszko fought (see p. 82), some as far afield as America. In 1856 the Austrians encircled the mound with brick fortifications, which have remained to this day. The popular RMF FM radio station broadcasts from the main building, which also houses the *FM Pod Kopcem Hotel*, a popular choice on account of the quiet, leafy surroundings (see *Where to stay*). Close by is the neo-Gothic **Chapel of the Blessed Bronisława** (1861), housing a small display of Kościuszko memorabilia. The only entrance to the mound is through the chapel (open May–Sept 09.00–19.00, Oct–Apr 10.00–17.00). Wind your way up to the top, where there is an open vista of Kraków, its Old Town sadly dwarfed by the chimneys of the huge Łęg power station, closed in on all sides by grey housing estates. The inscription on the granite boulder reads: 'To Kościuszko'.

Przegorzały

An eccentric, circular **villa**, built during the inter-war period, overlooks the Vistula from a hill in the suburb of Przegorzały (southeast). It adjoins a building erected by the Nazis in 1941 and modelled on Hitler's Alpine residences.

The complex is now used by the Jagiellonian University's Polonia Institute and includes a high-standard hostel for foreign students (see *Where to stay*).

From the terrace of the *U Ziyada* restaurant (see *Restaurants*) there is an excellent view over the river and the monasteries at Bielany and Tyniec. On a clear day you can even see the Tatra Mountains, some 100km to the south.

Beyond the city

1 • Wolski Forest, Bielany Monastery and the Villa Decius

To the west of Kraków (6km) lies the **Wolski Forest** (412ha), an area of hilly woodland and nature reserves. The various sites within the forest—the secluded Camaldolite Monastery in Bielany, the Piłsudski Mound, the skansen and Villa Decius—are linked by a network of well-marked trails and are all within easy walking distance of each other.

- **Transport** The best approach to the Wolski Forest is from the Zoo (bus no. 134 from the *Cracovia Hotel*; last stop). From here you can walk southwest to the Camaldolite Monastery, or north to the Piłsudski Mound and then northeast to the skansen and Villa Decius in the suburb of Wola Justowska.

  To get back from the Camaldolite Monastery, walk down to the hill to ul. Księcia Józefa and pick up bus no. 109 to the *Cracovia Hotel*, or nos 209, 229, 239, 249, 259, 269, all of which go to Salwator. From the terminus in Salwator take tram nos 1, 2 or 6 back to the city centre.

  To get back from the Villa Decius take bus nos 102, 152 or 192. These all go to the centre of Kraków.

  If you are travelling by car, be warned that at weekends the road leading up to the Zoo from Wola Justowska is closed to traffic (not buses or taxis); on weekdays a small toll is charged.

The Camaldolite Monastery ~ Bielany

The suburb of Bielany is situated in the southwest part of Wolski forest (about 7km from the city centre). Here, on a verdant hillside overlooking the Vistula, is the *Camaldolite Monastery (Klasztor Kamedułów), its twin towers visible on the horizon as one approaches Kraków from the west. Bielany derives its name from the white habits worn by the Camaldolite monks ('biel' means white).

Camaldolite monastery

The austere Camaldolite Order was brought to Bielany from Italy in 1603 by the Grand Marshal of the Crown, Mikołaj Wolski (only two monasteries belonging to this Order survive in Poland). As prescribed by the monastic rule, a suitably beautiful site was chosen for the church—a remote wooded hill, later known as 'Silver Mountain' (Srebrna Góra) after an exquisite set of silver cutlery which Wolski presented to the former owner of the land. Wolski himself supplied the Roman designs for the church. First to be constructed, though, were the monks' lodges (1605–09) in a large rectangular garden divided into plots. The nave, chancel and twin-tower stone façade followed in 1609–30.

• The church is open daily 08.00–11.00 and 15.00–17.00. Due to the strict monastic rule, women are forbidden to enter the monastery and, apart from attending mass at 07.00 or 10.00 on Sundays, can only visit the church on 12 days during the year (7 Feb, 25 March, Easter Sunday, Sun and Mon after

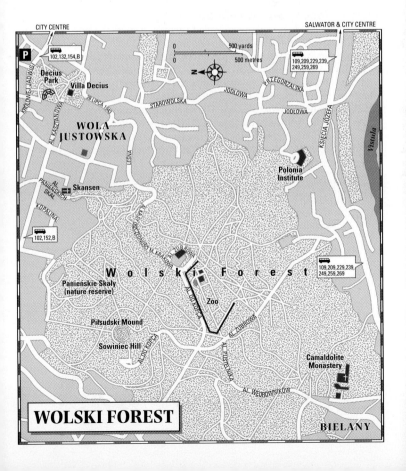

Pentecost, Corpus Christi, 19 June, Sun after 19 June, 15 Aug, 8 Sept, 8 Dec, 25 Dec).

You approach the site along a narrow path flanked by walls, with the church's broad monumental façade of white stone and black marble coming into full view beyond the gatehouse. The grounds are designed according to an early Baroque axial scheme: monastic buildings symmetrically flanking the inner yard and rows of monks' lodges at the back.

The church is one of the finest examples of early Baroque in Poland, its interior bearing striking similarities to Italian architecture of the period. The plain, tunnel vaulted nave is flanked by richly decorated chapels, with stuccowork (1622–42) and paintings by Tomaso Dolabella. Mummified corpses of monks are preserved in the church crypts. Wolski is buried in a tomb by the main entrance; his portrait, showing him in Sarmatian dress (see p. 137), hangs in the monastery.

Wola Justowska and Villa Decius

The green and affluent suburb of Wola Justowska borders the Wolski Forest to the northeast. It is named after Justus Decius (1485–1545), the royal secretary to King Zygmunt the Old, who in the 1530s commissioned Bartolomeo Berrecci to build the **Villa Decius** (*Willa Decjusza*), which stands in the park just off ul. Królowej Jadwigi. The present appearance of the building is the result of remodelling carried out in the 17C and 19C. Especially fine are the three tiers of arcaded galleries on the east façade. The recently renovated interior now houses conference rooms and the exclusive *Villa Decius* restaurant, where you can enjoy a meal to the accompaniment of live Renaissance music (see *Restaurants*).

A number of famous Cracovians live in Wola Justowska, among them the writer Stanisław Lem.

Villa Decius

Stanisław Lem

Stanisław Lem, science fiction author and futurologist, was born in Lwów (present-day Lviv in the Ukraine) in 1921. He graduated in medicine from the Jagiellonian University, and after the Second World War settled in Kraków permanently. One of the best-known and most frequently translated Polish writers, he won international recognition with such bestsellers as *The Cyberiad*, *Solaris* (filmed by Andrei Tarkovski), *The Star Diaries*, and *Memoirs Found in a Bathtub*. Lem goes beyond the standard fare of commercial science fiction. Under the guise of parody and humour, his novels explore the possibilities and limits of human knowledge; fantastic worlds and alien civilisations are used as a pretext to question the potentially dangerous consequences of human evolution. Inevitably, initial fascination with the possibilities afforded by advanced technologies gradually gives way to scepticism and pessimism.

In his futurological essays—including *Summa Technologiae* (1964), in which he predicted the emergence of 'virtual reality'—Lem poses questions about the future of civilisation and the links between science, ethics and culture. His most recent collection—*Megabite Bomb* (1999)—takes a wry look at the state of culture in the Information Age, and the ambivalent impact of the Internet.

Close to the Villa Decius (al. Panieńskich Skał, left off ul. Kasztanowa) is a small **skansen** consisting of a reconstructed 17C wooden church, a wooden inn with arcades, currently the priest's house, and a wooden granary of 1764 with characteristically large eaves, all brought here from villages in the Małopolska region. From the skansen a path leads up Sowiniec Hill (358m) to a mound raised in honour of Poland's benevolent pre-war dictator, Józef Piłsudski (1934–37). Also in the vicinity is a limestone ravine—Panieńskie Skały—with a nature reserve.

2 • The Benedictine Abbey in Tyniec

The *abbey (Klasztor Benedyktynów) is scenically perched on a limestone rock— the southernmost elevation of the Jura uplands—on the south bank of the Vistula river, 10km southwest of the city centre. The church is open to everyone, but visitors should ask for permission to enter the monastery.

• **Transport** To get there from the city centre, cross the river by the Dębnicki Bridge. Bus no. 112 goes from the square on the other side—Rynek Dębnicki— to Tyniec. A more attractive option is to take the boat from the riverside near Wawel Castle. The round trip (May–September only) takes 4 hours with a 30 minute stop to see the abbey. Unfortunately, there are plans to close the service, so it is best to check at one of the tourist agencies before you depart.

The Benedictine monks were probably brought to Poland from France in 1044. Recent archaeological discoveries suggest that their first church, a pre-Romanesque stone basilica, was built as early as c 1060–70. It is likely that the abbey, which dates from the same period, initially served a defensive purpose. In the 15C, a new, towerless Gothic church was constructed. A few fragments from it have survived—foundations, buttresses, two windows in the chancel, stairs and a founding tablet—but what you see today is largely Baroque (1618–22). The abbey was later surrounded with fortifications, but this offered little protection against the heavy attacks launched by the Confederates of Bar in 1772–73. It suffered even greater damage during a fire in 1831, after which only the church was rebuilt. The Benedictines returned to Poland during the inter-war period to begin reconstructing their abbey. Work is still in progress.

The abbey is reached along a winding road punctuated by two medieval gates. In the middle of the courtyard stands a well covered with a rustic timber cone (1620). The **church**, a modest, twin-towered structure, which lost its most valuable furnishings in the 19C, adjoins the partly ruined monastic buildings. Of note are the black marble high altar, designed by Francesco Placidi in the mid-18C, and the original Rococo pulpit in the shape of a boat. In the abbey buildings you might want to take a look at the medieval chapter house and cloisters, where there are fragments of Gothic murals. On the south side of the hill, behind a stone wall with two towers, stretches the 18C abbey garden.

Days out from Kraków

The suggested day trips to **Auschwitz**, **Wieliczka**, the **Pieniny Mountains**, **Lanckorona**, **Kalwaria Zebrzydowska**, the **Ojców National Park** and the castle in **Nowy Wiśnicz** are all within easy reach of Kraków. **Zakopane** merits a full two day's stay, especially if you intend to do any hiking or skiing in the **Tatra Mountains**. There are many other places of interest near Kraków and for those wishing to explore the Małopolska region, *Blue Guide Poland* will be more helpful.

Practical information

Getting there
By train

The places mentioned on the excursions are accessible by train except for the Ojcow National Park and Nowy Wiśnicz Castle, although it should be said that the train journey from Kraków to Krościenko is ridiculously long, and best avoided.

Most trains depart from Kraków Główny (see *Visiting the rest of Poland*), though a few leave from the Kraków-Płaszów station in the south of the city. There are trains between the two stations every few minutes. The train times given below were correct at the time of writing but may well change. Their purpose is only to give readers a rough idea of journey times and the frequency of services.

By bus

The Ojców National Park and Nowy Wiśnicz Castle can only be visited by bus (or car) and for mountain areas in general, bus travel is by far the best option.

All *PKS* buses leave from the main bus station (pl. Kolejowy), situated next to the main railway station.

Private mini-bus services

These leave from the ul. Worcella stop by the *Bar Smok* to Wieliczka (The Salt Mine) and other nearby towns and villages. Tickets are bought from the driver, not from the station ticket hall.

Bus times are not given as there are usually many companies operating the same routes. It is best to shop around at travel agencies and to check the advertisements posted at the stops by the main bus station.

AUSCHWITZ

Getting there
By train

Journey time: 1hr 30mins, unless stated otherwise.
Kraków–Oświęcim: 06.35, 08.05, 09.50 (Eurocity, 1hr) 12.33, 14.17, 14.36. You can get from Oświęcim railway station to the Auschwitz camp (2km) by local bus (frequent service) or taxi.

Oświęcim–Kraków: 12.30, 15.02 (Eurocity, 1hr), 15.36 (to Kraków-Płaszów), 16.29 (to Kraków-Płaszów), 18.07 (to Kraków Płaszów), 19.07.

By bus

Journey time: 1hr 30mins.
There are many daily buses from Kraków to Oświęcim, all of which stop

at the Auschwitz camp. Some tourist agencies in Kraków (see *Tourist information*) run special buses to the site.

By car

Journey time: 1 hr.
A4 motorway (toll) to Chrzanów, then road 933.

The industrial town of Oświęcim (50 km west of Kraków) is known primarily as the site of the largest and most notorious extermination camp in Europe—**Auschwitz-Birkenau**—where an estimated one and a half million people perished during the Second World War. In 1947 the grounds of the former camp, the largest cemetery in human history, were declared a memorial to the martyrdom of nations. The Polish Government turned the site into a museum, meticulously reconstructing all the evidence the Nazis had tried to destroy.

Auschwitz, the ultimate symbol of barbarism and genocide, remains the subject of controversy. Public declarations on the subject almost inevitably provoke outrage from one quarter or another. When the Polish Primate, Cardinal Glemp, allowed some Carmelite Nuns to set up a convent within the perimeter fence, he was swiftly admonished by Jewish organisations around the world for attempting to 'baptise the holocaust'. On the other hand, many Poles have publicly given vent to their belief that no one has a monopoly over suffering, and that films like *Schindler's List* or *Shoah*, far from helping Polish–Jewish reconciliation, have only served to reinforce naive and harmful stereotypes. Whatever the truth of the matter, there seems to be much wisdom in the words of the historian Norman Davies, that 'the dispute over who suffered most is the meanest of disputes.'

History of the camps

The first camp was erected in June 1940 as an internment centre for 10,000 Polish political prisoners, chiefly members of the intelligentsia and the resistance movement. The local population was removed to make way for a 'death zone' around the camp, whose purpose was to maintain the camp's secrecy and render escape impossible. In March 1941, Auschwitz was extended to accommodate 30,000 inmates. Once inside, each prisoner was assigned a tattooed number, a striped uniform, and a wooden bunk. No one was expected to live longer than three months. In October 1941, further extensions were made to accommodate prisoners from other countries subjugated by the Reich. Soon, the camp became an enormous death factory consisting of three parts: **Auschwitz I** (the original camp), **Auschwitz II—Birkenau** (constructed in 1941 in the nearby village of Brzezinka), and **Auschwitz III—Monowitz** (set up in 1942 near a factory in Dwory). Birkenau, the largest camp, had a capacity of 100,000 inmates. A special railway was built, with the tracks extending right up to the crematoria. Prisoners would be loaded off the cattle wagons onto a long concrete platform where the 'selection procedure' would take place. Those fit to work would be marched off to the barracks; the old, infirm, the young, and mothers with children would be stripped and led directly to the gas chambers, their corpses then burnt in open pits or incinerated in the crematoria. The gas chambers consumed their first victims on 4 May 1942 and it was then that the mass extermination of Jews began. At its peak, the Nazi war machine was able to slaughter 60,000 people during a single night, with a train arriving approximately every hour. Those who avoided the gas chambers were condemned to slave labour for the

Reich. Life in the camp was almost unimaginable: daily beatings, torture, executions, disease, mass starvation, cannibalism. Inmates were subjected to sterilisation and medical 'experiments'. When the Soviet Army liberated the camp on 27 January 1945, they discovered 7500 living people, including 90 pairs of identical twins whom the Nazis had used in the name of 'scientific research'.

The **museum** (open June, July, Aug 08.00–19.00; May, Sept 08.00–18.00; Apr, Oct 08.00–16.00; Dec, Jan, Feb 08.00–15.00) takes a 'no holds barred' approach and the experience can be distressing. Every gruesome detail of life in the camp is documented. You enter through the original iron gateway with its infamous slogan '*Arbeit Macht Frei*' (work makes you free). The prisoners barracks contain exhibitions devoted to daily life in the camp, living and sanitary conditions, as well as the fate of various nationalities. Blocks 4 and 5 present the story and evidence of mass extermination: a room of women's hair, piles of broken toys, collections of gold teeth, suitcases and artificial limbs, all precisely segregated by the Nazis, all revealing the insane bureaucracy of murder. Executions were carried out in the Block of Death. The bunkers underground, where prisoners were starved and tortured during interrogation, contain the notorious 'standing cells'. Beside the Block of Death is the Wall of Death, where the condemned were shot. Two of the grimmest places are the Crematorium I, and Assembly Square with its mass gallows. The cinema shows a film of the Soviet army liberating the camp in 1945.

A special bus service is provided for those wishing to visit the camp at **Birkenau** (3km). Here one gets an idea of the sheer scale of the Nazis' plans. The camp was actually subdivided into smaller sections housing men, women, Jews, Gypsies, etc. More than 300 prisoners' barracks were erected on the vast site, of which only 67 have survived intact. The rest were demolished or burnt by the fleeing Nazis, though the chimneys and the outlines of the foundations are still visible. The railway enters through the main gate, flanked by watchtowers, and proceeds towards the ruins of gas chambers and crematoria at the far end of the camp. About halfway along is the unloading ramp where the 'selection procedure' would take place. A Monument to the Victims of Fascism (1967) stands at the end of the track. Further to the right are two more crematoria, pits and pyres where corpses were burned, and a pond into which the ashes were dumped.

THE SALT MINE IN WIELICZKA

Practical information

Getting there
By train

Journey time approx 30mins.
Kraków–Wieliczka: 07.35, 12.30, 14.30, 15.30, 16.30.
Wieliczka–Kraków: 08.05, 13.01,

15.00, 16.00, 18.00, 19.40
By bus

Journey time approx 30 mins.
The best option is to catch one of the regular mini-bus services (journey time 30mins) from ul. Worcella stop by the *Bar Smok*. Some tourist agencies in

Kraków (see *Tourist information*) run guided tours of the Salt Mine.

By car

Road 4, heading southeast.

Wieliczka, 12km southeast of Kraków, is well worth a visit on account of its ancient Salt Mine (*kopalnia soli*). The mine predates the Polish state itself and was opened as a museum in 1950. Approximately 200km of tunnels and corridors stretch out in a vast web underneath the town. Such was the level of exploitation, that in the 19C cave-ins and flooding were common. A massive recent flood (1992) endangered the very existence of the historic site, and it was only thanks to special EU funds (Wieliczka was placed on the UNESCO World Heritage List in 1978) that enough water was pumped out in time to prevent total collapse.

History

Huge salt deposits were formed here 18–20 million years ago during the Miocene era, and were already being mined long before Wieliczka received its town charter in 1290. As early as the 11C the settlement here was known as *Magnum Sal*, or Great Salt. Kazimierz the Great encircled the town with walls, eleven towers and two gates. In this way he hoped to protect the precious deposits, which provided a staggering one-third of the revenue flowing into the royal coffers. It would be no exaggeration to say that the Wieliczka mine financed most of the architectural construction in Kraków and southern Poland during the Middle Ages.

A French visitor to Wieliczka in 1646 penned the following account: 'The salt mines at Wieliczka are no less superb than the pyramids of Egypt, and more useful. They are a commendable reminder of Poles' diligence, while the pyramids testify only to the tyranny and vanity of the Egyptians. The former may be called the children of the earth, the latter—the children of the winds. The vain loftiness of the one is no match for the usefulness depth brings to the other.'

In 1826, a spa was set up in the town when it was discovered that the salt waters had rich medicinal qualities. Patients afflicted with rheumatism, scrofula, pneumonia or tuberculosis, would wallow in salty mud mixed with bran, and then sweat out their ailments in a Russian steam bath. More recently, a small, subterranean spa hospital treating asthma and other respiratory diseases opened in the mine, at a depth of 211m.

Tours vary in length, but a standard one covers 3.5km of tunnels, and takes up to two or three hours. Some of the tours are in English, but to avoid waiting you should check the departure times at a tourist agency in alternatively, you can hire your own English-speaking guide for around 150 PLN. You are advised to bring suitable clothing, as the temperature below ground is around 13°C.

The exhibition area (open 08.00–18.00) is contained on levels I, II and III (64m–135m), reached by a long staircase. The remaining six levels, descending to a depth of 300m, are closed to the public.

The highlights, as you wander the long galleries, are the chambers containing **underground chapels**. Everything is made of salt—the altars, candlesticks, columns and pulpits, even the figures of saints. Two of the best chapels are St Anthony's, sculpted by the miner Antoni Kuczkiewicz, and the Holy Cross, both 17C. Truly breathtaking is the 19C Chapel of the Blessed Kinga, which took thirty years to carve. Religious services are held inside three times a year (24 July, 4 and 24 December). On your way to the underground salt lake you pass the largest chamber, famous for its excellent acoustics, and thus used as a venue for opera and concerts. The tour ends on level III, where there is a café, souvenir shop, and a **Mining Museum** (open 08.00–16.00), with a display of old tools and equipment. A genuine mine lift takes you back up the main Danilewicz shaft (1638) to ground level.

THE PIENINY MOUNTAINS

The spa town of Szczawnica, 127km southeast of Kraków, is the best base for excursions into the **Pieniny National Park**, which encompasses the scenic Pieniny Mountains. These partly wooded limestone peaks (Trzy Korony, 982 m, is the highest) are accessible along easy and well-marked hiking trails, which begin in the neighbouring village of Krościenko (4 km). The peaks drop steeply into the valley of the Dunajec river, a stretch of which marks the border between Poland and Slovakia.

Practical information

Getting there
By train

There is a train station in Krościenko, but from Kraków the shortest journey time is 7hrs 20 mins (!), leaving at 00.13 and changing in Zagórz.

By bus

Journey time: 3hrs.
There are a few direct daily buses from Kraków to Szczawnica. Alternatively, change at Nowy Targ (on the Kraków–Zakopane route) or Nowy Sącz. Many buses ply the short distance between Szczawnica and neighbouring Krościenko.

If you just want to do the raft trip along the Dunajec river, it is best to book this through *Cracow Tours*. If travelling alone, take the bus from Szczawnica to the wharf in Kąty (see below).

By car

Journey time: approx 2hrs 30mins.
Road 7, heading south (a dual carriageway up to Myślenice), followed by roads 968 (through Mszana Dolna) and 969

to Krościenko. **Warning**: If you're returning on Sunday evening or on a public holiday, it could take you as long as 4hrs.

Raft trips

The spectacular twists and turns of the river—in places the sheer rock faces of the gorge are 300m high—can be navigated on a raft steered by local highlanders. **Raft trips** through the Dunajec Gorge are organised by *Cracow Tours*, beginning at the riverside in Kąty and ending in Szczawnica. The 15km trip lasts from 2 to 3 hours depending on the water level of the river. Tours leave on Mondays and Thursdays and take up the best part of a day. The package includes lunch at the *U Walusia* restaurant in Krościenko. Tickets can be bought at most hotels, the Tourist Information Centre inside the Cloth Hall, and at the *Orbis*, *Intercrac* or *Jan-Pol* travel agencies (see *Tourist Information*). You must book in advance (by 15.00 on the day prior to departure).

Hiking

If you simply want to go hiking, pick up one of the trails into the Pieniny National Park from Krościenko or Szczawnica. The popular ascent from Krościenko to **Mt Trzy Korony** (yellow and blue trails) takes about 2hrs 15mins. Unless you leave Kraków very early, though, it may be difficult to squeeze a hiking trip into a single day. A better option may be to stay overnight in Szczawnica, where there are many guest houses and private rooms. South of the town there is a picturesque ravine cut by the Kamionka creek—follow the signs to 'Wąwóz Homole'. West of the Pieniny National Park you could visit the picturesque medieval castles at Niedzica and Czorsztyn, both described in *Blue Guide Poland*.

LANCKORONA AND KALWARIA ZEBRZYDOWSKA

The two places on this excursion are only 4km apart and can easily be visited in a single day. Lanckorona, the first stop, is a charming village with a Gothic church and castle ruins, but the highlight is the neighbouring pilgrimage town of Kalwaria Zebrzydowska, with its famous monastery church and calvary. Almost all the trains from Kraków to Kalwaria Zebrzydowska conveniently stop in Lanckorona, so getting between the two places is not a problem.

Practical information

Getting to Lanckorona
By train

Journey time approx 1hr.
Kraków–Kalwaria Lanckorona:
07.35 (journey time 1hr 30mins, changing in Kraków-Płaszów), 08.45, 11.16, 13.06, 14.26, 15.10, 16.15 (changing in Kraków-Płaszów).
Kalwaria Lanckorona–Kraków:
09.09, 12.22 (to Kraków-Płaszów) 13.35, 15.00 (to Kraków-Płaszów),
16.01 (to Kraków-Płaszów), 17.22 (to Kraków-Płaszów), 17.48, 18.51, 19.52.
By bus

Journey time: 1 hr.
There is only one morning bus to Lanckorona.
By car

Journey time approximately 1hr.
Head south on road 7 for about 20km and take the right fork signposted 'Bielsko Biała' (road 96). After Izdebnik turn onto a narrow winding road for Lanckorona.

Getting to Kalwaria Zebrzydowska
By train

Journey time: 1hr 20 minutes.
Kraków–Kalwaria Zebrzydowska:
07.35 (journey time 2hrs, changing in Kraków-Płaszów and Kalwaria Lanckorona), 11.16 (journey time 2hrs 20mins, changing in Kalwaria Lanckorona) 13.40 (changing in Kraków-Płaszów), 15.10, 16.15 (journey time 1hr 45mins, changing in Kraków-Płaszów and Kalwaria Lanckorona).
Kalwaria Zebrzydowska–Kraków:
13.24 (changing in Kalwaria Lanckorona), 14.53 (journey time 1hr 15mins, changing in Kalwaria Lanckorona and Kraków Płaszów), 16.22 (journey time 2hrs, changing in Kalwaria Lanckorona and Kraków

Płaszów), 19.36 (journey time 1hr 15mins, changing in Kalwaria Lanckorona).

By bus

Journey time: 1hr 20mins.
All buses from Kraków to Bielsko Biała, and some from Kraków to Cieszyn, stop in Kalwaria Zebrzydowska.

By car

Journey time: approximately 1hr.
Head south on road 7 for about 20km and take the right fork signposted 'Bielsko Biała' (road 96) for Kalwaria Zebrzydowska. From Lanckorona you can either return to the 96, or continue directly along the minor road for another 4km.

Lanckorona (36km southwest of Kraków) is a peaceful village situated well off the beaten track. The sloping, cobbled Market Square is lined with traditional 19C wooden houses, of which one (by the bus stop) contains a **Museum of Folklore** (tools, household items, handicrafts). Follow ul. Św. Jana up the hill to the Gothic **Church of St John the Baptist** (1336), beautifully set, but unfortunately accessible only on Sundays. Higher up are the ruins of a 14C **castle**, surrounded by a park, an ideal place for walks.

Once in **Kalwaria Zebrzydowska** (36km southwest of Kraków), watch out for the white signs marked 'Do Klasztoru' (to the monastery). Ascending the hill you will reach a square, its north side lined with one-storey houses with balconies. To the west stands the huge Baroque *monastery church of the Bernardines (Kościół Bernardynów) (1702), separated from the square by a row of stone statues of saints (1823) and a yard—the Paradise Square, with cloisters on its north and south sides. The majority of the monastic buildings are situated behind the church. They were built between 1603 and 1609 and are surrounded by partly preserved fortifications, of which two towers have been converted into chapels (the chapel of St Anne is the low square tower with a red tiled roof and lantern).

The broad, pedimented façade is dominated by two symmetrically placed towers, with three domed chapels abutting the church to the north. Inside, the spacious vaulted hall is lit by large plain glass windows, providing a sharp contrast to the dark, narrow and much lower chancel. The 17C organ loft is flanked by murals depicting the 17C Cossack leader Chmielnicki on a horse (north) and the Blessed Simon of Lipnica (south).

Be sure to walk behind the high altar to see the finely carved 17C wooden stalls. The altar itself is a bulky, rectangular structure, with four twisted columns supporting large pedestals on which frolicking angels are perched. The central painting of St Francis conceals a figure of St Mary, who is also portrayed in the garish murals covering the walls of the chancel. Another painting further east shows King Władysław Vasa (1632–48); on the north wall, Emperor Francis I of Austria (1804–35) is depicted attending mass at this very church. The stuccoed Zebrzydowski chapel, whose cream-coloured stone is enhanced by the mellow light entering through the large plain-glass window in the elliptical dome, has a marble altar with a miraculous painting of the *Virgin and Child* (17C). A door in its east wall leads to the chapel of St Anthony (1686), with a 17C painting of *St Anthony of Padua* in its altar.

Kalwaria is a popular pilgrimage spot, where thousands flock during Easter to watch the traditional **Passion play**, in which peasants from local villages act out the Crucifixion. The origins of this custom reach back to the early 17C, when

Mikołaj Zebrzydowski, struck by the similarity of the hills around Kalwaria to the landscape of Jerusalem, attempted to recreate the atmosphere of the Holy City by erecting 46 chapels and churches. His **Way of the Cross**, offering a pleasant walk through woodland, begins at pl. Rajski and proceeds west before turning full circle back to the north side of the monastery. Passing over the Mount of Olives, Mt Zion and Mt Moriah, it ends on Mt Calvary, upon which stands the **Church of the Crucifixion**, its interior (usually closed) adorned with four Passion paintings by Franciszek Lekszycki (1600–01). Some of the stations are tiny stone cubicles; others are churches in their own right.

THE OJCÓW NATIONAL PARK

To the northwest of Kraków lies a picturesque limestone terrain known as the Jura uplands, studded with medieval castles, caves and fancifully shaped rocks. The uplands stretch as far as the town of Częstochowa (see *Blue Guide Poland*), but their most attractive part is contained within the Ojców National Park (20km from Kraków), whose highlight is the royal castle at **Pieskowa Skała**. On parts of this excursion you follow the valley of the Prądnik river which flows through the Park. Only 17km long, the valley is an excellent example of the region's karst landscape, with its remarkable limestone needles, such as 'Hercules' Club' (see below), and 210 caves, some of which are home to large populations of bats. The valley is also exceptionally rich in flora, including several relict species.

Getting there

The best way of visiting the area is by car, but you can also reach Pieskowa Skała and Ojców by bus from Kraków. If travelling by car, leave Kraków along ul. Armii Krajowej. At the large roundabout keep straight ahead, following signs to Wrocław, then Olkusz. Turn left off road 4 in **Biały Kościół** (13km), following a sign to 'Jaskinia Wierzchowska'. After 3.5km, the last stretch of which has to be walked (yellow trail), you will come to the **Wierzchowska Cave**, where 900m of tunnels and 11 caves can be visited in summer (open 9 Apr–30 Nov, 09.00–16.00, guides available. The tour lasts approximately 1 hour). You can also walk to the cave from Ojców along the yellow trail (5km).

Despite what the map might suggest, do not turn right in Murownia, as the road is open only to buses further on. Instead, continue along road 4 to Jerzmanowice, turning right at the poorly visible signpost to Ojców (500m after Jerzmanowice). The winding, hilly road will take you to Sąspów and into the **Ojców National Park** (16km).

The hamlet of **Ojców** has a ruined medieval **castle** raised by Kazimierz the Great (1333–70). Like its sister castle in Pieskowa Skała (see below), its purpose was to defend the western border of the Polish Kingdom. Today, the only preserved structures are the chapel gate and an octagonal tower. From the car park, you could follow the black trail ('Szlak Łokietka') south for about 2km to see the **Łokietek Cave** (open 9 Apr–30 Nov, 09.00–16.00, guides available).

From Pieskowa Skała and Ojców there are easy hiking trails to other sites in the Park. All the trails are marked on the *Ojcowski Park Narodowy* map—an essential buy if you plan to do a lot of walking (see *Maps*).

Pieskowa Skała Castle

A few buses daily go between Ojców and Pieskowa Skała (6km). If travelling by car, head north from Ojców, signposted 'Olkusz' (road 733). On the way watch out for the **Chapel on the Water** (*Kaplica na Wodzie*) (1901), visible on the right (only open for mass on Sunday mornings). The road follows the scenic river valley. Soon, a tall limestone rock, aptly named 'Hercules' Club' will come into view. Experienced climbers may wish to scale the rock, but equipment is needed.

Hercules' Club

A less challenging prospect is a walk up the hill to see the Gothic and Renaissance **Royal Castle. The museum inside (open Tues–Sat 10.00–15.30, Sun 10.00–17.30, to 15.30 off season) is a branch of the Wawel collections and displays a motley of objects from various epochs and countries that Wawel could not accommodate.

More interesting than the exhibitions is the castle itself. Originally built by Kazimierz the Great in the 14C, it was expanded and remodelled several times afterwards, particularly in the 16C, when it received Mannerist arcades typical of the Italian style so dominant in Kraków at that time. Notice the Renaissance sgraffito and grotesque masks decorating the courtyard. A curiosity, especially popular with children, is the well in the courtyard, drilled into solid rock and reaching the level of the Prądnik river, which flows by the foot of the hill. There is a restaurant inside the castle. For lighter refreshments try the rooftop café, with good views over the castle and its environs.

THE CASTLE IN NOWY WIŚNICZ

Practical information

Getting there
By train

Journey time to Bochnia approx 40mins.

There is no railway station in Nowy Wiśnicz, but there are hourly trains from Kraków to Bochnia. Bochnia and Nowy Wiśnicz are 8km apart.

By bus

Journey time: 1hr.
There are several daily buses from Kraków to Bochnia, and many more from Bochnia to Nowy Wiśnicz.

By car

Journey time: 50mins.
Leave Kraków on the E40 heading east, a dangerous road with frequent accidents. Just before Bochnia (42km), turn south onto the 965 for Nowy Wiśnicz.

Nowy Wiśnicz, 48km east of Kraków, is an attractive small town, famous for its imposing *castle. Since undergoing large-scale restoration work, parts of the castle are now accessible to visitors (open Mon–Fri 09.00–14.00, Sat 11.00–15.00, Sun 12.00–18.00), though you have to follow the compulsory guided tour.

History

Though a castle probably existed here as early as the 13C, it was not until the estate passed into the hands of the powerful Kmita family that Wiśnicz rose to prominence. Piotr Kmita (d. 1553) fortified it with cannon and three angle towers of stone, decorating the interiors with paintings and murals. Soon Wiśnicz became a flourishing centre of Renaissance culture. A frequent guest was Queen Bona Sforza (see p. 78), the wife of Zygmunt the Old, after whom one of the towers (northwest) is named.

The estate changed hands in 1593, when Sebastian Lubomirski (d. 1649) purchased it for the sum of 85,000 Polish zlotys. In 1615–21, his son Stanisław—the most celebrated member of the clan, a man of fantastic wealth—employed Matteo Trapola to reshape the central block as a rectangle with three tiers of arcaded galleries around a small courtyard. The fake 'windows' on the north wall were one of the first examples *trompe l'oeil* painting in Poland. Giovanni Battista Falconi supplied the stuccoes for the new domed chapel. Outside, Trapola fortified the hill with a modern bastioned pentagonal wall, broken only by a sumptuous stone gate with scrolls and banded masonry.

In its heyday, the castle was inhabited by some 1000 people. Lubomirski also financed the construction of a fortified monastery for the Discalced Carmelites (see below) next to the castle, as well as a town hall and parish church in the village, both still there. Despite severe pillaging in the 17C by the Swedes, who took away 150 wagons of goods, and a fire in 1831 which made it uninhabitable, the castle has remained virtually unchanged in form since Lubomirski's day.

The guide will take you through the cellars and selected rooms in the residential wing. The rooms are mostly empty, though some sandstone (ground and first floor) and marble (second floor) portals have survived. Traces of Falconi's murals and stuccoes are discernible on the walls and ceilings, and are particularly well-preserved in the Chapel and the Tower of Bona. The single-storey Kmita House (16C)—the former kitchens—abuts the castle to the south. To the east, the adjoining domed chapel has five Baroque sarcophagi in its crypt of the Lubomirski family. The sarcophagi were transferred here in 1951 from the Discalced Carmelites' Church, which was bombed by the Nazis during the war.

Fragments of the church (the walls and portal) may be viewed from the courtyard of the former **Discalced Carmelites' Monastery** (1622–34), which, since the expulsion of the Carmelites in 1780, has been used as a high security prison, complete with Baroque entrance gate, bastion fortifications, and monastic cells! To get there, turn left up the hill from the castle. Ask at the porter's lodge for permission to enter the courtyard. You might also visit the small wooden house between the castle and prison. Built in the 19C, it was much frequented by the painter Jan Matejko, and now houses a biographical **museum** dedicated to him (open Wed–Sun 10.00–14.00).

ZAKOPANE AND THE TATRA MOUNTAINS

Zakopane (108km south of Kraków), Poland's best known resort, lies at the foot of the **Tatra Mountains**. It is a popular destination for day-trippers escaping the noise and fumes of Kraków, but it really merits more time, particularly if you want to go hiking. There are good tourist facilities, though in the winter and summer accommodation may be scarce, so it is best to book in advance.

Zakopane occupies a unique place in Polish culture. In the mid-19C, Kraków's and Warsaw's *bohème* paid frequent visits, some even settling permanently, and the town's popularity, or, some would say, snob appeal, continues to this day. The highlanders (*górale*) speak a distinct dialect, dress in an easily recognisable way, and set themselves apart from the rest of the country, taking special pride in their independence and their familiarity with the mountains, which inspire such awe among the *cepry* ('lowland folk', in highlanders' disparaging dialect).

In 1929 and 1939, Zakopane hosted the World Skiing Championships (but recent bids to stage the Winter Olympics here have failed); the cable car to the summit of Kasprowy Wierch became operational in 1936. In little over a century, the resort has been visited by practically all the luminaries of Polish art, science, religion and politics, from Maria Curie-Skłodowska, Henryk Sienkiewicz and Pope John Paul II (an ardent skier and mountaineer), to Lech Wałęsa.

The Tatras are the highest and only alpine range of the Carpathians, which form Poland's natural border on the south; two thirds are on the Slovakian side, including the highest peak—Mt Gerlach (2655m). Few visitors fail to be captivated by the majestic beauty of the mountains, whose unique landscape and wildlife is protected by the Tatra National Park. Several rare animal species are to be found, including the brown bear, chamois, golden eagle and black grouse, though their habitat is now under threat from the ever-increasing pressures of tourism. The Tatras are themselves subdivided into two district ranges: the High Tatras and the West Tatras. The former are craggy and precipitous, with many picturesque lakes and the highest peak on the Polish side—Mt Rysy (2499m); the latter are characterised by smoother rock formations and spectacular karst landscape with many caves—at 776 metres, Wielka Śnieżna ranks among the world's deepest. The major valleys in the Tatras run from south to north, and provide some of the best hiking terrain in the area.

Practical information

Getting there
By train

Kraków–Zakopane: 07.35 (changing in Kraków-Płaszów), 08.45 (journey time 3hrs 50mins), 11.16, 13.06 (journey time 2hrs 46mins), 14.46 (journey time 4hrs 50mins), 16.15 (changing in Kraków-Płaszów), 18.20 (journey time 3hrs).

Zakopane–Kraków: 06.06 (journey time 3hrs), 09.26 (journey time 4hrs, changing in Kraków-Płaszów), 11.32 (journey time 3hrs), 13.13 (journey time 3hrs, changing in Kraków-Płaszów), 14.23 (journey time 4hrs, changing in Kraków-Płaszów), 15.15 (journey time 3hrs 30mins), 16.40 (journey time 3hrs), 17.22 (journey time 3hrs 30mins), 18.17 (journey time 3hrs 20mins), 18.55 (journey time 3hrs 20mins), 21.26 (journey time 3hrs 50mins).

By bus

Numerous bus companies operate the popular Kraków–Zakopane line (journey time: approximately 3hrs). These include: *Frej*, 11 buses daily (reservations at the *Waweltur* office on ul. Pawia—see *Tourist Information*); *Szwagropol*, 7 buses daily, (reservations at the *Jordan* office on ul. Pawia—see *Tourist Information*); and *Lux*, 10 buses daily (tickets from the driver). All these buses leave from stops opposite the main bus station. State-run *PKS* buses leave from inside the station.

By car

Journey time: approximately 2hrs). The fastest road from Kraków to Zakopane is the 7 to Nowy Targ (a dual-carriageway up to Myślenice), followed by road 95 heading south. If you're returning on Sunday evening or on a public holiday, it could take you as long as 5hrs.

Tourist information
Ul. Kościuszki 17
(☎ 201 2211), or ul. Krupówki 12
(☎ 201 2429).
ORBIS. Ul. Krupówki 22
(☎ 201 2238/201 5051).

Telephone code
☎ (0–18).

Where to stay
Accommodation can be arranged through *TPT 'Tatry'* (corner of al. 3 Maja and ul. Kościuszki, ☎ 201 4000). There are scores of good, reasonably priced pensions, as well as rooms in private houses. Look for the signs '*noclegi*' (accommodation) or '*pokoje*' (rooms). The more adventurous could try one of the several mountain shelters, such as *Murowaniec* in Hala Gąsienicowa (☎ 201 2633), or the shelter in Morskie Oko (☎ 207 7609), but during high season (i.e. summer and winter) you are likely to be offered floor space only.

Hotels

✩✩✩

Orbis-Kasprowy Polana Szymoszkowa (☎ 201 4011). The best hotel in Zakopane, situated on the slope of Gubałówka hill. Car park, swimming pool, fitness centre, wheelchair access, tennis court, private garden, business services. 286 rooms, some with spectacular views over the Tatras. **$US86**.
Orbis-Giewont ul. Kościuszki 1 (☎ 201 2011). Located in the town centre. Car park (100m). 43 rooms. **$US56–64**.
Gazda ul. Zaruskiego 2 (☎ 201 5011). Central location, next to the main post office. Car park, swimming pool, tennis court. 55 rooms. **$US50**.
Biały Potok ul. Droga do Białego 7

(☎ 201 4380/201 4903). Car park, tennis court, swimming pool. 32 rooms. **$US40**.

☆☆

Pod Piórem ul. Jaszczurówka 30 (☎ 201 1001). Situated close to the town centre, 100m from the Jaszczurówka chapel (see below). Sun terrace, 11 rooms. **$US17–26**.

Dom Turytsy PTTK (tourist class) ul. Zaruskiego 5. Large hostel in the centre of town. 462 beds in rooms of 1 to 8 persons. **$US27** (double with bathroom).

Eating out

Bąk, ul. Piłsudskiego 6 (☎ 206 6216). Wide choice of traditional cuisine. Drink bar. Expensive.

Sopa, ul. Kościeliska 52 (☎ 201 2216). Regional specialities. Friendly service. Live highland music.

Chata Zbójnicka, ul. Jagiellońska (☎ 210 4217). Be prepared for a hearty welcome at the 'Robbers' Inn'. If you're wearing a tie, the owner will cut it in half and hang it from the ceiling! Lots of lamb dishes and an open hearth for frying sausages and highland kebabs.

Obrochtówka, ul. Kraszewskiego 10a (☎ 206 3987). Cosy cellar with good food and a friendly atmosphere.

Redykołka, ul. Kościeliska 1 (☎ 206 6332). Regional cuisine, including various smoked cheeses and lamb dishes. Live highland music.

U Wnuka, ul. Kościeliska 8 (☎ 206 6147). Restaurant of long tradition (1870), contained inside a large, historic interior. Regional cuisine. Live highland music.

Main post office

Ul. Krupówki 20 (corner of Zaruskiego).

Festivals

Usually in the last week of August, Zakopane hosts the **International Festival of Mountain Folklore**, which features dance, music and exhibitions.

History

Until the second half of the 19C, Zakopane was an impoverished, remote village at the foot of the inaccessible Tatras. However, by the mid-19C, its reputation as a fashionable retreat grew rapidly. Visitors began to arrive from Kraków, Warsaw and other Polish cities, lured by the magic of the mountains—their natural beauty, the fresh air and the exotic folk culture of the *górale*.

The **folklore** of the Tatras, and Zakopane itself, became inextricably woven into the fabric of Polish culture; it found its way into, or at least influenced, the work of the composers and artists Mieczysław Karłowicz (who died here in an avalanche), Karol Szymanowski, Wojciech Kilar, Henryk Górecki, Leon Wyczółkowski, and Władysław Skoczylas. Cultural influence has worked in both directions: Stanisław Witkiewicz, using elements of the native highlander style, created a unique, highly artistic and successful '**Zakopane style**' in architecture, which to this day gives the place its special flavour. The best examples are the **Pod Jedlami** house (ul. Na Antałówkę), which Witkiewicz designed in 1895–6, and the **chapel** in Jaszczurówka.

In the 1870s, Tytus Chałubiński, a Warsaw physician, mounted a vigorous campaign to bolster Zakopane's popularity further. Some years later, Count Władysław Zamoyski purchased large tracts of land in the vicinity (such as the area around the lake of Morskie Oko), and later bequeathed the land—as well as his entire fortune—to the Polish nation, thus laying the foundations for the Tatra National Park.

The town

Life in Zakopane centres around **ul. Krupówki**, which is lined with shops and restaurants. The funicular at its north end will take you to the summit of Gubałowka in 5 minutes (1hr 30mins walking distance, blue trail), where you can survey an excellent panorama of the Tatras. Also close to the north end of ul. Krupówki, across a creek, is the **Tatra Mountain Museum** (open Wed–Sun 09.00–16.00), which occupies an early 20C house (no. 10) designed by Stanisław Witkiewicz in the 'Zakopane style'. Close by, on ul. Kasprusie, stands the *Villa Atma*, where the composer Karol Szymanowski lived in 1930–35.

Further south, ul. Kasprusie becomes ul. Strążyska, bringing you to the bottom of the scenic **Strążyska Valley** (see below).

Perpendicular to ul. Kasprusie, at its north end, runs **ul. Kościeliska**, where some 19C peasant houses still survive, as well as the *Villa Koliba*, designed by Witkiewicz. Inside is a **Museum of the Zakopane Style** (open Wed–Sun 09.00–16.00). The street leads west to the Kościeliska Valley (see below). Further to the east, running roughly parallel to ul. Krupówki, is ul. Jagiellońska, at the north end of which are the bus and train stations. Also on this street, at no. 18b, is the **Hasior Gallery** (open Wed–Sat 11.00–18.00, Sun 09.00–15.00), devoted to the work of the renowned and controversial artist Władysław Hasior.

The mountains

Surrounding walks and cycle routes

To protect the natural environment of the Tatras, the hiking trails are carefully marked (look for coloured strips painted on rocks, trees or other objects). Do not stray from the trail, or you risk paying a heavy fine. There is a small charge for entering the Tatra National Park; car parks by the entrances cost about 1 PLN per hour. **Bicycles** can be used in the Tatra National Park only on specially designated routes:

- Siwa Polana to the mountain shelter in the Chochołowska Valley.
- Kuźnice to the mountain shelter in Kalatówki.
- Brzeziny to the Murowaniec mountain shelter.
- Siwa Polana to Bystre.

Walks

Some of the trails may be temporarily closed, especially during winter, depending on weather conditions. Several of the Tatra valleys are easily accessible. The mountains in the Western Tatras are also very safe, but the excursions tend to be long and exhausting. Good walking shoes, a small knapsack and a windproof jacket are a must even in summer (weather changes in the mountains can be sudden). The High Tatras should be attempted only by experienced hikers, and certainly not by anyone suffering from vertigo. The views are truly breathtaking, and the trails reasonably secure, but there have been fatal accidents. There are also trails for expert mountain climbers, which require special equipment. It is possible to hire a licensed Tatra guide (ask at the PTTK office, ul. Krupówki 12, ☎ 201 2429).

- **Strążyska Valley** (*Dolina Strążyska*). This is about half an hour from the centre of Zakopane. Walk up ul. Kaprusie, which becomes ul. Strążyska, and then follow the red trail (closed in winter). It offers excellent views of the mountains,

Tatra Mountains

particularly the Giewont range. The red trail continues to the summit of **Mt Giewont** (1894 m, 4hrs), on which a 15m iron cross was erected in 1901. Another possible route to Mt Giewont is from Kuźnice (see below) to Kalatówki, then across Hala Kondratowa and the Kondracka Pass—blue trail, 3hrs 30mins.

- **White Creek Valley** (*Dolina Białego*). Also half an hour from the town centre. Take ul. Grunwaldzka and turn into Droga do Białego; then follow the yellow trail. The yellow and black trails lead to the Kalatówki mountain shelter (2hrs).

- **Kościeliska Valley** (*Dolina Kościeliska*). This is perhaps the most popular walk (usually accessible in winter). Take a bus from the centre of Zakopane to Kiry (8km). The narrow, dark valley is the starting point for many attractive trails into the Western Tatras. You can visit several caves (well-marked and safe, provided you have a torch; black trail, 40mins to the **Frosty Cave**—*Jaskinia Mroźna*), wander along the 'streets' cut by water in the limestone rocks of the narrow **Kraków Ravine** (*Wąwóz Kraków*; so-named by highlanders who thought it resembled Kraków's Old Town), walk to the Ornak mountain shelter (1hr 30mins), or climb **Mt Ciemniak** (2096m).

- **Chochołowska Valley** (*Dolina Chochołowska*), further west from Kiry (black trail from the Kościeliska Valley, 2hrs, or by bus from Kiry to Hucisko). This is the longest valley in the Tatras, with a convenient mountain shelter (1hr) which can serve as a base for excursions into the Western Tatras. The most attractive trails lead to **Mt Ornak** (yellow and green; 3hrs), **Mt Trzydniowiański Wierch** (red; 2hrs 30mins) and **Mt Grześ** (yellow, blue and green; 4hrs).

The road (958) continues north for about 25km to the unmissable *Chochołów, a 16C village where fine 18C–19C wooden houses, typical of highlander architecture, have been preserved. The house at no. 75 contains a **museum** (open Wed–Sun 10.00–14.00; closed in November and December), featuring a mid-19C rural interior.

• **Kuźnice** can be reached from Zakopane town centre on foot or by bus (4km from ul. Krupówki). From there you can take the cable car (or walk) to **Mt Kasprowy Wierch** (1985m). During summer and winter tickets are hard to come by, so either arrive very early in the morning at the Kuźnice station or make a reservation two days in advance at the *Orbis* office on ul. Krupówki. Several attractive trails lead down, the most frequented being the one to Hala Gąsienicowa and the Murowaniec mountain shelter, which is a good base for several excellent trails into the High Tatras (closed in winter). The most scenic routes lead to **Mt Granaty** (2239m; blue and yellow trail; 3hrs) and to the **Zawrat Pass** (2159 m; blue trail; 2hrs 45mins).

• *Morskie Oko** (Eye of the Sea). This is a classic Zakopane excursion. During the summer, the trail can be crowded, but the stunning views amply justify the effort of getting there. Either take a bus or drive to the car park in Palenica Białczańska. From there you take a horse-drawn *doroshka* in summer, or a sledge in winter, or simply walk to Morskie Oko. The glacial lake, 862m long, 566m wide, and 1393m above sea level, is known for its striking greenish-blue colour, especially when viewed from the steep trial leading up to another lake—**Czarny Staw** (1580m above sea level)—at the foot of Mt Rysy. The mountain shelter by the north shore of Morskie Oko is a convenient base for excursions to **Mt Rysy** (2499m; red trail; 4hrs), the **Mięguszowiecka Pass** (red and green trail; 3hrs), and the **Szpiglasowa Pass** (yellow trail; 2hrs 30mins).

Glossary

Aedicule an opening framed by two columns supporting an entablature and pediment, originally used in Classical architecture.

Altarpiece an ornamental carving or painting above and behind an altar. Also, an architectural structure (eg. in form of a triupham arch).

Ambulatory a semicircular or polygonal aisle enclosing an apse or the rear of a chancel.

Apse the semicircular or polygonal rear wall of a chancel or chapel.

Architrave the lowest part of an entablature, or the horizontal frame above a door.

Art Nouveau a style in decorative arts and architecture that emerged in the late 19C as a reaction to *Historicism*, and characterised by undulating designs styled from nature.

Ashlar (ashler) a square-cut building stone, often used for facing masonry walls.

Atlantes columns, in the form of carved male figures, supporting an entablature.

Attic a low wall or storey above the entablature of a building.

Baldachin (*baldacchino*) a canopy, usually supported on columns, over an altar or tomb.

Baroque a style in European architecture that lasted approximately from the early 17C to the mid-18C, characterised by elaborate, opulent decoration, highly dramatic effects, and an emphasis on symmetry and illusion.

Basilica a building (often a church), usually with a nave and two or more aisles, the former higher than the latter, lit by clerestory windows.

Bema an elevated pulpit in synagogues, from which the Scripture is read.

Biedermeier a style of German furniture design (1830–50), a heavier version of the Empire style in France.

Black Madonna an icon depicting the Virgin with Child, the most revered religious painting in Poland, kept at the Paulite monastery in Częstochowa, northwest of Kraków.

Blind arcades a range of arches attached to a wall.

Boss an ornamental knob placed at the intersection of ribs in a vault.

Calvary an outdoor representation of the Way of the Cross, often in the form of chapels spread out over a hillside. There is a fine example in the town of Kalwaria Zebrzydowska (see p. 170).

Capital an element crowning a column.

Cartouche an ornamental panel in the form of a scroll, often inscribed with a coat of arms (armorial cartouche).

Caryatids female *atlantes.*

Chancel the east part of a church where the high altar is located; reserved for the clergy and choir, and sometimes separated from the nave by means of a rood screen.

Chapter house a meeting place for members of a monastery where chapters of the monastic rule are read, or a meeting place for cathedral canons.

Choir a part of the chancel reserved for singers of the divine service.

Classicism a style in art and architecture—particularly its late 18C manifestation—inspired by classical Greek and Roman models and characterised by balance, simplicity and restraint.

Clerestory the upper parts of the walls of a church above the aisles, containing windows. Wawel Cathedral has a clerestory, but they are otherwise rare in Kraków.

Coffering vault, ceiling or dome decoration consisting of sunken ornamental panels.

Collegiate church a church served by resident canons.

Composite an order that is a combination of Ionic and Corinthian.

Corbel a projecting block, usually of stone, supporting a cornice, arch etc.

Corinthian a column with a fluted shaft and elaborately sculpted capital.

Corpus the main body of a church.

Crenellation a battlement.

Crossing the space in a church where the nave, chancel and transepts intersect, sometimes covered by a dome

Crowning the uppermost part of a wall, façade, tower etc.

Doric a column with fluted shaft and an unadorned capital.

Drum a circular or polygonal wall supporting a dome or cupola.

Eclectic a mixture of various historical styles, common in the design of buildings in the second half of the 19C. A good example is the Słowacki Theatre (see p. 139).

Empire a version of classicism that originated in France during Napoleon's Empire (1804–15) and characterised by grandness, rich ornamentation and motifs of antiquity.

Entablature the band at the top of a column, comprising an architrave, frieze and cornice.

Frieze an ornamental band along the upper part of a wall, or in the middle part of an entablature between the architrave and cornice.

Gothic a style in European architecture that lasted approximately from the 12C to the early 16C, characterised by rib vaults, buttresses, pointed arches and large windows.

Hall church a church with the nave and aisles of equal height.

Hanseatic League a medieval union of primarily Baltic towns, but also

Kraków, established to protect their economic interests.

Hetman royal field commander.

Historicism the revival of historical (period) styles in architecture (1830–early 20C).

International Gothic (also known as 'Beautiful Style') the dominant style in European sculpture and painting from the end of the 14C to the mid-15C, characterised by realism of detail. The wooden *Madonna of Kruźlowa* (c 1410), in the National Museum (see p. 136), is a masterpiece of this genre.

Ionic a column with a fluted shaft and a capital adorned with *volutes*.

Jamb the vertical frame of an arch, door or window.

Keystone the central, uppermost stone of an arch.

Lantern a polygonal, windowed turret crowning a tower, dome or the crossing of a church.

Loggia a covered gallery, open on one side, as on the Cloth Hall (see p. 90).

Lunette a semicircular space in a vault or ceiling, or above a door or window, often decorated with a painting or relief.

Machicolation a narrow gallery projecting from the walls of a castle, with openings in the floor through which boiling tar or oil could be dropped onto besieging troops.

Magdeburg Law a system of municipal administration originally developed in Magdeburg in the 13C, and later adopted by other towns in Central Europe, Kraków among them.

Mannerism a late variety of the Renaissance style in art and architecture, originally developed in Florence and Rome and common in Europe during the 16C.

Mansard roof a roof with a double slope on each of its four sides; the lower slope is steeper and longer than the upper (common in the 18C).

Mensa a part of the altar in a Christian church (literally: table).

Monstrance a receptacle for the consecrated Host.

Nave the main part of a church, extending from the west entrance to the chancel and often enclosed by aisles to the north and south.

Order the type of column (shaft, capital, entablature and sometimes base).

Oriel a bay (projecting) window on an upper storey of a building.

Palatinate territory ruled by a palatine, equivalent to a modern voivodship.

Palatine a high-ranking royal officer.

Parapet a low wall along the edge of a roof, balcony etc., sometimes battlemented; the 'Polish parapet', as on the Cloth Hall (see p. 90), has a decorative cresting in place of battlements and completely conceals the roof.

Pediment a low-pitched triangular gable above a doorway or portico; a broken pediment is one that has a gap at the apex or base.

Piano Nobile the main floor of a palace or mansion, where the reception rooms are located.

Pier a heavy, usually square pillar, used to reinforce masonry.

Pietà a sculpture of the Virgin mourning the dead Christ.

Pilaster a shallow pier projecting slightly from a wall.

Pinnacle a small ornamented turret terminating a spire, buttress, pier etc.

Polyptych a set of four or more hinged and painted panels, used as an altarpiece.

Portico covered colonnade forming the main entrance of a classical building.

Predella a small painting or panel, usually in sections, attached below an altarpiece, illustrating the story of a Saint, the Life of the Virgin etc.

Putto (pl. putti) a sculpted or painted figure, usually nude, of a young male angel or cupid.

Renaissance a style in art and architecture that originated in Italy in the 15C, marked by the frequent use of domes and arcades, and by delicate, Roman-inspired decoration. The most original indigenous contribution to the style was the 'Polish parapet' (see above).

Retable an ornamental shelf at the back of an altar, often with carved central figures and painted wings.

Rococo a late form of the Baroque style in art and architecture that originated in Paris in the early 18C, marked by profuse ornamentation, lightness and grace.

Romanesque a style in European art and architecture that preceded the Gothic and derived its main impetus from the activity of monastic orders; typically, churches in this style are low, built of stone and characterised by round arches, thick walls and small windows. A good example is the Church of St Andrew (see p. 113).

Rood screen a screen below the rood, or crucifix, dividing the nave from the chancel of a church.

Rotunda a small, usually domed building on a circular plan.

Rustication large masonry blocks separated by prominent joints, used to give a rustic appearance to an exterior wall.

Secession the Central European version of Art Nouveau.

Sgraffito a method of producing designs on plaster by incising the top coat to reveal a differently coloured one beneath.

Skansen an open-air museum, usually displaying rural architecture.

Socialist Realism the official art and architecture doctrine of the Soviet Union and other communist countries, mainly during 1946–53, characterised by grandiose, monumental forms.

Stoup a vessel for holy water, usually situated near the west entrance of a church.

Stucco a fine plaster used for surfacing walls or for moulding architectural decoration and sculpture.

Tabernacle a cabinet-like enclosure containing the consecrated Host, usually placed at the high altar of a church

Tracery ornamental work of intersecting lines in the upper part of a window or blind arch, common in Gothic architecture.

Transept the part of a cross-shaped church between, and at right angles to, the nave and chancel.

Triptych a set of three hinged and painted panels, used as an altarpiece.

Trompe l'oeil literally, a deception of the eye; used to describe illusionist decoration, painted architectural perspectives, etc.

Tuscan a column with a plain (non-fluted) shaft and capital.

Vault an arched roof or ceiling.

Voivodship an administrative unit, equivalent to an English county.

Volute a spiral scroll found on Ionic and Corinthian capitals.

Westwork a form typical of Romanesque architecture, consisting of two towers linked by a gallery open to the nave.

Index

The Blue Guides

■ Ideal for touring the country or to accompany short breaks, this guide provides comprehensive coverage of all aspects of Austria, especially its rich history and culture. Full of fascinating detail about the lives and achievements of the country's rules, composers, artists and writers.

■ Nicholas T. Parsons
4th edition, 2000
448pp
ISBN 0–7136–4831–7
£15.99

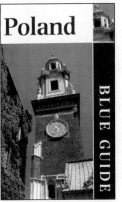

■ This vast country, stretching from the Baltic coast down to the Tatra Mountains and from Germany across to Byelorussia and the Ukraine, is compelling in its diversity. Teutonic castles, ancient palaces, cathedrals and wildlife reserves jostle for attention.

■ Jasper Tilbury and Paweł Turnau
1st edition, 2000
560pp
ISBN 0–7136–3899–0
£15.99

■ Immerse yourself in this entertaining guide to the art, history, literature and music of magical Prague. Discover the treasures of this ancient capital in eight carefully planned walks; and explores the countryside of Central Bohemia in days out from Prague.

■ Michael Jacobs
1st edition, 1999
224pp
ISBN 0–7136–4428–1
£10.99

If you would like more information about
Blue Guides please complete the form below
and return it to

Blue Guides
A&C Black (Publishers) Ltd
Freepost
Eaton Socon
Huntingdon
Cambridgeshire
PE19 8EZ

or fax it to us on 020 7831 8478
or email us at travel@acblack.co.uk

Name
....

....

Address

....

....

....

....

....